From Technical Professional to Entrepreneur

From Technical Professional to Entrepreneur

A Guide to Alternative Careers

David E. Dougherty

A Wiley-Interscience Publication

JOHN WILEY & SONS

New York   Chichester   Brisbane   Toronto   Singapore

Library of Congress Cataloging in Publication Data

Dougherty, David E., 1933–
  From technical professional to entrepreneur.

  "A Wiley-Interscience publication."
  Includes index.
  1. Industrial property—United States.   I. Title.

KF2980.D68   1986   346.7304'8   86-1501
ISBN 0-471-83042-9   347.30648

Printed in the United States of America

10 9 8 7 6 5 4 3 2 1

To
Beverly

Preface

The primary purpose of this book is to show you how to use technology in developing a business. To be more specific, the book provides a general overview of industrial property rights and shows you how to evaluate, develop, protect, and sell your ideas.

In providing an overview, I have consulted a number of distinguished patent professionals and entrepreneurs. I have worked closely with each of the patent professionals and consider them to be among the outstanding experts in our profession. It is true that they have many equals, and that my knowledge is limited to those lawyers with whom I have worked during the past twenty-five years. I hope that this book will help you as much as they have helped me.

The initial part of the book focuses on the techniques for screening, evaluating, and developing new technology. These techniques were developed by business executives and lawyers, and have been used by a number of corporations. These techniques include proper utilization of patents, trademarks, trade secrets, and copyrights, as well as defenses against unfair competition.

As a technical professional you will learn to answer questions such as: Is my idea patentable? How do I write and interpret claims, and more important, can a patent covering my invention help me make a profit? You will also learn that there are times when you should not seek patent protection, how to recognize those times, and what to do when you decide not to file a patent application. Actual case histories of inventors will help you to avoid costly mistakes that others have encountered.

In Part 2 of the book you will learn how to reduce the high costs associated with protecting your idea. In some cases you can avoid legal fees of $1000 to $5000 or more. However, you should recognize the value of a patent attorney and consider suggestions regarding the most efficient way to use their services.

As an engineer or scientist you will learn to understand the jargon that is frequently used by patent lawyers. You will also learn to think like a business-oriented lawyer.

In Part 3 of the book you will learn how to sell your inventions to established companies, and about difficulties encountered by others who have pursued this approach. In a way, you will learn to sell yourself and your technical abilities.

Much of the information presented in this book is applicable to the establishment of your own manufacturing operation. However, the actual establishment of your own manufacturing company goes beyond the scope of this treatise. Topics such as capitalization, advertising, site selection, or the like are not covered.

DAVID E. DOUGHERTY

Washington, D.C.
March 1986

Acknowledgments

I appreciate the contributions provided by the many capable engineers, entrepreneurs, executives, lawyers, and scientists with whom I have worked during the past twenty-five years. This book is based on their approach to business.

I am particularly grateful to Clare Garatti, who deciphered my notes, typed the manuscript, and made so many revisions. I am also grateful to William Lacey, who made the drawings.

D.E.D.

Contents

PART 1: EVALUATING AND DEVELOPING YOUR IDEAS   1

1. TAKING THE FIRST STEP   3

1.1. The Business of Developing New Technology   4
1.2. Taking Inventory: Identifying and Evaluating Your Ideas   7
1.3. What Is A Patent?   11
1.4. Is Your Invention Patentable?   12
1.5. Is A Patent Worthwhile?   13
1.6. Getting the Best Patent for the Least Money   14
1.7. Can Trademarks and Copyrights Help?   15
1.8. Summary   16

2. LAWYERS   17

2.1. Putting Things in Perspective   18
2.2. The Anatomy of a Lawyer   18
2.3. How to Select a Lawyer   19
2.4. When to Use an Attorney   22
2.5. An Attorney–Client Interview   23
2.6. Summary   26

3. THE BUSINESS OF MAKING MONEY   29

     3.1. The Importance of Patents   30
     3.2. The Importance of Broad Coverage   32
     3.3. Developing Value   35
     3.4. The Basic Rule of Integrity   37
     3.5. The Importance of Timing   37
     3.6. Summary   38

4. ESTABLISHING YOUR RIGHTS   39

     4.1. Ownership   40
     4.2. Written Records   40
     4.3. Witnesses   43
     4.4. Proof Is Required   44
     4.5. Beware of Employment Contracts   45
     4.6. Using Your Employer's Facilities   47
     4.7. Consider Your Helper's Contributions   48
     4.8. Summary   49

5. APPLYING MANAGEMENT TECHNIQUES   51

     5.1. General Concepts   52
     5.2. Managing a New Development   54
     5.3. Market Evaluation   55
     5.4. Technical Evaluation   60
     5.5. Patent Evaluation   64
     5.6. A Preliminary Search   66
     5.7. A Validity Search   69
     5.8. An Infringement Search   70
     5.9. A Collection Search   71
     5.10. Other Types of Searches   72
     5.11. Conducting Your Own Search   72
     5.12. Can You Rely on Trade Secrets?   73
     5.13. Time Is Money   74

6. DETERMINING PATENTABILITY   75

     6.1. General Concepts   76
     6.2. Statutory Requirements   77

6.3. Tests for Determining Patentability 79
6.4. Nonobviousness 80
6.5. Synergism and Aggregation 82
6.6. Substitution and Addition 83
6.7. Substitution of Materials 83
6.8. Abandoned Inventions 84
6.9. Statutory Bar: Public Use or Sale 85

PART 2: PROTECTING YOUR INVESTMENT IN THE FUTURE   87

7. THE ANATOMY OF A PATENT   89

7.1. General Concepts 90
7.2. Statutory Requirements 90
7.3. The Specification 91
7.4. The Claims 99
7.5. Summary 100

8. CLAIMS: THE SCOPE OF YOUR PROTECTION   103

8.1. General Concepts 104
8.2. The Purpose of Claims 104
8.3. Form of the Claims 108
8.4.   Types of Claims 109
8.5. Nonstatutory Inventions 113
8.6. Conclusion 113

9. CLAIMS: THE FINE EDGE BETWEEN BROAD PROTECTION AND INVALIDITY   115

9.1. A Practical Approach to Drafting Claims 116
9.2. Formal Requirements 117
9.3. The Preamble 117
9.4. Indispensable Elements 119
9.5. The Proper Use of Functional Language 120

9.6.   Generic, Species, and Markush Claims   121
9.7.   Proper Wording and Terminology   122
9.8.   Definite versus Indefinite Introduction   123
9.9.   Order of Elements   123
9.10. Antecedents   124
9.11. Dependent Claims   124
9.12. Subcombination Claims   127
9.13. The Problem with Prior Art   127
9.14. Claiming a Single Invention with Claims of
       Varying Scope   129
9.15. Words and Phrases in Claims Drafting   130
9.16. A Final Word on Drafting Claims   130

10. PATENT DRAWINGS   133

10.1. General Concepts   134
10.2. Formal Requirements   135
10.3. Flow Charts   138
10.4. Design Patents   138
10.5. Use of Photographs   138
10.6. Electrical Symbols   139
10.7. Conclusion   140

11. THE PATENT SPECIFICATION   141

11.1. The Title   143
11.2. An Abstract of the Disclosure   144
11.3. Background of the Invention   146
11.4. The Summary of the Invention   149
11.5. The Objects of the Invention   150
11.6. The Description of the Drawings   151
11.7. The Detailed Description of Your Invention   151
11.8. The Best Embodiment   152
11.9. Description of the Alternatives   153
11.10. The Operation of Your Invention   154
11.11. Conclusions   155
11.12. The Oath or Declaration   155

12. HOW TO FILE AND PROSECUTE YOUR PATENT APPLICATION   157

12.1. Formalities   158
12.2. Filing Receipts   159
12.3. Classification   160
12.4. The Information Disclosure   161
12.5. An Official Action   161
12.6. An Interview with a U.S. Patent Examiner   165
12.7. A Final Rejection   166
12.8. Filing a Divisional or Continuation Application   167
12.9. Interferences   167
12.10. The Notice of Allowance   169
12.11. The Final Fee   169
12.12. Issuance of Your Patent   170
12.13. The Effect of Fraud   170
12.14. Post Issuance Fees U.S.   171
12.15. Reexamination and Reissues   171
12.16. Foreign Filing   172

13. WORKING WITH YOUR ATTORNEY   175

13.1. Developing a Team Effort   177
13.2. Cost Effectiveness   177
13.3. The Preliminary Search and Opinion   178
13.4. The Preparation of Your Patent Application   178
13.5. The Prosecution of the Application   179
13.6. Participation in the Sale of Your Invention   179
13.7. Contractual Negotiations   180

14. TRADEMARKS   181

14.1. What Is a Trademark?   183
14.2. Selecting a Trademark   183
14.3. Avoid Conflicts with Established Competitors   185
14.4. Using Your Trademark Properly   186
14.5. The Strength of a Trademark   187
14.6. Registering a Trademark   188

14.7. Trademark Prosecution, Opposition, and Affidavits under
       Sections 8 and 15   189
14.8. Cancellation and Other Proceedings   190
14.9. Other Considerations   191

PART 3: SELLING YOUR IDEAS   193

15. SELLING YOUR INVENTIONS   195

15.1. Selecting Your Target   197
15.2. Don't Pay Something for Nothing   200
15.3. Consider the Use of a Consultant   200
15.4. How to Prepare for an Initial Presentation   201
15.5. Structuring a Presentation   203
15.6. How to Make an Initial Approach   205
15.7. Getting an Appointment   206
15.8. The Initial Interview   207
15.9. The Debriefing   209
15.10 The Second Presentation   209
15.11. Continued Business Negotiations   211
15.12. The Key Elements for Success   212

16. ENVIRONMENTAL INFLUENCE
AND THE ROLE OF STRATEGIC PLANNING   213

16.1. The Environment for Small Business   214
16.2. The Environment and the Large Corporation   215
16.3. Strategic Planning in a Large Corporation   217
16.4. Using Strategic Information to Sell Your Ideas   218
16.5. Corporate Strategy for R&D   219
16.6. Tactics and Reconnaissance—Valuable Aids in
       Selling Your Idea   221
16.7. The United States, Its Environment and Terrain   222

17. CONTRACTS   225

17.1. Key Issues   226
17.2. Royalties   228
17.3. Minimum Royalties   230
17.4. Other Forms of Diligence   231
17.5. Legal Issues   231
17.6. Time Is of the Essence   233
17.7. Further Obligations   233

18. THE ART OF NEGOTIATION   235

18.1. Introduction   236
18.2. Selling: An Integral Part of Negotiations   236
18.3. Developing a Successful Negotiating Attitude   237
18.4. Preparation for Negotiation   238
18.5. Negotiations with a Large Organization   239
18.6. Dealing with People   240
18.7. Patience in Negotiations   241
18.8. Developing Creative Solutions   242
18.9. Closing the Sale   244
18.10. Implementing an Agreement   244

19. LITIGATION AND THE ENTREPRENEUR   245

19.1. An Introduction to Litigation   246
19.2. Litigation and the Large Corporation   247
19.3. Litigation and the Entrepreneur   249
19.4. Damages   250
19.5. Reissues and Reexamination   251
19.6. Alternative Forms of Dispute Resolution   252
19.7. When All Else Fails   252
19.8. Settlement   254

20. CREATIVITY—A VALUABLE ASSET   255

21. GETTING STARTED   259

APPENDIXES   261

A. Invention Submission Letter   263
B. Invention Submission Form   265
C. Confidential Agreement   269
D. License Agreement (Exclusive)   273
E. License Agreement (Nonexclusive)   281
F. Manufacturing, Sales, and Trademark Agreement   285
G. Joint Development Agreement   297
H. Joint Venture Agreement   303
I.   Distributor Agreement   311
J. Consultant's Agreement   323

INDEX   327

From Technical Professional to Entrepreneur

PART 1

EVALUATING AND DEVELOPING YOUR IDEAS

1

Taking the First Step

Every one has good ideas. It is what you do with them that separates the successful entrepreneur from the idle dreamer.

1.1   THE BUSINESS OF DEVELOPING NEW TECHNOLOGY

If you have the ability to solve technical problems, you have the potential to become an entrepreneur. You can use an invention as a basis for your own manufacturing business or you can sell inventions to companies that need new products and processes. After all, new products are the lifeblood of small businesses, and large companies need new technology to meet their profit goals. You can also use your technical developments as a basis for selling your services as a consultant.

Consider the work of Peter Shaffer, Ph.D., who is a scientist and an entrepreneur. He earned his doctorate in inorganic chemistry at Pennsylvania State University in 1955. Then, after three years at DuPont, he went to the Carborundum Company and spent the next twenty three years working there as a materials scientist. And then in 1981, after the Carborundum Company was merged into the Kennecott Copper Company, Dr. Shaffer and his friend, Keith Blakely, left Carborundum to found a new company, Advanced Refractory Technologies, Inc.

Their new company was based on an inventive concept that provided a foundation for growth. Peter said, "The idea was to use a continuous furnace for the direct production of fine refractory powders. Essentially, it just didn't make sense to use an Acheson furnace to make giant crystals and then break them up. Why not put the material into a furnace, hold it there for a controlled time and then quench it in order to get the fine powder that they wanted?"

Peter and Keith also identified a market niche. In fact, Peter tried to interest Carborundum in this technology, but without success. But then, Peter and Keith recognized that the fine powder market was very small, perhaps only several millions dollars a year. Nevertheless, they recognized a need and went ahead with their new business. After only a few years, their company has grown and now has sales of over $3 million a year.

Peter Shaffer attributes much of their success to the fact that he and Keith complement one another. He said, "I never would have started a business without a partner like Keith. Keith is the businessman, financially oriented and a neat dresser, while I'm the idea man. In fact, I'm still a scientist." But Peter Shaffer is more than an idea man. Peter Shaffer is a doer, a scientist, and a tenacious worker who sticks with a problem until he finds a solution.

As a scientist, Peter Shaffer learned a lot about patents and trade secrets. He said, "DuPont sent me to a course on patents which gave me a good foundation. And then I learned a lot more from Karl Brownell, director of patents at Carborundum. Karl helped me to get six patents. I know that many of the things that Karl emphasized have helped me with our work at Advanced Refractory Technologies."

Now, if you want to follow Peter Shaffer's example and convert your technical development into a source of income, make a realistic appraisal of yourself and your ideas. Begin with a self-evaluation and develop a goal-oriented philosophy. You can be successful, as successful as Peter Shaffer and many others like him, if you develop a goal-oriented philosophy and apply the techniques suggested in the following chapters.

But before going further, consider the difference between an idea and an invention. An invention is an idea or a concept that is new, useful, and nonobvious to a person of ordinary skill in the art to which it pertains. And while you cannot obtain a patent on a concept, you can on an invention.

As an entrepreneur, you should also recognize the importance of a good attitude. For example, Peter Shaffer had confidence in his idea and himself. He also had enthusiasm. "I'm not a worrier," Peter said. "If I work on a technical problem and can't solve it, I'll just have to find some other way to get around it." And in starting a business, Peter relied on Keith Blakely's abilities, and developed new skills. In essence, he had a positive attitude and learned to sell his ideas and himself. You can do the same thing because most of these skills are easy to learn. With continued practice they can help you to succeed.

So assuming that you want to develop new technology as an entrepreneur, recognize the importance of avoiding procrastination. Do it now. Getting a job done well usually takes hard work and perseverance. Chester Carlson, the inventor of electrostatic printing (xerography), worked hard and had perseverance. After being turned down by a number of companies, he convinced the people at the Battelle Development Corporation in Columbus, Ohio, to work on the development of his invention. They overcame a number of technological problems and made hundreds of millions of dollars.

Selling your ideas requires effort. Dr. Shaffer said, "If you are not ready to eat, sleep, and live with your new company, don't start your own business." He went on to say, "I'm not saying that we live at the office or even spend sixteen hours a day there. We don't. However, we do work some strange hours. I may mull something over in my mind all night and then jump in to work on it early the next morning. Realistically, I guess that we are never not working."

Selling new inventions is an uphill battle, and at times it may seem more like trying to climb a mountain. But if you convince yourself that you have a good idea, you will have taken the first step toward selling it. Until you sell yourself on your own ideas, you can't sell them to anyone else.

You should also accept the fact that promoting your ideas will usually require a financial investment. In the case of Peter Shaffer, he and Keith Blakely went to a venture capitalist and started their own company. They included modest salaries for themselves as a part of the cost for starting a business. However, those of you who do not want to start your own manufacturing company, and do not have access to a venture capitalist or an angel, can reduce your out-of-pocket costs if you are willing to accept new challenges.

Peter Shaffer recognizes that time is a limited asset. In essence, this may merely mean eliminating the wasted hours in front of a TV, and using that time constructively. There is one other approach to saving time that can help an entrepreneur. You can learn to use your periods of higher productivity, such as early mornings if you are a morning person, or late evening if you are a night person, to become more effective. Just plan to use your peak periods to work on your project. Remember that time is a precious and limited resource and that you should use your time effectively to develop new technology.

Now, in considering your own business, look a little closer at the concept of developing and selling your inventions. Developing and selling your inventions allows you to concentrate on your favorite projects. You are your own boss and can use whatever hours for work you like, provided, of course, that those hours fit into your other schedule.

As an entrepreneur, you will devote considerable time to a project before it generates income. Therefore, you will probably have to work for a salary to meet your everyday needs. Chester Carlson devoted full time to the development of his invention for a while, but found it necessary to return to work. In fact, he worked for many years before his xerography inventions paid off.

It is true that very few inventions are as successful as xerography. However, whether you have a pioneer invention or a minor improvement, your success will depend on good business practices such as planning, organization, and accounting. Studies have shown that farmers who keep good records make more money than those who do not. Similarly, lawyers who keep good records make more money than those who do not. Therefore, it is safe to assume that you will do a better job if you keep a careful record of your efforts.

As an employee of a large corporation, Peter Shaffer learned to use an engineering notebook. He learned to record his progress on technical projects, to write down concepts for improving existing products and processes, and to keep a record of his experiments, including those that didn't work. Now, as an entrepreneur, he is even more diligent in keeping a record of his work.

"Everything that I do, think, or say goes into my notebook," Peter explained. "I even include a record of my stock transactions. I keep a bound notebook open on my desk and have found that a 150 page notebook lasts me about three months. From my notebooks, I can reproduce everything that I've done since we founded our business. I consider them so important, I have them microfilmed as soon as I complete them and keep the two microfilms in separate locations." The importance of engineering notebooks and the proper procedures for their use is covered in more detail in Chapter 3.

You may think that once you refine the technical aspects of an invention, you can sell it to industry or through distributors and that they will overcome any marketing problems. In reality it is not that easy. You will usually have to convince the consumer or a corporate executive to buy your invention. If you want to sell your invention to a corporate executive, you must show that executive how to use your invention to make money. It is true that selling inventions to a company is difficult and requires careful preparation. However, this approach is feasible in some cases, as explained in Part 3.

As an entrepreneur, think in terms of objectives rather than activities. An objective may be to complete a working model of your device or to complete a subassembly. In a way it is like writing a book. You just take one small task, like one paragraph, and complete it, rather than trying to work on the entire project.

1.2 TAKING INVENTORY: IDENTIFYING AND EVALUATING YOUR IDEAS

Let's look at your inventions. You probably have several good inventions. Your first problem is to separate the patentable inventions from those that are not patentable. In some cases an unpatentable idea may offer business opportunities; however, you need to know whether or not a patent on your invention will help you to launch a business or make a profit. You also need to know if somebody else already has a patent that could prevent you from using your idea on a commercial scale. Focus your efforts on the more readily salable inventions and remember that you are operating a business for profit.

Try to identify which one of your ideas or inventions has the highest income potential.

In Peter Shaffer's opinion, "The most difficult problem that we faced as entrepreneurs was a lack of resources. We had to learn to prioritize and tighten our belts. Many new entrepreneurs try to work on too many things. And if they don't retrench and carefully select projects, they fail. And yet, if you concentrate your efforts and learn to live within your resources, it is a lot more fun."

Contrary to popular belief, corporate managers are not always far-sighted individuals. They are frequently preoccupied with short-term profits. What this means to you is that many corporate managers are interested in producing sales and profits this year or next rather than investing in an invention that offers a five year payback.

There are, of course, a few executives who are interested in long-term projects. For example, products such as the laser, holography, and transistors, required twenty-five years or more to reach commercial success. But it is extremely difficult to convince a potential licensee to pay you a large amount of money for an unproven invention.

Nevertheless, the long-term potential for a basic invention may be much greater than the potential for a minor improvement that can be brought to the commerical stage within one to two years. However, the development of a basic invention will probably require a total commitment from the individual who wants to develop it.

In considering patents, Dr. Shaffer said, "I view patents somewhat negatively, and yet, I have a lot of respect for them. I don't go very far with a new project until I see the results of a patent search. I review the information in the prior art patents. And in most cases, I can use some of the information and figure out how to avoid their claims."

He went on to say, "We can't risk infringing somebody's patent because we don't have the time or the money to waste on patent litigation. The high cost of litigation also discourages us from seeking United States patents on many of our developments. And when you consider our limited resources, we don't see any justification for foreign patents. In essence, we consider each project on its own merits, and whenever feasible, we rely on trade secrets."

Trade secret protection may work for Peter Shaffer, but the use of a trade secret approach is not always appropriate. The sale of a product may disclose your secret. Even if you have a secret process, a competitor may be able to discover it by reverse engineering. Therefore, as an entrepreneur, remember that each case should be evaluated on its own merits.

Don't rely on trade secrets if you hope to sell an invention to a large corporation, because many corporations refuse to receive information in confidence. They insist that any outside inventor rely on his or her patent rights for any remuneration for the invention.

And then there are men like John Gentner, president of AMF Wyott, Larry Fie, President of AMF American, and Franz Deutsch, Director General of Tyrolia Freizeitgerate G.m.b.H. in Austria. These fine executives are patent conscious. They have each developed and marketed new products under licenses from outside inventors.

These three executives are also interested in foreign patents because they market their products internationally. For this reason, they will authorize filing for foreign patents if the inventor's rights have not been lost. Therefore, as an independent inventor or entrepreneur, try to license your inventions before the foreign rights are lost, and before spending your own money for foreign patents.

One success story is that of Walter Sharp, a school teacher from Columbus, Ohio, who was teaching typing. As he observed the young typists, he saw that many could type rapidly and yet, because of frequent hesitations and particular weaknesses, they were ineffective. Walter could only determine each student's particular weaknesses, (slow carriage return, weak fourth finger, etc.) by observing that student's actual typing. This presented a problem, a problem that was also aggravated by the student's nervousness when Walter watched over a shoulder. But only by pinpointing each typist's weaknesses, could Walter assign drills to strengthen those areas.

Walter thought that there ought to be a better way to analyze his students' problems. Being creative, he invented a typewriter with a motor on the platen, so that the platen would rotate slowly as a student typed. Whenever a student who was using one of Walter's special typewriters hesitated, a vertical space would appear to indicate the weakness. In addition, the slope of the line was a measure of typing speed and allowed a student to see any progress from a glance at the work.

Walter talked with a patent attorney who, after conducting a patent search, filed a patent application. Walter licensed his invention to a typewriter manufacturer. But when the manufacturer had a corporate reorganization, Walter took his invention to the Battelle Development Company in Columbus, Ohio.

The engineers at Battelle worked with Walter and did some additional development work to refine his idea. Battelle then licensed Walter's patent to Scientific Advance, Inc. (SAI). And SAI hired Walter as a consultant and introduced the product to the commercial market.

Larry Little, a diary chemist in St. Louis, Missouri, is another example of an inventor who succeeded. Larry was intrigued by the production of cottage cheese and sour cream. He knew that there had to be a better way to make these products than by using the old-fashioned culture process. In that process, cream was inoculated with bacteria, and as the bacteria grew, it produced lactic acid, which then reacted with the milk solids to form curd for cottage cheese or sour cream.

Larry thought that he could add lactic acid directly and actually produce cheese curd and sour cream in a much shorter time if he first added stabilizers. After many experiments, Larry produced sour cream in about four hours as opposed to fifteen to sixteen hours by the culture method. Larry encountered a number of other problems. For example, he encountered a serious problem in obtaining state and federal approval. Dairies that processed and sold food products could not use Larry's process without proper approvals. Besides, they probably could not sell the sour cream if the federal regulation required that they label it as "imitation."

These hurdles were overcome, and the process was licensed to the Meyer Blanke Company of St. Louis. Larry went to work for Meyer Blanke, but eventually returned to his own consulting business so that he could devote more time to the development of a process for producing cottage cheese.

One reason for Larry Little's success was his attention to detail. He also recognized the importance of patents and contacted a patent attorney during the early stages of his work. They developed a portfolio of patents that were extremely helpful in licensing Larry's processes.

Larry Little is a unique individual. He worked on new ways to make sour cream and cottage cheese during the same time period, but did focus most of his attention on the production of sour cream. He worked primarily on sour cream partly because he thought that the technical problems were easier to solve, but more important because he knew that the producers of sour cream would be more likely to accept a new process than the producers of cottage cheese.

You can also make money, as many others have, from unpatentable ideas. For example, a number of years ago, Betty Graham, an executive secretary and part-time artist in Dallas, Texas, recognized the difficulty in erasing a typing error. She knew that when she didn't like what she painted, she merely painted over it. Putting these two concepts together, she thought that a secretary could use a finely tapered brush and a small dab of white paint to cover an error. She selected a water-based paint, tried it, and found that it was far easier than erasing.

She contacted a patent attorney but was told the idea was not patentable. In effect, she was applying the everyday practice of a sign painter on a small scale. She developed a formula for a superior product and kept her formula secret. She also ran an advertisement in a secretarial magazine and was deluged with orders for her product. Her product, known as Liquid Paper ® correction fluid, is found in many offices today.

Today, many companies manufacture and sell typewriter correction fluid as a result of one woman who recognized a problem, a solution, and a need. She evaluated her patent rights, kept her formula a secret, and registered her trademark with the U.S. Patent and Trademark Office. This trademark became the symbol of a high quality product and a very valuable asset.

This example shows that an individual with confidence in an idea and a willingness to pursue its development can succeed even without a patent. So, as an entrepreneur, don't overlook products with potential even if you can't get a patent. However, don't overlook the advantages that are offered by the patent system.

1.3   WHAT IS A PATENT?

A patent, or "Letters Patent" as it is frequently called, is an official document that gives an inventor the right to exclude others from making, using, or selling an invention. However, this right to exclude others is limited to what is covered by the patent claims. In addition, a U.S. patent is limited to the geographical territory of the United States and to a period of seventeen years from the date that the patent is issued.

While other countries also grant patents for limited periods of time, the costs of obtaining foreign patents should be weighed for each foreign country versus the potential benefits. Many entrepreneurs, like Peter Shaffer, believe that foreign patents are often worthless to an American individual. On the other hand, many business executives want foreign patents. Therefore, as an entrepreneur, restrict your investment in foreign countries to those countries in which there is a high probability that a licensee will pay for them.

Now patents have limitations. They do not assure you of making money. They do not assure you of a right to make, use, or sell your own invention because someone may have an earlier patent or patents that would be infringed by practicing your patented invention. In that case, you might be able to prevent the other patent holder from using your invention, but he or she could also prevent you from using the earlier invention.

Consider the case of a patent on a grinding wheel having a particular type of abrasive that works best when pressed against a workpiece with a great deal of force. This type of wheel may require a reinforced center section. So, someone who had previously obtained a patent on a reinforced center section could stop you from using a reinforced center even though its use is necessary for the successful use of your invention. And you could prevent the other patent holder from making a grinding wheel that uses your type of abrasive.

1.4   IS YOUR INVENTION PATENTABLE?

35 USC 101 provides, "Whoever invents or discovers any new and useful process, machine, manufacture, or composition of matter, or any new and useful improvement thereof, may obtain a patent therefor, subject to the conditions and requirements of this Title." You may also obtain a patent if you have developed a novel ornamental design or a new plant. Because only certain types of novel plants are patentable, the criteria for patenting plants is not discussed in detail in this book.

Before you apply for a patent consider the business aspects of patents. For example, if your inventions aren't marketable, they will have little or no value even if you have a patent. Ask yourself if somebody would pay a premium price for a product that incorporates your invention. Think in terms of what corporations want and what they are willing to pay for in a salable product or a process that will give them a competitive advantage. And when you consider the patentability of your ideas, remember that mere ideas, mental concepts, systems of doing business, and principles of nature are not patentable.

If your invention is new and useful, assume that it is probably patentable. It may be patentable even though a patent examiner (an employee of the U.S. Patent and Trademark Office) may say that your invention would be obvious to a person of ordinary skill in the art. It is true that one of the patent law's criteria for patentability is based on the invention's being nonobvious to a person of ordinary skill, and that this is an important concept in patent law. The problem with this criteria is that it is frequently misapplied. Besides, it is difficult to define who a person of ordinary skill is. And then there is the tendency to say that something is obvious based on hindsight. For example, many creative inventions appear obvious after they have been disclosed and fully explained. So don't leap to a conclusion that your invention is obvious.

It is often difficult to determine whether or not an invention would have been obvious to a person of ordinary skill in the art at the time that the alleged invention was made. However, if you can show that there has been a long-felt need for your invention, you can argue that if it had been obvious someone would already have done it.

Now as an entrepreneur, consider whether the cost of obtaining a patent is justified. Remember that the key question is whether or not your invention can be used or sold for a reasonable profit.

1.5   IS A PATENT WORTHWHILE?

C. Marshall Dann is a partner in the Philadelphia law firm of Dann, Dorfman, Herrell, and Skillman and a former U.S. commissioner of Patents and Trademarks. He is also a former president of the American Intellectual Property Law Association and a member of the executive committee of the International Patent and Trademark Association and a former chief patent counsel at DuPont.

According to Marshall Dann, "There are many factors that affect the value of a patent. Certainly, you will have to consider the scope of the claims. Are they [the claims] broad enough to give you a commercial advantage? And, of course, the value of a patent depends on the size and value of the commercial market."

In a way, the value of a patent depends on you and what you do with it. It depends to a large degree on your ability to sell your invention and yourself. In other words, don't be misled by the popular myth that if you invent a better mousetrap, the world will beat a path to your door. Unfortunately, it just doesn't happen.

Now, as a first step in evaluating a patent on your invention, consider the market potential for the invention. Then consider the effect of price on this market. Can you really offer a product at a competitive price? Can you produce a product at a lower cost than a competitor?

Assuming that you have a viable business opportunity, consider the probable scope of a patent on your invention. Ask whether or not the scope of your patent will stop a competitor from marketing a colorable imitation of your invention. Understand the scope or breadth of your patent; such an understanding is vitally important to technical entrepreneurs and is treated in more detail in Chapters 8 and 9.

Your patent also has an intangible value. For example, a patent suggests that you are a creative individual. It also proves that you are astute enough to protect your ideas. These characteristics are valued by many corporate executives with whom I have worked. Actually, a patent may even help you to get a job, to sell your invention, and perhaps, if you are persistent enough, to become financially independent.

1.6 GETTING THE BEST PATENT FOR THE LEAST MONEY

Marshall Dann said, "An inventor should regularly review his work, compare it with what has been disclosed in the prior art, and see what can be protected. After all, an inventor's knowledge can help him to get the best patent for the least money. But in most cases, he will need a patent lawyer."

You should engage a patent lawyer because there really is much more to patent law than taking your invention and putting it into the proper form for the U.S. Patent and Tradmark Office. You should distinguish between merely getting a patent issued by the U.S. Patent and Trademark Office and obtaining a valid patent that will be upheld by the courts. The problem is that in many cases the U.S. Patent and Trademark Office issues a patent that is subsequently held invalid. In effect, the court is overruling the Patent Office and holding that the idea wasn't patentable.

There are many reasons why the courts find patents invalid. It is frequently just a matter of searching the remote corners of the technical literature to find some prior art that anticipates an invention. After all, you can't expect a patent examiner to know everything that has happened in a field of rapidly expanding technology. However, if there is a commercial incentive to attack your patent, a competitor will extend a search into university libraries, review doctoral dissertations, and search through foreign literature.

What you want to do is obtain a valid patent and assure yourself of the strongest legal position possible. Therefore, conduct a thorough review of the literature yourself, do a computer search, write a clear description of your idea, and explain how your idea differs from the earlier suggestions found in the literature. Then ask your patent lawyer for advice. Make certain that you give your lawyer the facts and ask if the lawyer recommends a more thorough search by a patent professional.

In general, the more you do to prepare for a meeting with your attorney, the more money you will save.

1.7 CAN TRADEMARKS AND COPYRIGHTS HELP?

"The value of a trademark frequently depends on what you are selling." Marshall Dann said, "I believe that trademarks on apparatus or equipment can be valuable. But it probably wouldn't be worthwhile to obtain a trademark if you are selling bulk chemicals."

Trademarks such as "Coke," "Kodak," "DuPont," and "Holiday Inn," have tremendous value. However, this value has been developed through actual use and with the aid of massive advertising. What this means to you is that someone may have to spend lots of money to develop a valuable trademark. This is particularly true in the consumer markets. Nevertheless, a good brand name for your product can be valuable if you take steps to protect your trademark and if you avoid a number of common mistakes.

In essence, a trademark is a work or a symbol that is used to identify a certain manufacturer's goods. In other words, a trademark is a brand name that will distinguish your goods from those of a competitor, serve as a guarantee of consistency of quality to your customers, and serve in an advertising capacity to help in the sale of your products.

Some people think that it is simply a matter of selecting a clever trademark and then registering that name with the U.S. Patent and Trademark Office. However, there are rules for selecting and using trademarks, requirements for registration, and the possibility of infringing on the rights of others. These rules and requirements are considered in more detail in Chapter 14.

Now, you should recognize that your rights in a federal trademark are established by actual use of the mark on a product.

Copyrights are completely different from trademarks. Copyrights give the copyright owner an exclusive legal right to reproduce, publish, or sell the matter and form of the work. Copyrights protect an author or composer from having literary, dramatic, musical, or artistic works copied without the artist's authorization. Walter Sharp (introduced earlier as the inventor of a device for teaching typing) recognized the value of a copyright. Walter wrote the text material that went with his invention. This material was protected by copyright and licensed with his idea to a manufacturer. Copyrights are also important to computer programmers. In fact, there are a number of recent treatises on copyrights and computers. For example, you are referred to *Legal Care for Your Software* by Daniel Remer, (Addison Wesley, 1984).

1.8 SUMMARY

In summary, don't overlook the value of your inventions. And remember, what you do with them is what really counts.

Recognize that getting started is half of the battle. All you have to do is take positive action now.

2

Lawyers

Consider the role of the lawyer, what this professional can and will do for you and to you, and what it will cost in dollars and anguish.

2.1 PUTTING THINGS IN PERSPECTIVE

You should be apprehensive about discussing your ideas with someone else. You may feel even more apprehensive about talking to a lawyer. But you cannot operate in a vacuum, and you need to communicate with others. This may seem like a dichotomy, but there is an easy solution.

Don't talk to others about your inventions until you have protected your rights. However, to protect these rights, you may need an attorney. But don't contact an attorney until you are prepared. Once you are prepared, your initial meeting with a lawyer should proceed smoothly and be inexpensive. You can usually obtain an estimate for an initial consultation before you schedule the meeting.

2.2 THE ANATOMY OF A LAWYER

Many lawyers specialize in the same way as medical doctors. Some lawyers are general practitioners, but in reality, such lawyers concentrate on "family practice," such as the drafting of wills, adoptions, real estate transactions, and the like. They may be helpful in setting up a corporation; however, they usually are not qualified to protect your invention.

General lawyers can't protect your invention because they are not licensed to practice before the U.S. Patent and Trademark Office. A patent lawyer is analogous to an opthamologist. For example, today's patent lawyer has a technical background, probably graduated from an accredited law school, and has been licensed to practice law as a general lawyer. Then, after additional training and testing, such a lawyer has been licensed to practice as a specialist.

And then there are patent agents. Most patents agents are not lawyers; however, they are licensed to practice before the U.S. Patent and Trademark Office. They are licensed to prepare patent applications and represent inventors in Patent Office proceedings. In fact, many are well qualified and quite knowledgable about patent law. And almost all of them have a college degree with a major in engineering or some other technical field. Some of them have attended and even graduated from law school, but limit their practice to the work normally done by an agent. The patent agent is analogous to an optometrist who, although not a medical doctor, is trained to determine whether you need glasses and to prescribe glasses for correcting impaired vision. However, patent agents are not permitted to practice law, that is, to prepare license agreements.

You should also recognize that in any profession there are many well-qualified professionals, but there are also a few who are not as good as others. What this means to you is that you should look for a patent professional who will be enthusiastic about getting a patent on your invention. Now, assuming that your invention is patentable, finding an attorney who believes in your invention is a first step toward convincing the U.S. Patent and Trademark Office that your invention is patentable. An attorney who is negative about patentability may accept narrow claims instead of arguing for the broadest possible patent protection. This is obviously something you need to be concerned about.

2.3 HOW TO SELECT A LAWYER

In a way, selecting a lawyer is a lot like getting married. It's like marriage because it is only after the passage of time that you will know if you made a good decision. "Finding a good patent lawyer should be pretty easy," according to Marshall Dann of Dann, Dorfman, Herrell and Skillman. "Assuming that an inventor does not have any contacts in the patent profession, he can contact a general lawyer with whom he does have confidence. Then, all that he has to do is ask the general lawyer to make a few inquiries. The inventor can ask the lawyer to check the credentials of a particular lawyer in a legal directory, and, in this way, can find out the number of years of experience, technical background and identify a few of the patent lawyer's clients. Another approach would be to contact the American Intellectual Property Law Association in Washington D.C. and ask for a list of patent attorneys who are available to represent clients in your area. But look for someone who has a fair degree of experience."

As Marshall suggested, you probably want a patent lawyer with at least three to five years experience. You should find a patent lawyer who has licensing experience and some experience in litigation. After all, you might want to obtain a license under some other patent or figure out how to avoid infringement. Then, of course, you might want to license your invention to a manufacturer or need help with a subcontract to have it manufactured by an established manufacturer. And if you license your invention, you will want to structure the license to insure the commercialization of your invention.

As previously stated, a persistent attorney can frequently obtain a patent on a marginal invention. However, an experienced attorney should counsel you on the scope of the patent claims. Ask yourself if your claims will present a serious impediment to a competitor, and if your patent can be sold to an industrial company. If your patent will not present a serious impediment to a competitor and cannot be sold, it probably is not worth your time and effort.

However, do not decide against seeking a patent prematurely. Consider, for example, any benefit of listing patent pending or a patent number on a commercial product. Will such a notice discourage copying? Can you obtain a tax advantage by selling a patent? What this boils down to is that you want an attorney who will give you good practical advice.

Another easy way to find such an attorney is to start with the "Directory of Registered Patent Attorneys and Agents," which is available from the U.S. Department of Commerce in Washington, D.C., or from one of their local field offices. Then try to find a lawyer in your area since there are advantages in meeting face-to-face with your lawyer. You should also try to select a lawyer who will have time for you when you need assistance. For this reason, you may not want to select a lawyer who is primarily engaged in litigation unless there is some other attorney in the firm who will be available when needed.

Stanley H. Lieberstein, author of *Who Owns What's In Your Head* (Hawthorn Books, 1979), is a successful patent lawyer who practices in New York City. Stan says, "Probably the best way to find a patent lawyer is by talking with other inventors, preferably with inventors who have successfully developed their inventions." There is no question that this is an excellent way to find and evaluate a patent lawyer. However, if you don't know a successful inventor or don't feel comfortable with a recommendation, you will have to take another approach.

Another approach for finding a lawyer is to use the Roster of Attorneys or a legal directory such as Martindale Hubbell (available at most law libraries). Look for the name of a corporate patent counsel in your area. If you can't find a corporate patent counsel, look for an attorney who is employed by a large corporation. Then ask that attorney to recommend a patent lawyer. The advantage of using a corporate patent counsel (head of the department) is that he or she probably has more experience in working with outside counsel.

Telephone the corporate patent counsel's office and explain very briefly who you are and what you want. For example, "Mr. Johnson, my name is Jane Doe. I'm an independent inventor and obtained your name from the Roster of Attorneys. Would you be so kind as to recommend a local patent lawyer who could assist me in preparing a patent application?"

You might continue, "If you can spare a couple of minutes, I'll explain that my invention is mechanical in nature and that I would prefer an attorney with at least several years of experience. If possible, I would like one who has licensing experience." Some attorneys base their recommendations on friendships rather than professional qualifications. Therefore, ask if the counsel with whom you are speaking has had any work done by this attorney.

Most corporate attorneys will take the few minutes required and offer one or more recommendations. To be thorough, you can call a second corporate attorney and repeat the process. If the second recommends the same lawyer as the first, you can be reasonably assured that the proposed lawyer does quality work.

In selecting a lawyer, consider the advantages of working with one who is a member of a law firm as opposed to a sole practitioner. A member of a firm can confer with partners and bring many years of experience to bear on an unusual problem. And you may be able to work with a younger attorney who charges less for his or her time, and yet obtain the benefit of a more experienced attorney when necessary. On the other hand, a sole practitioner may give you more personal attention. In general, a lot depends on you; you should select an attorney with whom you feel comfortable.

If you want to obtain the best lawyer for the least money, consider using a retired corporate patent lawyer who maintains a small private practice. Such attorneys are probably receiving a pension, and yet continue to work on a limited basis. These lawyers do not usually have an elaborate office, and are frequently willing to do work for an individual. Many of them have a wealth of experience, and know how to deal with corporations. You should not, of course, expect anyone to work for nothing, but should seek the best value for your money.

A few corporate patent lawyers maintain a small outside practice. They offer many of the same advantages as a recently retired lawyer, but should refuse to work on any project that is in the same field as their corporate client.

Don't contact any lawyer if you know that lawyer is currently working for another client in your field. After all, an attorney cannot accept a new client if there is a conflict of interest with another client. For example, if your invention is in the field of abrasives, an attorney who is doing work for the Norton Company's Abrasive Division would not work for you. Fortunately, you can easily avoid this problem by asking a direct question.

Just ask if a prospective lawyer has any conflict that will prevent him or her from working in your field.

2.4   WHEN TO USE AN ATTORNEY

As an entrepreneur, use your lawyer during the planning stages because problems can be more readily avoided then than at some later date. For example, it will be easier to change your design to avoid an infringement problem before you have tooled up for production.

But don't contact a lawyer until you have carefully thought through your invention, written a concise description of it, and committed yourself to developing and selling it. Then, when you prepare for an initial consultation with your lawyer, reflect on the real purpose of contacting this professional. Remember that you are a businessperson, and that your goal is to make money. Ask yourself if this lawyer can help you to make money. Can such legal counsel help you to avoid a serious problem such as an expensive lawsuit? If the answers are no, don't contact the lawyer.

In general, look at the market potential for your idea before contacting a lawyer. For example, a number of years ago, a young inventor asked me about obtaining a patent on his invention. The proposed device was designed for archers and particularly for those who entered competition. The young inventor had a model of his invention and pointed out that it could be sold for a low price. It was also apparent that the idea could easily be copied. In other words, individuals could make their own devices at a small price.

After considering the costs of obtaining a patent and the number of devices that he would have to sell to pay for the patent, the inventor decided to try to sell his device without the benefit of a patent. I suggested that after making an initial offer to sell a device according to his invention, he would have one year to prepare and file a U.S. patent application, but he would lose his right to obtain foreign patents in most countries. This inventor was willing to sacrifice those rights in order to evaluate the market.

Generally, the costs for obtaining foreign patents are substantial and should, whenever possible, be passed on to a licensee. Nevertheless, you should not disclose your invention to the public or offer a product encompassing your invention for sale until you have carefully considered foreign protection. Foreign filing decisions are frequently difficult and are covered in more detail in Section 13.2.

2.5 AN ATTORNEY–CLIENT INTERVIEW

John Brown (a pseudonym) was a typical inventor/entrepreneur. He thought that he had made an invention, but was not certain how to develop it. John knew that he wanted some type of protection, such as a patent, so that he could manufacture and sell his product without competition from others.

In reality, John was a little afraid of contacting a lawyer. His invention was very personal. He could almost taste the riches it would produce. However, there was a chance that a lawyer might think him foolish, dash his hopes for a better life, and charge him some exorbitant fee in the process.

John needed sound advice, and because of his determination, he overcame his trepidations. He had already spent time in the library and had not found any mention of a device such as the one he imagined. He also did some library research on analogous developments, and was convinced that there was a multimillion dollar potential for his idea. He assumed that a patent on his idea would greatly enhance its value.

Selecting an attorney was not difficult for John. A friend, an engineer with one of the local companies, had worked with a local patent lawyer and had praised her work on several occasions.

John telephoned the lawyer's office at about 9:15 A.M. He chose the time carefully, assuming that the lawyer would be in her office and yet would not be in conference before 9:30 A.M. John told the secretary his name, explained that he was an independent inventor, and wanted to talk to Ms. Waters about representing him.

The secretary put the call through to the attorney. John said that he had an invention in the abrasives field and would like to make an appointment to discuss it if the attorney did not have a conflict in this area.

In talking with the lawyer, John was a little more specific about his idea, but did not try to discuss the details. He hastened to add, "Before making an appointment, I would like to know how much time you suggest, and how much it will cost." Ms. Waters answered without hesitation that she would allow thirty to forty-five minutes and that the cost would not exceed $50.00. (Some lawyers charge more or less for an initial consultation, while others have an hourly billing rate and charge you for whatever time you use.)

Don't be embarassed to ask about costs. No one buys an automobile without asking the price. In fact, one of your key objectives in the initial consultation is to obtain a clear understanding about charges, fees to be incurred, and method of payment.

Most patent lawyers charge by the hour, but will do certain jobs for a fixed fee. To do this, your lawyer needs to know more about your invention and its complexity. The lawyer will also need to know how much support you can provide. For example, can you explain your technical knowledge clearly? If you can define your invention in clear and concise terms, the lawyer's work can be done more easily.

Your lawyer should also consider your interests before discussing costs. Are you interested in selling an idea and getting the broadest claims possible, or do you want whatever comes easiest? You are the client and your decisions will affect not only the scope of your claims, but also your costs for legal services.

After establishing a fee for the initial consultation, John and his lawyer scheduled an initial appointment. Then John started to prepare carefully for the meeting. He prepared a checklist that included all of his questions. John still felt slightly uneasy. Nevertheless, he was taking positive action and intended to see this thing through to success.

John arrived at the lawyer's office a little early. He didn't want to be late, and planned to review his notes once more before the meeting. The secretary was pleasant, told John that Ms. Waters would be with him in a few minutes, and offered him a cup of coffee. The office appeared business-like, and the secreaties seemed busy. The reception area was spacious, and based on the names listed on the firm's directory, served six lawyers. Current issues of the *Wall Street Journal, Business Week,* and other business publications were available.

Within a few minutes, John was ushered into Ms. Water's office. The lawyer walked forward extending her hand and said: "Good morning, Mr. Brown, my name is Roberta Waters. Let's sit over here," indicating a couch. Ms. Waters offered John a cup of coffee and then asked how she could be of service.

John stated that he had an idea for an improved grinding wheel, had researched the literature, and believed that it might be patentable. In answer to Ms. Water's questions, he explained that the use of a new type of abrasive grain in combination with a filler produced a tremendous improvement in metal removal and a longer lasting wheel. He explained his invention, how it worked, and how it differed from those devices that were already on the market.

During the discussion, John noticed that the attorney's desk was neatly arranged, businesslike, and that the office, while quite comfortable, was not overly elaborate. Neatness suggested efficiency and John liked efficient people. Had the office been poorly appointed, John would have been uneasy about the lawyer's ability. On the other hand, if the office was overly sumptuous, it might suggest that the lawyer charged very high fees to pay for it.

Ms. Waters explained the advantages of a patent search and its costs. She compared the value of an inexpensive search to that of a high quality search and made her recommendations as to how much should be authorized and the name of the Washington firm which she used for searches.

Ms. Waters estimated the probable costs for filing and obtaining a patent and said that she charged $125.00 per hour for her time, and that it would take about twenty hours to prepare the application. She said that she had written a few applications in as little as ten hours, but in veiw of the complexity of the present invention, she would estimate twenty hours and would not charge in excess of $2500 to prepare the application. A government filing fee, a minimum of $170, would be required, and it would cost about $200.00 for a patent draftsman to prepare appropriate drawings. Ms. Waters explained that her estimate of the government fee was based on the fee for an independent inventor and on an estimate that the application would have no more than twenty claims and no more than three independent claims.

Ms. Waters reviewed a tentative timetable for a patent search, preparing a patent application, and the need to file an amendment. John asked about contacting potential customers and was advised about how such contacts could be made, the type of presentation that should be prepared, and the advantages of delaying such contacts until after a patent application had been filed.

At the end of the conference, John asked if the attorney thought that a search was justified, and whether the lawyer thought that he would be able to sell his invention to a corporation. Ms. Waters said that John's invention appeared promising if someone else had not already patented it. She disclaimed any expertise in marketing, but stated that if the results stated were verified, she knew several companies that might have an interest in evaluating his invention.

At the end of the meeting, John authorized an expenditure of $300 for a patent search and an opinion. He could have reserved that decision, but had confidence in Ms. Waters and wanted to get started. He also gave Ms. Waters a check for $300 as a retainer when authorizing the search.

Ms. Waters had explained that the costs for a patent search could vary substantially and that many corporations routinely authorized $500 to

$600 for a more thorough search to avoid the possiblity of preparing an application that is anticipated by or unpatentable in view of the prior art. Ms. Waters explained that the $500 to $600 authorization usually covered a limited right to use search in which the searcher looked for any patents that might be infringed by the proposed invention. She said a thorough infringement search would cost much more, but did not recommend such a search at this time.

Now, when you consider the fees charged by an attorney, you should not be overly concerned about whether its $75 or $175 per hour. This may seem surprising and may appear to violate the rule for getting the most value for your money. However, in many cases, the more experienced lawyer is more efficient and will take less time to do a job. Nevertheless, you will consult with a lawyer a number of times and should know what the charges will be. One good rule is to avoid a "cheap" lawyer, but to use a lawyer's time wisely.

Your patent application will probably cost between $1000 and $5000 to file. For example, a typical patent application in today's market tends to run about $2500−$3500 for a fairly straightforward invention, according to a senior partner in an east coast law firm. The range in cost is attributable to the complexity of the invention, the closeness of the prior art, and whether the invention is "basic" to the art or a sophisticated improvement in a highly developed art. Nevertheless, it will probably cost more to have a "prestige" New York City firm prepare an application than it will to have the same work done by a competent midwestern patent lawyer.

John did inquire about a contingent fee but learned that such fees were not usually accepted by patent lawyers. In general, patent lawyers charge either a set fee or an hourly rate for filing applications. Nevertheless, you may want to ask about contingent fees, since a few lawyers may be willing to work for a share of your future income. In my experience, I know several patent lawyers who have taken cases on a contingency basis. However, they were highly selective and based their acceptance of a case on their estimate of an applicant's business ability.

2.6 SUMMARY

The time you spend in selecting a lawyer is a good investment. By asking others about their experiences with a patent lawyer, you will avoid wasting money on an interview with someone you don't like. However, if based on your initial interview, you don't like a lawyer, don't hire that person.

Remember, that you are selecting a key member of your team and that your lawyer can help you to obtain a good patent and to sell your invention.

Contacting a lawyer will cost money. Therefore, don't contact a lawyer until you have carefully and concisely defined your invention. Prepare a list of specific questions to make certain that you use your lawyer's time efficiently.

Remember that you may have a salable invention and that the role of your lawyer is to help you to protect your investment and avoid future legal problems. A good lawyer can also relieve you from worry, so that you as an entrepreneur can concentrate on developing and selling your inventions.

3

The Business of Making Money

If it's not a money maker, don't file a patent application.

3.1 THE IMPORTANCE OF PATENTS

Dr. H. Joseph Gerber is the president of Gerber Scientific, Inc., a company that he founded not long after he conceived his first invention while a junior at Rennselear Polytechnic Institute. After thirty seven years, Gerber Scientific has annual sales of about $200 million and Dr. Gerber has over 200 patents in his name.

"We started with an investment of $3000," Dr. Gerber said, "and an unconventional idea. Today, we are a small, high technology entrepreneurial company with over 800 patents issued or pending." He went on to say, "Many engineers overlook the value of patents. In fact, a number of years ago, a colleague and I did not file for a patent. And then, a few years later, we had to take a license from a third party who obtained a patent on the same invention. That is only one of the reasons why I am a firm believer in the importance of patents."

Joe Gerber has learned a lot about patents over the past thirty seven years. "At first," he said, "we were reluctant to license any of our patents. Actually, we looked at our patents as a way to protect our products and processes. We viewed patents as one of the few allowable monopolies. But then a German machine tool company wanted to take a license under one of our patents that we used for drafting machines. As a result, we learned that licensing our inventions could be very profitable."

Dr. Gerber believes that "Research and development is the lifeblood of a high technology company" and that "If an invention can be licensed it will help pay for its development." He also believes that "Licensing helps a company earn income from foreign markets where the company is not doing business. And, at times, you might want to think in terms of a cross license." Joe said, "Cross licensing offers a unique opportunity to expand a potential market." However, he cautioned, "Cross licensing requires the counsel of an experienced lawyer."

So when you consider the value of your invention, remember that its value to a large degree will depend on what you do with it. In other words, in considering whether or not to file a patent application, decide whether you want to manufacture and sell products, or if you will try to sell your invention to an industrial company and collect a royalty on the products that they use or sell.

As a manufacturer of a patented product, or as an owner of a patented process, you may be able to sell your products with a 40–50% or greater gross margin and make considerably more money than you could from a

5% royalty. In this case, the value of the patent would be measured by your ability to keep a competitor out of the market.

There are problems associated with these higher margins, however. For example, a competitor may copy your product. Therefore, you want to assure yourself that your patent will be effective in limiting competition. You should also bear in mind the high cost associated with patent litigation. In essence, a patent lawsuit can cost each side hundreds of thousands of dollars. And the only way to justify the high cost of litigation is with profits.

Fortunately, some companies respect valid patents. And the Federal Circuit Court of Appeals is finding more patents valid and infringed than some of the other circuit courts did in the past. This should further discourage a competitor from copying your invention.

However, even relatively narrow patents can have significant value for a small manufacturer. For example, you can use them to raise capital and attract distributors, and then you can prevent others from selling a slavish copy of your product. You might also keep some competitors out of the market since they will not assume the risk of patent litigation.

A number of patent lawyers suggest that patents can have a "defensive" value because others may assert their patent rights against you. And then you can suggest a cross license as a way to obtain a license with a more favorable royalty. However, the real value of a so-called defensive patent relates to a subsequent sale of the business and relates to tax considerations that go beyond the scope of the present work.

Patents may be detrimental to a small business. For example, some entrepreneurs believe that the time and money devoted to patents could be better spent in developing a business. This may be true in some cases, particularly where a small manufacturer tries to enforce a marginal or weak patent. You could rely on trade secrets, but don't overlook the costs of maintaining a secret. For example, you could lose sales because some companies will not accept information in confidence.

Now consider the alternative of licensing your idea to a large company. In this case, there is an advantage in having broad coverage. In this case, the value of your patent is the difference between what you can sell your idea for with a patent and what you can sell it for without a patent. And recognize that it is very difficult, if not impossible, to sell an unpatented idea to a large corporation.

Many individuals submit inventions to large companies and receive form replies. Essentially, such a reply states that the company will not recieve any information in confidence and that the individual submitting the invention must rely solely on patent rights for any remuneration. Sometimes you can avoid this type of reply by a carefully drafted letter, which is discussed in Chapter 15. However, you will probably still have a problem unless you have filed your patent application, and are willing to rely on your patent rights as a basis for any payment by the corporation.

Corporations normally use a form reply that is a nonconfidential disclosure agreement. They do this to protect themselves against a claim that they are using someone's idea without paying for it. For example, suppose someone submits an invention that the corporation is already working on. In this case, the corporation would reject the submission and refuse to make any payment to the outsider who submitted the invention until he or she obtained a patent. Besides, if you don't have a patent, what do you have to offer the corporation?

Business executives who run corporations are concerned, and at times almost paranoid, about a competitive advantage. For example, they will not usually pay a 5% royalty on their products if a competitor is free to sell the same product without any payment. However, if you have a patented process by which a company can save thousands of dollars, as compared to their competitor, the company should pay you a percentage of the savings. In the latter case, you may want to develop a strategy that allows you to grant subsequent licenses since lower manufacturing costs might benefit an entire industry and generate more income for you.

Therefore, when you want to sell an invention, think like a corporate manager. Compare the expected profits from your product with the cost of developing another. Compare the manufacturing costs using your process with the costs associated with conventional processes. And if your invention offers a significant profit potential, be realistic. Ask for a fair share of the profit or savings. After all, business managers are concerned about the risk of losing their investment if the product fails or if some competing product reduces their profitability. You can help them reduce their risk by obtaining a strong patent. Nevertheless, you should offer a licensee an opportunity to keep a majority of the profits.

3.2   THE IMPORTANCE OF BROAD COVERAGE

Many lawyers will tell you that "A strong patent is the only kind that is worthwhile." They say, "It is the strong patent, not the weak one, which industry seeks and for which industry pays well." Don't be misled by this familiar argument.

The terms "strong patent" and "broad coverage" are frequently used interchangeably. There is a subtle difference, however. A strong patent suggests that the patent is valid and will be enforced by a court. On the other hand, a broad patent is characterized by an invention that represents a major advance in technology. But even if you have not made a major advance in your field, recognize that even a minor improvement may be economically significant, and may be extremely valuable to industry.

Joe Gerber attributes much of the success of his company to the fact that "We are innovators and have very good patents." He also said, "We have many basic patents." They have basic patents because Joe has the ability to identify problems that need solving. For example, he said, "We targeted the apparel industry with the aim of automating it." As a result, they obtained a basic patent on the way to cut thick piles of material.

But Don Banner said, "A broad patent is great, but you may have difficulty in litigating it. In fact, I view broad claims as a mixed blessing and would prefer the narrowist claim which covers every practical way of doing something or which covers the commercial version."

Don Banner is a good friend with a wealth of knowledge about patents. Actually, Don has so many impressive credentials that it would be difficult to list them. However, to list a few, Don is a partner in the Washington, D.C., law firm of Banner, Birch, McKie and Becket. He is a former U.S. commissioner of Patents and Trademarks, former general patent counsel at Borg Warner, former president of the American Intellectual Property Law Association, The Association of Corporate Patent Counsel, and the International Patent and Trademark Association, and is also a distinguished professor of law at the John Marshall Law School.

Don knows that the strength of a patent may change very suddenly. For example, if you own a strong patent, you might expect a sizable advance payment for an exclusive license. But a prospective licensee would probably initiate a thorough search of the prior art. And, if that search disclosed an early reference that suggested your invention, the presumption of validity of your patent would be weakened and its value diminished.

For example, The Tappan Company of Mansfield, Ohio, obtained two U.S. patents on pilotless ignition systems for gas ovens. In those patents, they claimed a system that included a silicon carbide (solid state) igniter in combination with a thermal valve as a replacement for a pilot light in a gas stove (U.S. Patent Nos. 3,870,457 and 3,968,785). Tappan then sued Caloric, another stove manufacturer, alleging infringement of their patents. In preparing the defense, the attorneys discovered prior art that suggested the features claimed by Tappan. The suit was then settled.

Don Banner explained why many patents have been held invalid by the courts or weakened by subsequent searches. He said, "Essentially, the examination of a patent application is a comparative process. The patent examiner compares what you claim with the prior art that he is aware of." Don went on to say, "There is really little or no difference between the courts' standards of patentability and the standards of the United States Patent and Trademark Office. It is just a matter of finding the best prior art. And, if there is a large commercial market, a competitor will have the incentive to search through the remote corners of the technical literature in an attempt to invalidate a patent."

As Don explained, "There is tremendous pressure on our patent examiners to reduce the backlog of pending patent applications and to issue patents more quickly. And, it is only the integrity of the examiners that maintains the quality of their examinations." What this means to you is that you should conduct a thorough search of the prior art and call the most pertinent prior art to the examiner's attention. After all, the only patent worth having is a good patent, that is, one that has been examined in view of the most pertinent prior art.

Don Banner believes in the patent system. He said, "In my opinion, the patent system is the only defense that the little guy has against the large corporation. For example, a little guy can compete in a real sense if he has a valid patent that covers a commercial product or process. Don mentioned the Square D Company as an example. He said, "Back in the 30s, John Jackson invented and patented an entrance circuit breaker. And his patent enabled the Square D Company to compete with General Electric and Westinghouse. Jackson's invention helped the Square D Company to grow and to become the successful company that it is today."

Now, in lay terms, broad coverage refers to a patent that will not only prevent a competitor from making exact copies of your patented device, or colorable imitations thereof, but also from making something quite different that functions in a similar manner. This broad coverage is appealing to a corporate manager, it may prevent a competitor from coming out with a competitive product.

But narrow patents also have value. For example, the Pangborn Division of the Carborundum Company (now a part of SOHIO) in Hagerstown, Maryland, obtained a patent on a curved vane throwing wheel (U.S. Patent No. 3,872,642). A throwing wheel throws abrasive particles against a workpiece. The patent covered the optimum curvature, that particular curve that produced the best results. Since there were earlier disclosures of curved vanes in the prior art, Pangborn could not prevent their competitor from using such vanes. Pangborn did, however, prevent a competitor from using the optimum design and therefore gained a competitive advantage.

As an inventor, you should recognize one caveat. A competitor who determines that a device can be manufactured and sold while avoiding your claims will probably make that device. Likewise, if the licensee who is manufacturing and selling your product determines that your claims can be avoided, the licensee may do so, and discontinue payments to you.

However, Don Banner said, "In my experience, major corporations will go out of their way to treat an individual fairly." The author has had the same experience.

But if you held a patent on a typewriter correction fluid in which the fluid evaporated more rapidly than water, a licensee might manufacture and sell a water-based product without paying any royalty to you. In fact, many manufactures followed that approach, and learned that the product was not very popular. But if your patent was limited to carbon tetrachloride as a carrier, a licensee might change to another solvent, such as trichlorethylene, have a satisfactory product, and discontinue royalty payments.

3.3 DEVELOPING VALUE

Knowledge is the key to developing your invention. In other words, you should know more about your invention than anyone else. Make use of your computer to search the prior art. Find out what others have done in your field. Then list all of the advantages and disadvantages of your invention from a technical and marketing viewpoint. Learn everything that you can about competitive products. And consider the scope of your invention and, when appropriate, conduct simple experiments to find out if your invention is applicable to other fields.

Start a filing system and keep your clippings and notes on marketing separate from those of a technical nature. Collect marketing information that will establish the size of the market. For example, if your product will be sold to motorcyclists, you should find out how many motorcycles are sold each year. You should consider trends such as a preference for light weight motorcycles versus the larger touring machines.

In reality, an invention development business is based on selling yourself. You must be positive, enthusiastic, and knowledgeable. When you sell your idea to a group of financiers or to a large corporation, it will probably be reviewed by a number of people before it is accepted as a commercial product. What you have to do is pass your enthusiasm on to at least one person, and give that supporter the ammunition needed to sell your invention to others. If you have factual, accurate information, it is more likely that you will sell your invention.

Now in selling an invention, emphasize those features that are most important to your customer. For example, as you study the market, you will learn that certain features are more important to one company than another. You should also be sensitive in order to determine what it is that is most important to a company or individual. For more information on selling your inventions and yourself and on negotiating techniques, the reader is referred to my earlier book, *From Technical Professional to Corporate Manager,* (John Wiley and Sons, 1984).

You can enhance the value of an idea by tailoring it to the needs of a particular business. During the development of an idea, learn everything that you can about those companies that are your potential customers, and design a sales effort that shows how your development fits into each company's business. And to develop the maximum value in your idea, select companies that will do the best job in marketing your invention.

You can also improve your patent position by writing a clear, concise, and complete description of your invention. By distinguishing your invention from those in the prior art, you will be more effective in convincing a patent examiner to issue a good patent on your invention. You will also be more effective in selling your ideas.

Leslie O. Vargady, a prolific inventor, is an expert in the field of optical measuring instruments (metrology). Shortly after coming to this country, Leslie made an invention and consulted his company's patent attorney. A search was conducted and a patent application prepared. Mr. Vargady saw a defect in the claims. Leslie knew that the proposed claims would cover a device that had been sold many years ago in Germany. The claims were redrafted based on the inventor's knowledge, and a strong patent was obtained.

After you or your attorney prepare the patent application, it will be filed in the U.S. Patent and Trademark Office, and examined by a patent examiner. The examiner's job is to determine that your application is in the proper form and that your claims are not anticipated by prior art. Then your knowledge may be required to explain how your invention differs from the prior art that is cited by the examiner.

In considering the value of your patent, keep the breadth of the claims in mind as you pursue the further development of your invention. For example, if you make changes during your development work, verify that those changes are adequately covered by the claims in your patent application. In some cases, it may be necessary to refile your application as a "continuation-in-part application" to cover your latest modifications. In other cases, you may have made an improvement on your invention that justifies a separate application. However, this type of decision should only be made after consultation with your patent lawyer.

The steps contemplated in the previous paragraph can make a significant impact on the salability of your invention. Nevertheless, as a businessperson, you must keep your eye on costs and compare the value of additonal work with the expected return on your investment.

Some years ago, I was asked to evaluate the patent portfolio of a small company. That company had obtained over fifty patents. I reviewed each of their patents and found that not one single claim covered a commercial product. It was obvious that there had been a failure in communications between marketing and the attorneys who filed the patent applications.

3.4   THE BASIC RULE OF INTEGRITY

Donald Banner has a basic rule about integrity in the U.S. Patent and Trademark Office. He tells his students, "Don't play games with the Patent Office." He tells them that they should be "the soul of integrity." Don tells them this because he knows that "Getting something that you don't deserve is asking for trouble."

Don also points out, "You can help yourself by making certain that the patent examiner is aware of the most pertinent prior art. For example, you should file a prior art disclosure statement which lists the most pertinent prior art that you are aware of."

Integrity in dealing with the U.S. Patent and Trademark Office also means that, if you perform a number of tests to illustrate how your invention differs from the prior art, you are obligated to report all of the facts. Do not suppress results that might tend to disprove your arguments. To do so might destroy whatever value you may develop in your invention.

3.5   THE IMPORTANCE OF TIMING

Time is of the essence in most patent proceedings. For example, if you offer a product embodying your invention for sale or publicly disclose it prior to filing a patent application, you will lose your patent rights in most foreign countries. And if you fail to file the application within one year of the disclosure or offer you will lose your U.S. rights as well.

Also consider the effect of timing on the sale of your idea. It will probably take about a year or perhaps a little longer from the date of filing a patent application until you receive your first office action from the U.S. Patent and Trademark Office. Actually, the U.S. Patent and Trademark Office tries to issue a first action well within one year and may achieve the goal in some areas.

"You should contact a company just as soon as you have filed your patent application," according to William Webb, a prominent Pittsburg patent lawyer. The advantage of an early sale is that further development costs will be paid by the licensee. Besides, it is desirable to pass any foreign filing costs on to your licensee and at the same time, let the licensee participate in the decision for foreign filing.

3.6 SUMMARY

It is up to you to make the most of what you have. If you are enthusiastic, persevere, and take a businesslike approach to selling inventions, you can succeed.

And in developing your invention, further development work should be accompanied by a regular patent review. Also, remember to analyze the market carefully and direct your attention to the needs of the marketplace. If you do this, you may have the basis for your own manufacturing company, or perhaps select a licensee and establish a long and mutually rewarding association.

In essence, know your product, understand your market, and sell successfully.

4

Establishing Your Rights

*Before you spend any money on a patent application, make certain that you own the invention.**

Stanley Lieberstein

4.1 OWNERSHIP

Do you own what is in your head? Do you own any inventions that you make? "You do unless you have given your rights away," according to Stanley Lieberstein. "The problem is that you may have inadvertently forfeited your rights by signing an employment contract or by using your employer's facilities to work on your invention," according to Mr. Lieberstein. Another potential problem is that someone else may have made the same invention. That other inventor may have already reduced it to practice, filed a patent application, or even obtained a patent.

Therefore, determine who owns your invention before you invest your time and money to develop it. And then, assuming that you own it, you will want to protect your rights. Now, to evaluate your rights, review any employment contracts that you have signed, and consider the importance of your written records.

4.2 WRITTEN RECORDS

Your rights will probably depend on your written records. Therefore you should keep good records. Follow the advice of Peter Shaffer (see Chapter 1) and keep these records in a safe place. And don't throw them away, even after you obtain a patent on your invention. Now, if you have not already started to keep an engineering notebook, buy a bound notebook with sequentially numbered, lined, but otherwise blank pages. These notebooks are similar to the ones given to engineers by large corporations. In corporate practice each volume is numbered, and all engineers are provided with their own notebooks. However, don't use a company notebook for your personal work. Buy your own notebook, since it is a minor expense and an excellent investment. Besides, it is probably tax deductible.

Now, If you work as an engineer or scientist for a large corporation, you should have learned that an engineering notebook is a diary of your technical activities. You probably know that the company provides engineering notebooks and instructions on their use because it is cost-justified by the value of the written records. And, if you read Chapter 1, you know that Peter Shaffer believes that his notebooks are extremely valuable to him as an entrepreneur.

Therefore, recognize that the development of your invention is a serious business and should be conducted in an orderly manner. Recognize that accurate records are indispensable. They should be complete and, in the field of invention development, kept on a daily basis. In keeping a record of your activities include your successes as well as your failures.

To keep a record of your invention, write a description of your idea and all of its features, and make a sketch or drawing that illustrates the idea as well as how it works. For example, if you were the inventor of U.S. Patent No. 4,445,688 to Frillici et al., you might have recorded your original concept as follows:

> This morning, I was considering the problem of "break-in" with plastic coated bowling pins and had an idea that a woodcore with an ionomer resin coating could result in a bowling pin with improved characteristics.
>
>   Signed:
> Witnessed: Dated:

This record, like all of your records, should be in ink. Then, after completing a daily record, sign the entry in the notebook and date it. And the initial description of your invention should be witnessed. However, the proper use of witnesses is described in more detail in Section 4.3.

You should also recognized that records are not a substitute for a patent application, but are a valuable adjunct. Just remember, your records may make the difference between receiving a large income and the loss of your invention. In other words, take the time that is required to keep good written records.

In maintaining your records, keep track of the hours that you worked on each project. If your work is interrupted for a period of time, such as a hospitalization, this fact should be recorded in your notebook. There is one good reason for keeping a record of your time and any interruptions in your work. The reason is that if your application is involved in an interference proceeding, a record of your efforts may make the difference in winning or losing the interference. Your records may make the difference between getting a patent on your own invention and infringing someone else's patent. And as an entrepreneur, you should also include a list of any incidental expenses that you incurred in developing your invention.

Stan Lieberstein said, "In order to protect your rights, make certain that your written description of your invention speaks for itself." Make certain that your written description does not require an oral explanation. Describe your experiments in detail and report your results accurately. Stan advises, "Describes all tests, measurements, designs, and drawings in a manner so that a person of ordinary skill in your field can understand what you have done."

There is one other fact that ought to be recorded and witnessed. When you actually make a device that incorporates all of the features of your invention or use your invention, record this fact and have the entry witnessed and dated. In doing so, use care in defining each feature that is incorporated in your device. Use care because this "reduction to practice" is one of the most important facts in establishing your rights to your invention.

For example, you might after further work on the ionomer coated bowling pin record a reduction to practice as follows:

Today, I mixed ionomer resin pellets (Surlyin 1707 with 2% by weight of titanium dioxide pigment) and injection molded two preforms which corresponded to the exterior configuration of one half of a bowling pin (viewed endwise). A precisely contoured maple core was then placed between the 2 preforms and molded on our laboratory press at a temperature of 300° to 350°F and under a pressure of 45 tons. The resin coated core was cooled to about 120°F, removed from the mold, deflashed, cleaned, and painted with epoxy paint.
Signed:
Witnessed: Dated:

Later, you would record further details from your test results. In doing so, record the composition of Surlyn 1707 as well as other ionomer resins that should be tested and details of the processing parameters in making additional pins.

Stan Lieberstein said, "Your records should show when your work was done, who did the work, and the date of the written record." He added, "Don't change your records or leave spaces in your notebook for future insertions. And if you take photos, record that fact, and when the prints are obtained, insert them in your notebook on the day they are received."

Keeping good records is really very easy. Just maintain a daily log, and at the end of each day, make an appropriate entry. Or, write up an experiment and record the experimental data as it is obtained. Then, at the end of the day, sign your name and the date. Don't put off your recordkeeping until tomorrow.

Many patent lawyers would advise you to be as accurate as possible, since any ambiguities in your records could cost you the rights to a valuable invention. Use commercial designations for describing components when possible. If, for example, your invention includes an electrical amplifier, your written record might read: A Bogen model DB 230 amplifier was connected in series to a . . . Such a description would be more complete and accurate than: An amplifier was connected to . . .

Your description should teach another person how to practice your invention. Remember that another person may be unfamiliar with your invention and that your description should explain your invention in a way that can be clearly understood. The problem is that your idea may be so clear in your own mind that it is easy to forget essential details that are necessary to give someone else a complete picture. Use care and avoid this problem.

Another advantage in keeping good records, one that is seldom mentioned by patent lawyers, is that it will enable you to go back and review what you have done in the past. At times, it may help you to understand why an experiment didn't work or keep you from repeating earlier mistakes.

4.3 WITNESSES

"Your uncorroborated records will probably be insufficient to establish your legal rights," according to Stanley Lieberstein. Therefore, select a witness who will be available to corroborate your records. Your witness should also be impartial, so do not use a co-worker if there is a possibility that person might be a co-inventor. If a court determined that the co-worker was a joint inventor, they might consider such testimony to be self-serving.

If, however, a co-worker is serving in the role of a technician or mechanic, and all work is being done under your direction and control, that co-worker could be the most likely witness. In this case, you should have your co-worker keep an accurate record of all progress, and you should occasionally witness his or her entries.

Ask your witnesses to sign their names and the date with a statement "witnessed and understood." And make certain that the witnesses do understand your disclosure. At some future date they may be called on to testify in a court or patent office proceeding and should be able to testify that they witnessed your record and understood it at that time.

So, in selecting witnesses, choose two so that at least one of them will be available at some future date. You should also select witnesses who will respect your rights and keep your information confidential.

Of course, the use of two witnesses may increase the likelihood of a premature disclosure. Therefore, you should pursue the development of your invention with diligence. Do everything that you can to get your patent application prepared and filed as soon as possible.

4.4 PROOF IS REQUIRED

At times, you may have difficulty in proving that you are entitled to your invention. For example, in those cases where two people file patent applications that claim the same invention, the U.S. Patent and Trademark Office will declare an interference. An interference is a complex proceeding to determine which inventor will receive a patent. However, you can improve your chance of obtaining a patent if you keep good records. Then you can use those records to prove that you were the first inventor.

You can frequently win an interference if you can prove that you were the first to reduce your invention to practice. However, if you were the first to conceive the idea, but the second to reduce it to practice, you can still win the interference if you can prove that you were diligent in your development work. For example, the U.S. Patent and Trademark Office rules require that an inventor involved in an interference proceeding state "The date after conception of the invention when active exercise of reasonable diligence toward reducing the invention to practice began."

Now, in considering how your rights are affected by a reduction to practice, it is necessary to introduce two new terms: "generic" and "species." A generic claim can be defined as a general claim, one that covers the invention as broadly stated. The species claims are each directed to a specific embodiment of your invention and are more limited, or narrower, than the generic claim.

One example of a generic claim relates to a pilotless ignition system for a gas stove. The generic claim calls for a thermal valve and an "igniter" connected in series to the thermal valve. A species claim would call for a specific type of igniter, such as "a silicon carbide igniter" or, in another claim, a "molybdenum disilicide igniter."

One reason for distinguishing between these terms is to illustrate the importance of adequate records. For example, you may have to prove when you reduced each species of your invention to practice. And, if all of your work was done on a single species and that of the other party on a different species, you may not be entitled to a generic claim. Therefore, you should experiment with several embodiments of your invention to adequately support your rights to a generic claim and should keep good records of your experiments.

A patent interference proceeding is one of the more complicated legal proceedings that you might encounter. However, those of you unfortunate enough to be involved in an interference should review *Patent Interference Law and Practice* by Maurice H. Klitzman (Practicing Law Institute,

1984). This book covers the essential aspects of patent interferences, and even though it is intended for lawyers, it is a readable text that can be understood by a technical professional. However, please note that the procedures are quite complex and that you should always rely on competent counsel for advice in this area. In addition, the rules for interference procedures were changed in 1985. Nevertheless, the book is still worth reading.

In addition to the rights that may be won or lost in an interference proceeding, your rights to an invention may be affected by a contract. For example, in some government contracts, all patent rights that are first conceived or first reduced to practice under the contract become the property of the U.S. government. Therefore, if you have made an invention and filed a patent application on it, you could still lose your rights if you enter into a contract with the government before reducing your invention to practice.

You should not be misled by a "constructive reduction to practice." When you file your patent application, you will effect a constructive reduction to practice. In an interference proceeding, a constructive reduction to practice is treated in the same way as an actual reduction to practice. However, the constructive reduction to practice may be ineffective for preserving your rights under government contracts. Therefore, get legal advice before you sign a contract.

4.5   BEWARE OF EMPLOYMENT CONTRACTS

Most major corporations will require you to sign an employment contract. These contracts require an inventor to assign his or her inventions to the employer. The contracts are frequently presented with a plethora of other papers such as insurance papers, pension program, documents for security clearance, and the like, so that many employees sign the contracts without adequate consideration. Don't make this mistake.

In fact, employment agreements are carefully drafted legal documents that have been prepared by the company's lawyers. The purpose of the contract is to protect the company's interests. The problem is that few people question the scope of their agreement. Stan Lieberstein says, "In a few cases, the agreements are overreaching and require an employee to assign all of his inventions to the company instead of limiting the employer's obligation to those inventions relating to the work done for the company."

However, you can usually avoid problems if you read your agreement before signing, and if in doubt, consult with your lawyer. In any case, make certain to get a copy of your agreement. Don't lose it or discard it. Remember that this is a legal document that affects your rights.

Stan Lieberstein said, "Don't ask your new employer's lawyer for advice about your employment contract since he represents the company and cannot ethically represent you. His loyalty belongs to his client. However, if you are concerned, contact your lawyer."

There is another important provision in most employment contracts. That provision states that you will be given confidential information. The contract will also require you to keep this information confidential. Many engineers overlook this obligation or fail to recognize the legal liability for a breach of this obligation. As an entrepreneur, the last thing that you need is a lawsuit by your former employer that alleges that you have misappropriated confidential information.

Many agreements have a provision where you can exclude inventions that you made prior to the agreement. Under this provision, you can exclude a field in which you are doing independent work. And if the field is adequately defined and outside of your employer's field of interest, you should have no problems. However, few companies would accept an exclusion of any development in the chemical field, particularly if you are a chemical engineer. If, however, you exclude work on the electro-chemical deposition of chrome, you would avoid problems with most companies unless you were hired to work in that specific field.

Make any changes in your employment contract before you sign the agreement. You should also be cautious about signing any agreement if you are already working on an idea. Even though the agreement may be limited to products or processes relating to the company's business, you might be surprised to learn that the scope of their business includes your area of interest. To be safe, exclude all of your previous ideas. Besides, by listing numerous ideas, you are showing that you are a creative individual.

A number of companies provide for the assignment of your inventions even though you make the invention after termination of your employment. This type of provision may seem to be unreasonable. Nevertheless, if you sign the agreement, you may be bound by its terms. However, it may be appropriate for you to ask for a consulting fee to be paid during any such period. For example, you might suggest a consulting fee equal to one or more months pay per year for each year of the obligation. The rational for this suggestion would be that the agreement limits your ability to work for someone else during the term of the consulting contract. Besides, the company should pay you for your time in submitting inventions to them after termination of your employment.

Before leaving the subject of employment contracts, consider your obligation to keep information confidential. In view of this obligation, don't divulge any of your company's confidential information to outsiders or use any such information except for the company.

Then when you leave an employer, make certain that you return all of the company's files, memoranda, information, and the like to the company. This step might avoid the possibility of some future claim that your rights were dependent on the use of their material. It will also help to establish your reputation for integrity.

As an entrepreneur, take reasonable precautions to avoid disputes with your employer. At the very least, they will take time, and they may require the use of legal counsel. Don't sacrifice your rights, and don't spend your money needlessly.

As a prudent business person, read any agreement carefully before signing it. Ask questions before signing, and if you have signed an agreement, keep your copy in a safe place. If it was lost, obtain another copy. Don't rely on what you think your agreement says or on someone else's agreement.

Of course, you may need to consult with an outside lawyer to determine if you are obligated to assign an invention to your employer. For example, you might ask if an invention relating to an electric lawnmower made on an employee's own time belongs to the employer, a large aerospace company. In one such case, the employee was hired to work on the design of an airplane, and yet, according to the terms of the inventor's contract, the employer owned the lawnmower invention. Remember, don't guess when your rights are involved.

There is one other rule to consider before leaving the subject of employment contracts. The situation arises from time to time and usually involves a disgruntled employee. In essence, don't try to hide your idea and quit your job with a plan to develop the idea on your own.

4.6   USING YOUR EMPLOYER'S FACILITIES

"In the absence of an agreement, an employer acquires title only if the invention falls within the scope of the employee's duties," according to Stan Lieberstein.

Even when an employee acquires title, the law does give certain rights to an employer. Stan Lieberstein says, "If you have an invention, don't use your employer's facilities or materials to work on your invention. Do your work at home and on your own time." The reason for this is that if you use your employer's facilities or materials to develop an invention, your employer will obtain a royalty free license (a shop right) to use your invention. This license lasts forever and is not extinguished by the sale of the business.

You may think that this isn't a bad deal, particularly if your employer has extensive facilities. However, the shop right would preclude you from granting some other manufacturer an exclusive right to make, use, and sell products covered by your patent. And without an exclusive license, a prospective licensee may reject your offer of a license.

Just remember, the development of your idea is a business. And as an entrepreneur, you should make certain that you own an invention before you invest your time and money in its development.

4.7 CONSIDER YOUR HELPER'S CONTRIBUTIONS

It may be difficult to determine who the actual inventor is at the time of filing a patent application because your original invention may not be patentable. For example, it may have been one of your helpers who suggested an alternative or some modification that encompasses the patentable subject matter. In other cases, you may learn that what you thought was your invention turns out to be a joint one.

Generally, if you have an invention and do all of the work on its development, you will be the sole inventor. If, however, you come up with an idea that looks like a significant invention, but someone else also works on the idea, that person may make a valuable improvement. And if a patent search indicates that the broad concept is unpatentable, the only invention might reside in the improvement.

Some years ago, Dr. Robert J. Meltzer was asked to develop a fiber optic device that would encode a person's signature. The concept of translating portions of signature to different locations was straightforward; however, to reproduce the devices would have been expensive. Bob overcame the problem of high cost for reproduction, invented a low cost fiber optic device, and was awarded U.S. Patent No. 3,145,247.

Then Dr. Meltzer questioned whether or not the same result could be achieved by lenses at a lower cost. He had an idea to use a screen of glass rods that, when placed over a signature, would distort it beyond recognition. Then, after photographing the result, the rods would be placed on the photograph, and the image received would be a reproduction of the original signature.

Dr. Meltzer had invented and actually reduced to practice an optical cryptographic device. The problem was that is wasn't quite good enough for the proposed application, which was to encode the signature on a bank passbook or credit card. The solution appeared to lie in the use of a screen of spherical lenses in place of the glass rods (cylindrical lenses). But for some reason, the spherical lenses didn't work. Dr. Meltzer discussed the problem with an associate, John Ferris, who suggested the addition of an objective lens in the optical system. A device was built according to John's suggestion and it worked. Robert Meltzer and John Ferris were joint inventors and obtained U.S. Patent No. 3,178,933 on their optical cryptographic device.

4.8   SUMMARY

If you want to protect your rights, written records are essential. So if you don't have a written description of your invention yet, write one now. Don't wait until you read the balance of this book. Time may be of the essence.

And when you write the description of your invention, write legibly and keep your records in ink with an appropriate sketch to establish a clear meaning for your description. Carefully record in a bound volume the date of your original idea, dates of drawings, the date when you started to make a device according to your invention, the date of its completion, dates of tests, and results.

Remember that your rights depend on your records, which should begin with the moment of conception.Records that are witnessed by competent individuals may be your key to success. Work diligently to obtain a reduction to practice, and as soon as you are convinced that your idea is viable, seek patent protection.

But before doing anything else, assure yourself that you have the right to file for a patent on your invention. Clarify the status and obligations imposed by any employment contracts. Don't lose your rights by using your employer's facilities or by seeking the aid of a less-then-scrupulous invention promoter.

Those of you who would like a more thorough review of your rights versus those of an employer can read: *Who Owns What's In Your Head* (Hawthorn Books, 1979), by Stanley Lieberstein.

5

Applying Management Techniques

Your goal as a manager should be to produce the maximum return from your investment.

5.1   GENERAL CONCEPTS

Thomas W. Butler, Jr., is the dean of engineering at the Oakland campus
of the University of Michigan. He was formerly vice president of research
and engineering at AMF Incorporated and co-author of *Planned Innovation* (the University of Michigan, 1981). Tom has spent over twenty-five
years in new product development.

Tom Butler believes, "New products are the lifeblood of any firm." And
yet, he said, "it is very difficult for an entrepreneur to launch a successful
company based on new technology." However, he admits, "It can be done."

The basic problem, according to Tom, "Is that most independent inventors don't understand market needs. For some reason, they just will not
take a market-oriented approach. And then, too, many entrepreneurs
focus on invention instead of innovation." He said, "An invention is a
solution to a technical problem, while innovation is the commercially
successful use of the solution." He went on to say, "If they obtain an
in-depth understanding of market needs, focus their efforts on innovation,
and use systematic and efficient procedures, they can succeed."

Now as an independent inventor or as an entrepreneur, you should
understand and apply management techniques in developing your invention.

"Return on investment is only one measure of management efficiency,"
according to Tom Butler. However, it is a good technique for evaluating an
invention development program. This means that you should estimate the
amount of money required to bring your invention to the commercial
market. You should also include some value for your time. Then apply
discounted cash flow for calculating the present value of your projected
future income. And if there is a reasonable return on your investment,
continue with your development efforts.

Now when you consider return on investment, don't underestimate
inflation. For example, assuming that inflation may return to 14% per
year, the present value of $100 one year in the future at a 14% inflation
rate will be $86. And since the rate of inflation is compounded over the
years, the value of the same $100 projected five years in the future will
be only $51,94.

Your business analysis should include risk, since there is always risk
with any new development. Thus, your investment in the early stages of
development should be given a greater weight than an investment during
the later stages when your invention is ready for marketing.

Don't, like so many inventors and managers of new product development, underestimate risk. Be realistic. But be optimistic and enthusiastic

about your invention, because if you are not, you will probably fail to sell your invention. Don't be discouraged, as there is a relatively simple rule that many business executives use when they consider risk and inflation. They apply a discounted cash flow of 20% or greater to compensate for risk and inflation. This means that your investment of $100 today would, five years from now, have a value of $40.19. In other words, you would have to generate $248.82 at the end of five years to break even on today's $100 investment.

This brief introduction to return on investment and risk analysis shows how a financial manager would look at an investment in your venture. It also provides a relatively simple evaluation technique for your own financial investment.

But don't limit your analyses of a potential business to actual costs. Consider your investment in time and what it takes to launch a new business. As Peter Shaffer said, "Be prepared to live with your business twenty-four hours a day, seven days a week."

And don't overlook the advantages of starting your own business. For example, you can frequently get started with a small capital investment. In essence, you have a good invention and a willing worker. Assuming that there is a market need, you can use your own capabilities and minimize the actual money that you invest.

Using your time effectively and as efficiently as possible is a good rule. You can do this if you keep track of the hours spent in actual work on your development, and then assign a reasonable hourly rate for your worth as a measure of your investment. If for example, you normally earn $20 per hour, use that figure for evaluating your investment. If you can earn time and one-half during off hours, the higher value would be appropriate. And don't overlook the effect of taxes in considering your investment and potential return. After all, as an entrepreneur, you are interested in after-tax dollars.

You can also profit from the tax advantages that are inherent in your business. For example, you can convert your time into money and yet, by properly structuring the sale, your income may qualify as capital gains. This means that the income from your business may be subjected to a lower tax than ordinary income. However, the tax laws are complex and constantly changing. For these reasons they are not discussed in detail.

Nevertheless, you should recognize the benefit of capital gains treatment and whenever possible structure the actual sale of your invention to maximize after-tax income. This is true even if you establish your own manufacturing business and hope to sell the company some time in the future, or if you develop an invention and license it. And as you become more successful, obtain the services of a tax lawyer or accountant.

Now, in seeking an early pay-off from an invention, do not lose sight of the long-range potential. It is almost impossible to sell an untried idea for a million dollars. However, you can maximize your return from the sale of your inventions if you are willing to compromise. For example, if you have put forth a reasonable effort to protect, develop, and test an invention, you should obtain some initial payment at the time of selling it. You will also want a reasonable royalty on future sales. For example, a 3−5% royalty is usually reasonable.

There is one other approach to licensing that is worth considering. If you decide to license your invention, seek an arrangement under which a licensee will pay you as a consultant during any development period that precedes commercial sales. But remember, your primary concern is to assure the commercial success of your invention. More details on business terms and arrangements are covered in Chapter 17.

Now, before going further, recognize the importance of minimizing your own investment. Minimizing your investment can be accomplished by transferring the development expenses to an industrial licensee as soon as possible. This means that you should do the least amount of work that is necessary to sell your invention. Then, if you couple this concept with a consulting agreement, you can be paid to develop your own invention.

5.2 MANAGING A NEW DEVELOPMENT

Many major corporations consider the commercial potential of an idea before investing their money in a patent application. Such corporations review hundreds of ideas each year and their managers realize that only a few will become commercially successful. Tom Butler said, "You should not be discouraged by this poor batting average because you can do far better if you screen your inventions based on market needs."

In corporate practice, the initial screening of ideas involves an evaluation of the market potential, and then a technical economic feasibility study. A corporate evaluation also includes a patent search to determine whether the company can obtain a patent on the idea, or if infringement problems will be encountered when the company markets a product. Many companies today, as suggested by Tom Butler, put more emphasis on the marketability of the new product than on its technical merits. The argument in favor of this approach is that, if the product doesn't sell, all else is irrelevant.

As an entrepreneur, you do not want to follow all of the practices used in large companies. Nevertheless, if you understand their approach, you can structure your presentation to convince a particular company to invest in your invention.

In order to sell your invention, consider how a large company functions. And then sell yourself and your invention by emphasizing the company's needs. In this way you can use their financial resources to promote your invention. Don't overlook the fact that small companies are also interested in new products and can be approached in a similar manner. And while small companies may be less sophisticated than their larger competitors, many of them make up for any lack of sophistication with good judgment and an aggressive style.

But before proceeding with the development of your invention or its sale, construct a business plan. This business plan is for your own use and also for use as a selling tool. This plan should include an executive summary, market strategy, technical considerations, patent and legal, production and financial sections.

As you work on your business, keep a file for each of these various segments. Then information can be filed and be at hand when needed. One approach to a business plan is to use a loose-leaf notebook with manila dividers for each section.

5.3   MARKET EVALUATION

In many cases you can evaluate the market potential for your invention in a very short time at a relatively low cost. It is true that sophisticated market research is expensive, but in most cases it will not be needed to sell your invention. If it is needed, such expensive research can usually be deferred until after you have sold your invention to someone who will pay for the study.

Ask yourself: What is it that you really need to know? You need to know the size of your potential market. How is it defined? How can you best reach those people who will buy a product that incorporates your idea? What type of distribution system will you use and how much will it cost?

Never underestimate the difficulty in marketing new products. For example, William S., president of a small communications company, addressed this problem. He had sold sophisticated electronics equipment for a major corporation and assumed that he could easily sell the simplified equipment for his new company.

The problem was that the new company, unlike Bill's previous employer, did not have an established reputation. Customers questioned the new company's ability to provide spare parts or back up a guarantee. Through perseverance, Bill overcame this problem and built a successful company.

As a general rule, spend at least three days in your public library before you spend your first dollar in developing an invention. And when you go to the public library, think in terms of Tom Butler's advice. He said, "Use care to define a market segment and then focus your attention on meeting the needs within that segment." He also suggested, "Identify those forces which will drive your business. For example, what will be the effect of higher energy costs, legislation, and toxic waste disposal? What will be the effect of new legislation to reduce the levels of tetraethyl lead in gasoline? Just remember, you need an in-depth understanding of the market and then focus your efforts on your customers needs."

Now, those of you who want a better understanding of these concepts and a better understanding of market screening, trend analysis, and the like should read *Planned Innovation* by F. R. Bacon, Jr. and T. W. Butler, Jr. (University of Michigan, 1981).

As an entrepreneur, you should become familiar with the available marketing tools if you want to license one of your inventions. In that case, you can ask your licensee to conduct market research as part of their obligation. And if the company does those studies, make certain that you receive a copy of the findings. If you believe that market research will really help in selling your project, you can suggest that a part of the payment for the study be treated as an advance against future royalties or for an option to enter into a license agreement. There is also the advantage to you that, if the company terminates your agreement, you will have more to sell to a subsequent licensee.

You can also obtain meaningful information by working with an industrial company. For example, when you first try to sell your invention, you can obtain information about marketing from your prospective licensee. Listen to and remember what is said during the initial meeting. And then, if the company offers to look into the market, cooperate by working with them. When you go to the library, try to identify potential customers for your invention. For example, start with *Thomas' Register,* which lists companies by product. Then analyze your prospects. Top sales people stress the importance of qualifying a prospective customer. See, for example, *How to Sell Anything to Anybody* by Joe Girard (Simon and Schuster, 1977). Your job is to qualify those companies that are most likely to buy your inventions, and then concentrate your efforts on the best candidate.

You can also learn about marketing from industrial publications. In reviewing industrial publications use the reader inquiry cards to obtain information about similar products and their properties. Also, look for information on products that will be replaced because of your idea.

Now in evaluating a market, don't underestimate the ability of your competitors. For example, if your product displaces theirs, they may modify their products, lower their prices, increase advertising, or take some other step to protect their share of the market.

There is one other approach to consider during your library review. Consider the successful commercialization of similar products. For example, if you had had the initial idea for a motor home, you might have drawn an analogy between motor homes and boats as an illustration of market potential. A less apparent analogy would be in-ground swimming pools, which are somewhat less expensive, but do compete for a family's recreational expenditures. In either of these examples, you may have overlooked the potential for sales to corporations that use motor homes as traveling showrooms.

The point to remember is to list all of the potential applications for your invention. Analyze the potential market for each application and then try to estimate the time required to commercialize that application. And, as Peter Shaffer suggested, don't spread yourself too thin. Be realistic about your resources. And analyze timing in the same way as potential market size. Read case histories and find a product that has some similarity to yours. Then use these analogies to sell your inventions.

When you are considering the market potential for your invention, don't overlook the value of trade associations and U.S. government statistics. For example, if your product relates to home swimming pools, there is a wealth of information available from the Swimming Pool Manufacturers Trade Association that shows the growth in sales over a number of years. Similar information would be available on automatic skimmers, swimming pool chemicals, and other related products.

In some cases, a telephone request will produce a wealth of information because many trade associations have general information that they will send out on request. You can identify an appropriate trade association by checking your local library for a list of trade associations and then call or write to the ones in your area of interest.

The key to conducting effective library research is to obtain the assistance of a librarian. Recognize that many librarians have a wealth of knowledge and an ability to find information. However, first look in the subject card index and obtain background information. Many librarians are eager to help you, but it is a matter of courtesy to do what you can before asking them for assistance. Assume that you will use the library frequently and will need additional help. For this reason establish a good working relationship with the library staff. "Please," and "Thank you," are small words and a small price to pay for important information. Don't forget to use these words often.

As you go through a preliminary market evaluation, establish the size of the potential market. In many cases these figures will be fairly easy to establish. For example, information from the Bureau of the Census will give you the number of families in the United States and in various regions. In addition, the number of households, number of families with a certain level of income, number of automobiles, motorcycles, farms, and many other facts are readily available from government statistics. However, it is up to you to obtain the information and use it in selling your inventions. Then use the information to show that you have facts, rather than mere speculation. Remember that, in the words of an effective sales person, the most difficult job is to sell yourself. By knowing and using facts, you will establish your credibility.

Of course, there are times when you may have to resort to speculation. If, for example, the Bureau of Tourism reports that 12,000,000 tourists visit Niagara Falls annually, you can only speculate on how many would pay x dollars to attend a particular attraction. You could, however, learn how many visit a small museum that costs 25 cents and the number who pay several dollars to visit an aquarium. Knowledge of the latter figures would be more convincing to a business executive than a guess that 10% of the tourists might attend a particular attraction.

One important question to consider is: Does a market really exist for your invention? Or will it be necessary to create one? Consider the market for motorcycles after World War II. The primary market was for the large U.S.-built machines. And yet the Japanese created an entirely new and much larger market for their light weight motorcycles. Creating a market is expensive and almost impossible for an individual, but if the potential is there, the rewards may be very large.

In general, estimate marekt growth conservatively and take into account government intervention. If, for example, your product requires approval by the Food and Drug Administration, you will be confronted with another hurdle. And you may not have the resources to prove that your product does not have any adverse side effects.

Price determination is another consideration. Sometimes, price is related to cost and at this stage is, at best, an approximation. Nevertheless, markets are usually price sensitive. Therefore, consider what the market will bear. In general, try to estimate price sensitivity based on the pricing of competitive products, and learn all that you can about an industry's pricing structure in your area of interest.

In 1960, a company was developing an instrument for fitting contact lenses and asked a well known research institute to conduct a study of the potential market. The initial study indicated that there would be a large market that was only slightly price sensitive between $1700 and $2500. However, the study failed to disclose the difficulty in selling to the ophthalmologists and optometrists. In fact, at that time, most of the equipment for eye testing was sold by two major companies, each of which provided favorable financing. The product for fitting contact lenses failed because the company did not understand marketing and pricing within the industry.

You may have difficulty in finding information on pricing. However, you might be more successful at a university library. Those schools that have an MBA (Masters of Business Administration) program frequently have a more extensive business library. These libraries will probably have a number of studies on pricing in various industries.

Unfortunately, there is very little information at a library on how much to charge a corporation for a patent license. However, suggestions for pricing a patent license are found in Part III of this book.

Now when you evaluate a consumer product don't overlook the high cost for consumer advertising. If there is an advertising agency nearby, take one of the associates to lunch and ask for an opinion on the costs for launching a hypothetical new product. At lunch, discuss typical costs for introducing a new product on a local, regional, or national scale. You should learn what will be required to convert your idea into a commercial success, but don't be discouraged by advertising costs; just be realistic.

For example, Lee Scott of Denver, Colorado, developed a new furniture polish in 1925. He thought that his mixture made the furniture look better than any other product on the local market. He named his product "Scott's Liquid Gold" and started to sell bottles of it to his neighbors. Two years later he sold his business to Rose and John Hartman.

Rose Hartman assembled a sales force of Denver housewives and in the next twenty-five years sold about 15,000 bottles of Scott's Liquid Gold. When she reached her seventies, her eyesight began to give out, and she was forced to sell her business (bottles, corks, and Lee Scott's secret formula) for $350.00 to Jerome J. Goldstein and his two brothers.

Goldstein gradually began to expand his business. After spending $7500 for local advertising in 1953, sales reached $19,000 and then, with additional advertising, grew to $179,000 in 1969. In 1970 advertising was increased to $688,000, which generated sales of over $1 million. Advertising was again increased until it reached $10 million. At that time Scott's Liquid Gold was being promoted on popular TV programs such as Johnny Carson, Mike Douglas, and David Frost. As a result, sales reached $16 million annually.

This case illustrates the fact that an individual can successfully launch a consumer product and build a company based on that product. It also illustrates the high cost of advertising. And, unless you have the ability to manage a marketing oriented business, seek expert help. With expert help you may be able to sell your business for considerably more than Rose Hartman received from Jerome Goldstein.

When you visit the library, find out if they have a copy of the *Manual of Patent Classification of the United States Patent and Trademark Office* and a subscription to the *Official Gazette*. Both are available at many large libraries.

The *Official Gazette* (published weekly) includes the title and a representative claim for each new U.S. patent. The patents are grouped into general and mechanical, chemical, electrical, and design sections. They are also classified by a class and subclass as set forth in the *Manual of Classification*. For example, if your interest is in surgical devices, you would look in the *Gazette* for all new patents issued in Class 128. Most inventors will find that it is worthwhile to review at least one or two *Official Gazettes*.

One or two copies of the *Official Gazette* will give you an indication of the type of developments that are being patented. Besides, once you have identified a specific field of interest, you can limit your review to those classes in the *Gazette*. Then you can review several months' *Gazettes* for an overview of new developments in your field.

5.4   TECHNICAL EVALUATION

"There is a lot of good technology around," Tom Butler said, "and there is a lot of available money. But when you come down to it, it is very difficult to get money to develop new technology." He added, "A number of states, counties, and regions have tried to remedy this problem and attract high technology companies to their areas." He also said, "A number of corporations are also taking a minority interest in new ventures. However, for an individual to get started, he will have to have a lot of persistence. He will also do a lot better if he can find an angel for the initial financing."

There is one particular problem in raising the initial capital for a new venture that is based on new technology. The problem is, "Most venture capitalists don't have the expertise to evaluate new technology," according to Paul Erlandson. Paul Erlandson is a partner in the Connecticut Venture Management Corporation, which deals with a full range of services to start up ventures. He has over forty years experience in new technology development and is responsible for over forty patents.

Paul said, "A technical evaluation frequently involves a second opinion. And the problem is that an individual who works with a venture capital company may have to review several business plans a day. He just doesn't have the time or resources to get a second opinion. Besides, it's a lot easier to base his investment decisions on an established cash flow, something that he can understand."

Paul went on to say, "Today, there is more hope for an entrepreneur since a number of venture capitalists are starting to consider new technology." In fact, Paul questions whether today's large corporations are flexible enough to cope with the rapid changes in technology. He also believes, "When you want to sell technology, you need a technologist. You need someone who can bridge the gap between the technologist and the financier."

Now if you want to sell your invention, according to Paul Erlandson, you will have to demonstrate the following points: "You will have to show that your technology is sound, that it is really proprietary, and that you can get good patent protection. You should also know who else is working in the field. After all, there are not many investors who would want to compete with IBM in the computer field."

Paul Erlandson added, "Be prepared to show the expected product life. How long will it take to commercialize your invention? How long will it be before your product becomes obsolete? Does it require FDA approval?"

There are two more tests that Paul suggested: "Does the technology fit within the existing skills of the group which hopes to commercialize it? After all, it can take anywhere from ten to thirty years to learn a completely new business. Therefore, you should make certain that your group has the knowledge to operate in the chosen field." And as a last test, Paul would ask, "How well is the technology documented? Has there been a thorough patent search? Has anyone reviewed the foreign art?"

Paul added, "If you incorporate this type of technical information into a good business plan, you will have something to talk about."

Now consider the essential features of a technical evaluation. First, make certain that your idea works. This may seem simple, but a number of individuals thought that they had invented perpetual motion machines and believed in the operability of their devices. One such inventor even built a working model. The problem was that each cycle required the manual assistance from the inventor. He was confident that a larger model with improved bearings would overcome this problem.

In your role as an entrepreneur, you want an objective evaluation on the technical economic feasibility of a proposed product. The problem is that a second opinion by a technical institute would be expensive. However, you should be able to conduct a number of experiments and document your work to show technical feasibility.

Generally, a large corporation screens ideas based on whether they will work and the projected cost of producing a product. If you can provide the corporate managers with a good analysis along these lines, you will probably clear the first hurdle. Next, assuming that your idea clears the first hurdle, it will be evaluated by engineering. A company engineer will break your proposed product or process down to its component parts, evaluate each part, and analyze the best way to produce it. The engineer may come up with a modified product. You should also perform this same type of analysis.

An initial review of the technical literature should help to "flesh out" your idea. For example, a review of the books on mechanical design may enable you to substitute one mechanism for another. You may want to suggest alternatives, such as a rack and pinion assembly or a worm drive for a steering mechanism. Become familiar with the various alternatives that are applicable to your invention. It's possible that you can use some of the alternatives to modify your idea and extend its applicability to other fields. Besides, you can use the additional knowledge to sell your invention.

And then, in analyzing your idea look at each element and consider how it could be replaced or modified. As a general rule seek an approach that is least expensive. Remember, it's easier to sell a change that will result in lower costs. In general, do whatever possible to simplify your design. Avoid complex machinery and consider the manufacturing costs. Recognize that a manufacturer will want a 40–50% gross margin on its products. In addition, there must be a profit for the wholesaler and retailer.

For example, consider the case of an inventor with an improved spark plug. The inventor may believe that this improved spark plug would sell for a premium price. However, upon looking at the pricing structure of spark plugs, the inventor might be surprised to learn that in 1960, a spark plug which retailed for $1.10 was sold to an automobile manufacturer by the same company for eight cents. At that time it would have been virtually impossible to convince the manufacturer to invest in a replacement that would cost fifty cents to manufacture.

Nevertheless, there are circumstances when a manufacturer will pay a premium price to avoid manufacturing problems. For example, a paper company paid thousands of dollars for ceramic suction box covers to replace wooden covers that cost several hundred dollars. They did so because the ceramic ones saved them thousands of dollars in maintenance costs.

As you read the technical literature in your field, jot down ideas that are applicable to your invention. At the end of each day, record your progress in your engineering notebook. You should also be developing a more refined product. In patent jargon this is called "the preferred embodiment" of your invention. It should be disclosed in your patent application and then used in your sales presentation.

At this stage, you will probably want a drawing of your invention. It is true that some inventions cannot be illustrated by a drawing. For example, chemical compositions, processes, and even a number of inventions in the general and mechanical fields will not require a drawing to explain their operation. Don't rush out to hire a draftsman to illustrate your idea. All that you want to do is to describe your idea clearly, illustrating each element of your refinements and how it works.

Then, in reviewing your work, learn what others have done in a similar field and be objective in recognizing technical problems. For example, one young engineer evaluated an invention for the foundry industry and predicted a prosperous future. His initial calculations were based on a market penetration of 10% of the casting business. However, a more detailed analysis showed that the invention was only applicable to 10% of the industry so that his projected penetration was reduced by a factor of 10.

His evaluation was also based on the cost of a valve and an assumption that only one valve would be needed for each casting. The assumption was wrong, since it failed to include the cost of installing the valves and in some cases more than one valve was needed. The final problem with his analysis was that he based the projected savings on the cost of the scrap metal that would be saved. In fact, the scrap metal was remelted so that the only savings were the costs of melting rather than the cost of the metal. Be realistic, and consider whether your invention has true commercial potential.

In your evaluation, don't overlook the cost for capital equipment to produce a new product. If possible, show that your invention can be made on existing equipment and without a major plant expansion.

One of the problems relating to invention evaluations is that it's easy to show that a new development has limited potential. In fact, many engineers are so negative that they will reject almost anything. For example, in the late 1960s, a technical expert at the Battelle Development Company thought that sophisticated evaluations would reject an invention like xerography. So be positive, but realistic, and don't dwell on all the reasons why something will not work.

Next consider the possibility of a working model. If you can produce a working model, you can be more effective in selling your invention. Nevertheless, if you are not a skilled machinist, don't spend your money to build a working model. If possible, delay the production of the model until you have sold the invention and can use the licensee's money for its further development.

You should also defer consultations with technical experts until after you file a patent application. However, after filing an application, you might find help at a university. For example, a number of universities and research institutes offer an invention evaluation service. And even though such services are provided for faculty inventions, some of them are available to the public as an aid to community businesses. Besides, you might find a university professor who will give you that second opinion on technical feasibility at a reasonable cost.

By now, you know if you have a good invention, one that is patentable, technically feasible, economically sound, and with commercial potential. Your next step is to evaluate patent coverage.

5.5 PATENT EVALUATION

Robert P. Whipple, president of Whipple International Development Company of Sherman Oaks, California, and former president of the Licensing Executives Society, has over twenty years of experience in new product development. In fact, Bob specializes in new business development based on technology. Bob says, "The two most important things an inventor can do to develop an idea are: First, he must develop a proprietary position, and second, clearly establish in his own mind its economic validity." He cautions, "Don't mislead yourself."

In other words, your future income may depend on your patent rights.

And, as an entrepreneur, you know that an invention is valuable if it produces a benefit for which someone is willing to pay. But many companies will not pay for something if they can get it free, or if after they pay for it, a competitor can take the idea without paying for it. "The advantage of a patent is that it gives the little guy a chance to compete with a large corporation," according to Don Banner.

Generally, find out what others have done in the field of patents. Has someone already obtained a patent on your idea or one that is very similar to yours? Can someone prevent you from using your idea? A corporate employee can usually obtain answers to these questions by asking the Patent Department to initiate a patent search and render an opinion on the patentability of the idea. However, as an individual inventor, you will have to pay for this type of an evaluation or do it yourself.

The question is: How can you get the best possible patent evaluation for the least amount of money? Let's assume that you have already utilized your library resources and looked through several *Official Gazettes* and the technical literature without finding a disclosure of your invention. Let's assume that you have already conducted a computer search and reviewed the results. Also assume that you did not find anything that anticipated your invention. At this stage you will probably want a patent search.

If you live in the vicinity of Washington, D.C., you could conduct your own search in the public search room at the U.S. Patent and Trademark Office at Crystal Plaza in Arlington, Virginia. If not, you will either have to go there or pay someone else to do the search.

You probably want to know how much a search will cost. In most cases, an initial search of reasonable quality will cost between $150 and $300. But don't be misled by advertisements for patent searches at a much lower cost. A cheap search is analogous to a sign in a motorcycle shop which read, "If you have a $10 head, buy a $10 helmet." Obviously, the quality of a $10 search leaves much to be desired. You should also be cautious so that you don't pay $100 to $150 for a search that is done by a subcontractor for $5 to $8.

In reality, you have three alternatives for obtaining a high quality patent evaluation. The first is to make a trip to the U.S. Patent and Trademark Office, check the *Manual of Classification,* take the "shoes" (bundles of patents) in the most appropriate class and subclasses, and look at each of those patents. Write down the patent numbers of the most pertinent references and order copies from the U.S. Patent and Trademark Office.

This approach is not recommended for the average inventor because the

Manual of Classification is complex and because patent searching is an art. It is a fact of life that a good searcher knows where to look, which class and subclass are pertinent, and charges considerably less for the time spent than an attorney. Generally, a good searcher provides a valuable service for a reasonable price.

Therefore your second alternative is to hire a patent searcher directly. To do so, consult the list of attorneys authorized to practice before the U.S. Patent and Trademark Office. Telephone one and ask for the name of a Washington search firm or individual they would recommend. That organization can then be contacted for a quote on conducting your search.

Probably your best approach at this time is to consult a patent lawyer. In Chapter 2, you read how to select a patent lawyer and how to set up the initial meeting. By following this procedure, you will establish the cost for an initial consultation. The attorney should also quote a price for a patent search and an opinion.

Don't be bashful. As an entrepreneur, you want answers to specific questions. Ask how much of the initial cost is for the search. If your patent attorney quotes $250 will the searcher be paid $150 or $200? Find out what the searcher charges per hour and ask for ten to twelve prior art patents that show the state of the art in your field. Ask your attorney for an opinion as to whether a search is justified. Usually, the costs for a preliminary search and opinion in the mechanical field is about $250 to $350. The same services in the chemical or electrical field might typically cost an additional $100.

Now, if a search does not disclose prior art that anticipates your idea, you will probably want to file a patent application. On the other hand, if someone has a patent that dominates your idea, you may elect to discontinue your efforts. What you want are facts so that you can make an intelligent business decision regarding any further efforts and expenditures in protecting your invention.

Before leaving the area of patent evaluations, recognize that there are several types of searches that you can use in evaluating your ideas.

5.6 A PRELIMINARY SEARCH

A preliminary or novelty search is used to determine whether or not your idea is patentable. This type of search is relatively inexpensive and should help you to determine whether the costs for filing a patent application are justified. In considering a preliminary search, think about who will do the search and what the searcher will look for.

J. Ernest (Ernie) Kenney probably knows more about patent searching than anyone else that I know. Ernie is a senior partner in Bacon and Thomas, an Arlington, Virginia, law firm that goes back about seventy years. The firm was originally located in Washington, D.C., but moved to Arlington when the U.S. Patent and Trademark Office moved to that city. As a senior partner in the firm, Ernie has trained and supervised a staff of patent searchers for over twenty-five years.

Ernie Kenney said, "A good patent searcher has to have an eye for detail and an exploratory mind. He needs a deep sense of satisfaction from researching ideas and technology." And, when it comes to technical qualifications, Ernie said, "The Peter Principal is true. In other words, the best of searchers will fall down on the job when they get outside of their field of expertise."

Now it is true that many professional patent searchers are technically trained. Many searchers are university graduates, some are law students, and others are former patent examiners. Nevertheless, a searcher's job is to find the closest prior art and to send you or your attorney a report on what has been found. In other words, the searcher doesn't usually render a legal opinion, but should state why he or she believes that the cited references are pertinent. The reason for this is that most searchers are not lawyers and most searches are conducted for patent lawyers. And many patent lawyers prefer to look at the prior art and render their own opinions.

Ernie Kenney said, "A searcher's ability is not always dependent on formal education. For example, I know some excellent searchers who do not have a college education, and then, some engineers don't make good searchers." However, he cautioned, "A searcher is limited by his ability to understand the technology. What I am saying is that you don't need an engineering degree to work in the mechanical arts, but you do need an ability to visualize what is shown in a drawing. And then, in the chemical and electronics fields, you do not need this ability to visualize, but you do need more formal education in the field."

Ernie went on to say, "And even if you have the formal education and an ability to visualize something in concrete form, you still need supervision and training to become a good searcher. In fact, it usually takes about a year of training to become a competent searcher."

Ernie would probably be the first to point out that there are exceptions to the one year rule and that some searchers are quite proficient after only three to six months. He did say, "Of course, if you are already knowledgeable in a specific field of chemistry, such as polymer chemistry, or a specific field in electronics, you could become quite proficient in searching that specific field in a relatively short time." So, if you are trained in a specific field you could do your own searches with a minimum of training.

Now, if you have completed your library research and had a preliminary search conducted without finding a disclosure of your invention, your invention is probably patentable. Keep a copy of the search report and the prior art patents. You will use this information for preparing and prosecuting your patent application and also for future sales presentations.

In the event that the prior art patents do not seem relevant, review the field of search. Refer to the *Manual of Patent Classification* to satisfy yourself that the most pertinent classes were covered. You might also ask if the patent searcher checked the references cited in the most pertinent patent that was found. Issued patents (except for very early ones) include the references that the patent examiner relied upon in examining that application. In many cases, examing these references will lead to a more pertinent reference.

It is important to recognize the limitations of a preliminary search. A preliminary search is not an extensive study of the prior art. In other words, a patent searcher will spend between four and twelve hours on a preliminary search. The length of time depends on the complexity of the subject, and on how well the patents are classified. For example, some fields are poorly classified and it is necessary to search through numerous subclasses to adequately cover the field of interest.

As a business person you can estimate the cost of your search as about 10% of the cost of preparing and filing a patent application. In a sense it is an insurance policy against preparing an application on an old idea. Besides, the search will help you and your attorney to build a strong foundation for your business. By analyzing what others have done, you will be able to draft the broadest valid claims possible.

In 1958, a major corporation made a serious error. The problem began, as it frequently does, with their budget. The patent budget was overextended and efforts were made to minimize further expenditures for the balance of the year. Instead of authorizing $150 or more for an infringement search, they decided to limit all outside searches to a $40 preliminary search.

On the basis of the $40 search, the company built a plant. And, when they opened that plant, they received a written notice that they were violating someone's patent. The cost of defending that suit was substantial and could have been avoided by a better search. In a way, a search is like an insurance policy. If you are building a small garage, a small policy should be adequate, but when a mansion is involved, you want adequate insurance.

The question of patentability is treated in more detail in the next chapter. Nevertheless, consider the results of your search as an additional input to your technical and marketing evaluation. For example, you may learn that the broad concept contemplated by your invention is old. However, if the broad concept is old, ask yourself why the earlier suggestions have not become a commercial success. Your idea may include the key to solving a problem that was not overcome by the earlier patents. Besides, evidence of a long-felt need supports the patentability of your idea.

And then, of course, if your search fails to disclose any close references, ask your searcher whether an extended search might be justified. Ask what classes and subclasses the searcher would suggest for further searching and the estimated cost. Later, if you decide to license your invention, you can discuss the search results with your potential licensee and suggest that they initiate a search in the additional subclasses. But ask for a copy of the results and emphasize the importance of working together to establish the strongest possible patent.

5.7 A VALIDITY SEARCH

A few years ago, one of my clients was accused of infringing a patent. In fact, the company was sued in a number of different countries and charged with infringing a U.S. patent and its foreign counterparts. These suits had been pending for about a year when I joined the company. And, when I reviewed the files, I was concerned because the prior art that had been uncovered was not very good. Yet, our trial counsel assured me that a number of extensive searches had been done in the United States and in foreign countries.

I took a copy of the patent and one of our devices to Ernie Kenney and asked for a thorough validity search on the patent. Ernie analyzed the patent and the key element (a spring assembly) that no one had been able to find. He analyzed how the assembly worked and then broke it down into its components. And when Ernie's searcher clearly understood what he was looking for, he conducted a validity search. As a result of his clear understanding and his knowledge of searching, he found an early (1903) patent that showed that same spring assembly in a box. The suits were then settled and hundreds of thousands of dollars saved. This money was saved because Ernie made certain that his searcher understood what he was looking for.

Essentially, a validity search is more extensive than a preliminary search. And it is designed to locate any patents that might adversely affect the claims of a patent or application. In addition, as illustrated by the previous example, a request for a validity search is initiated to locate prior art that is better than the art found by the patent examiner during the prosecution of the patent application.

Some corporations also request a validity search on a patent application before they invest in an invention. If they do, ask for the results and call any pertinent references to the attention of the patent examiner.

5.8 AN INFRINGEMENT SEARCH

An infringement search is like any other search, a review of the prior art. However, in this case, the searcher reads each claim in every patent in the pertinent subclass. It is a thorough search and is relatively expensive. The purpose is to determine whether a new product will infringe someone's patent.

There is one advantage in doing an early infringement study. If you find an infringement problem, you can redesign your product to avoid the problem or discontinue your efforts. And in some cases you may conduct a valdity search on the infringed patent and if successful, ignore the patent.

Ernie Kenney said, "The need for an infringement search is often dependent on the client's knowledge of the market place. For example, if an entrepreneur has an exotic computer control and is really knowledgeable about the market place, there is less need for an infringement search at the early development stage. In fact, they probably don't need an infringement search until the product is fully developed in its commercial form. But as soon as the final design of the commercial version is ready, an infringement search should be done."

Realistically, your decision to conduct an infringement search is based on economic considerations. For example, as a business person you want to know if you will have a patent problem when you sell your product. Besides, a cost of several thousand dollars for an infringement study may be far less than the cost of retooling to avoid the problem. This cost is certainly far less than the cost of a lawsuit.

Therefore if you decide to manufacture and/or sell a product, you should consider investing in an infringement search. However, in some cases there is a less expensive alternative. That is a state of the art search or a collection search.

5.9   A COLLECTION SEARCH

"It is frequently advisable to start out with a novelty and state of the art search," according to Ernie Kenney. "In this way you will get knowledge of all of the prior art for just a little more money than for a preliminary search. Then you can put your efforts into commercializing your invention." However, Ernie went on to say, "Then update your search to include any refinements which you incorporate in a commercial product. For example, if you purchase an off-the-shelf item as a component for your device, there is probably little need to update the search. But if you design an exotic valve which is essential for a commercial product, you had better conduct an infringement search before you build your plant."

In essence, a collection search is really an extensive preliminary search. But ask a patent searcher to send you a copy of every patent that relates to a particular subject. As you might imagine, there are times when the search will disclose a lot of patents. However, you can reduce the number of patents by limiting the search to a more specific field or by limiting it to patents that have issued in the past seventeen years.

One good thing about a collection search is that it will give you an extensive review of what has been done in a field. In addition, some of the patents may suggest solutions to problems that you have not yet overcome.

Another good thing about a collection search is that it is cost effective and a searcher need only read the patent title or glance at the drawing to determine whether or not it is a pertinent reference. In general, a corporation might authorize $350 to $750 for a collection search. This estimate does not include the cost of patent copies, which might easily add an additional $500. Because of this you should ask for an estimate of the number of patents, and at times you may decide to narrow your field of interest.

Some years ago, a client requested a state of the art search for all unexpired patents on brassieres and learned that there were over 750 unexpired patents in this field. If, however, the client had been interested in a strapless design, the number of patents ordered could have been greatly reduced. Nevertheless, in cases involving a major corporate development program, the cost for patent copies is a minor consideration.

As an entrepreneur, consider the cost of a collection search but don't overlook the cost of analyzing the patents. It is not usually necessary to ask your attorney to analyze all of these references. However, your attorney should screen the references before preparing an application.

There is also one caveat in obtaining a collection search and a large number of prior art patents. Inventors and their attorneys are obligated to disclose "pertinent" prior art to the patent examiner. If through inadvertence you fail to point out the pertinence of a reference that is in your possession, that is tantamount to fraud. Fraud is a basis for uneforceability and a basis for awarding large sums as damages. It could also result in your having to pay the other party's litigation expenses.

Nevertheless, you can avoid serious problems if you are candid in dealing with your attorney and the U.S. Patent and Trademark Office. Besides, you can usually help yourself and avoid future problems by learning as much as possible about your field of interest.

5.10   OTHER TYPES OF SEARCHES

There are two other types of searches that may be useful to an individual inventor. Both are relatively inexpensive and yet will frequently produce valuable results for a minimal expense.

An assignment search will tell you whether or not a patent has been assigned to an individual or company. If, for example, you are aware of a small company that is producing a particular product, you can determine which, if any, patents have been assigned to that company.

Also, in those cases where your library research has identified individuals in your field, you can look in the Patentee Index, that is, you can conduct an index search to find out if those individuals have obtained any patents and to identify those patents.

5.11   CONDUCTING YOUR OWN SEARCH

As an initial screening, you can conduct your own computer search of the prior art. However, a computer search is not a substitute for a professional search. In fact, Ernie Kenney said, "A computer search is a valuable adjunct, but will not disclose the older patents even though they may be the most pertinent. And, at times, you will need considerable expertise to limit the number of patents without eliminating those that are pertinent. For example, a computer search only matches words and will include any patent which has those words in the patent text. Actually, computer searches can be effective, but you will need skill to conduct them effectively."

To conduct a patent search, use the index in the *Classification Manual* to select those subclasses that appear most pertinent to your field of interest. This may be more difficult than it sounds, but with practice becomes easier. Then, after selecting the class or subclass from the index, you will turn to the class in the manual and try to determine which other subclasses might be pertinent. And when you have a list of subclasses, go to the stacks in the U.S. Patent and Trademark Office and pull a number of "shoes" (bundles of patents). Return to a desk and page through the patents, noting those patents that appear pertinent. Never remove a patent from the shoe, and use care that each patent is kept in its proper order.

If you fail to find pertinent references, it is likely that you are searching in the wrong subclass. Don't be discouraged, because it is sometimes difficult even for an experienced searcher to find the right subclasses. Consider for example, a search on a folding bicycle frame. The index suggests Class 280, 200+. However, it is not until subclass 274 that you find "frames and running gear." Proceeding on to subclass 278, you will find "extensible and knock down." Then, further along you find another subclass No. 287, which also relates to "extensible and knock down frames." Finally, subclass 298+ relates more specifically to "pivoted and extensible frames."

At this point, you can go to the stacks and look in the various subclasses to see which appears most pertinent. You will note that in the first shoe, or bundle, of patents in each subclass there is a definition of the class and subclass, which should indicate whether or not you have the most pertinent subclass. There is also a manual including these descriptions in the Search Room, which will enable you to compare the definitions of the subclasses.

There is one other approach, which is probably far better for you if you want to conduct your own searches. Select a search firm and offer to pay them to show you how to conduct a search. In this way you will learn how to be an effective searcher, and you may want to work with that firm on future inventions.

5.12   CAN YOU RELY ON TRADE SECRETS?

The concept that you can keep your idea a secret may be viable, as illustrated by the example of Peter Shaffer. However, as an entrepreneur the concept is not always practical. Nevertheless, consider trade secrets as a complement of patent protection.

The only sure way of keeping something secret is not to tell a single person about your inventions. But if you keep your idea a secret, you can't sell it. In other words, if you intend to manufacture a product yourself, and if your process for making the product will not be disclosed by a sale of the product, you can probably rely on a trade secret.

The problem is that many people do not understand trade secrets. In many cases they think something is a trade secret even though it is in the public domain. Just remember, a trade secret is something that is not known by the public or by other persons who are working in your field. And a trade secret must be something more than that which is obvious to an ordinary worker in the field.

You should also consider the cost of maintaining trade secrets. To do the job right requires a reasonable security system. It probably requires something like the ones used by the U.S. Department of Defense for handling classified material.

Even the best of the systems can fail. For example, Celanese Corporation learned that a trusted plant manager with an unblemished twenty-six year record at the company had obtained copies of their technical documents. The plant manager, earning in excess of $50,000, sold to a Japanese company a set of fifty-eight rolls of microfilm with over 12,000 engineering drawings and over 90,000 pages of research and development reports.

Trade secret litigation is difficult and usually expensive. For this reason, many managers favor patent protection whenever possible. However, when the patentability is doubtful, it is desirable to keep secret as much information as possible. To do this, you must limit access to buildings and locations to authorized personnel, keep files locked, and keep unauthorized personnel out of the area. This may be difficult, but you should do all that you can to keep a competitor from copying your ideas.

5.13   TIME IS MONEY

Your patent rights may depend on your diligent efforts to produce a working device. For example, someone who is developing a similar idea may obtain patent rights that are superior to yours and, in fact, may preclude you from using or selling your own invention.

It is also important to consider the cost of any delays on your own income. For example, you will have invested considerable time and some money in developing an invention. What you want to do now is to convert the negative cash flow to a positive cash flow. In other words, it is time to manufacture and sell products or to license your invention. And if you decide to license your invention, it is time to stop using your own money and start using someone else's for future development costs.

6

Determining Patentability

*Whoever invents or discovers any new and useful process, machine, manufacture, or composition of matter or any new and useful improvement thereof may obtain a patent therefor . . . .**

*35 U.S.C. 101.

6.1   GENERAL CONCEPTS

Auzville Jackson, Jr., is principal associate of AJ Associates, and is an engineer, patent and trademark lawyer, corporate and foundation executive, inventor, adjunct university professor, and entrepreneur. He is also counsel to the firm of Luedeka and Neely in Knoxville, Tennessee. And before he became counsel to that firm, he was vice president of technology and chief patent counsel for Robertshaw Controls in Richmond, Virginia.

Auzville Jackson has served as an expert witness and continues to do consulting work in the areas of strategic planning, emerging technology, and corporate development. Auzi is a busy individual who recognizes the importance of patents.

In Auzville Jackson's opinion, "there are two approaches for determining patentability. First, you look at patentability as a business-oriented lawyer. And, second you look at patentability as a patent lawyer."

Auzi said, "As a patent lawyer, ask if the idea is novel, and useful. And then, after studying the prior art, ask: What are the chances of getting a good claim? Will the claim be significant?"

Recognize that, "If you have an invention which is commercially important, it is frequently up to the patent lawyer to figure out how to get protection," according to Mr. Jackson. After all, the U.S. Government has granted over 4,400,000 patents, and foreign governments have issued many more. And it is likely that an invention disclosed in one of those patents may be similar to your idea. What this means to you is that you probably need an experienced patent lawyer to review the prior art and render an opinion on the patentability of your invention.

However, there is one way for you to screen your inventions for patentability before seeking a professional opinion. Ask yourself: Have I ever seen a commercial product that incorporates my concept? If not, why not? Assuming that your concept is a good one and that someone will buy a product based on your concept, why isn't a product being offered for sale?

And then, after you have obtained a preliminary search on your invention, carefully review the prior art. Read each prior art patent carefully and consider all of the alternatives suggested. On closer analysis you may find significant differences between your invention and the prior art. It is frequently these differences that form the basis for patentability. And these patentable features may make the difference between commercial success and scientific curiosity.

Auzville Jackson suggests that you consider patentability as a business-oriented lawyer. "Of course," he said, "if you can obtain broad basic protection in an emerging technology, you will have something really exciting.

However, the importance of patentability is more frequently dependent on what you will do with your invention. For example, will you use your invention to manufacture and sell products or will you try to license your invention?"

Auzville Jackson is not optimistic about selling ideas. He said, "If you want to sell an invention, you need a prototype. You need a prototype because companies don't usually buy raw ideas. Besides, you don't usually make much money from selling inventions."

Now, as you consider the importance of patentability, do not become preoccupied with cost justification. Auzi said, "Over the years, I have seen so many valuable secondary benefits attributed to patents. For example, I attribute high morale, prestige, and even credibility to an organization's patent position. And, in some cases these intangible values outweigh the dollar value of a patent."

What this boils down to, according to Auzville Jackson, is that "As an entrepreneur, you need to ask yourself, from a practical viewpoint, what type of protection do I need, and will it contribute to the success of my venture?"

6.2 STATUTORY REQUIREMENTS

There are statutory requirements that determine whether or not your concept is patentable. For example, Title 35 of the U.S. Code Section 101 provides that "Whoever invents or discovers any new and useful process, machine, manufacture or composition of matter or any new and useful improvement thereof may obtain a patent." Your concept probably falls within one of these categories. Nevertheless, take a few minutes to look at each category and determine where your invention fits within the framework of the statutory language.

"Process" is synonomous with method and means a series of steps or operations for obtaining a physical result. In many cases you can and should describe your invention in terms of a process. For example, if you have a new chemical product, you should write a claim that covers that product. However, you should also consider claiming a process for producing a chemical product. Now, would you think of a telecommunication system as a method for transmitting information, an electrostatic copier as a method for producing copies, or a furnace lining as a method for insulating furnaces. If you start thinking along these lines, you can enhance your patent protection.

Patent lawyers try (when appropriate) to include one or more method claims in most patent applications. For example, U.S. Patent No. 3,497,072 to C.R. Cannon is entitled "Reverse Osmosis Membrane and Method of Manufacture." The method is defined in the following steps: forming a cellulose solution, casting the solution, evaporating the solvent, immersing the cast membrane in water to form a swollen structure, and annealing to form a membrane.

Don't underestimate the importance of method or process protection. Actually, one prominent patent lawyer said, "They [method claims] can be enormously valuable for basic mechanical inventions as well as for other types of inventions." He went on to say, "Method coverage is one way of patenting something that is old as all-get-out, but which is being used for a new purpose. Besides, method coverage has some real nifty uses."

But there are limitations to method claims, and at times it will be inappropriate to define your invention as a method. For example, a method generally requires some physical result to be patentable.

Now consider the advantages of defining your invention in terms of a process. By defining your invention as a process, you form the basis for charging a royalty on throughput. And, using electrostatic copying as an example, you can see the advantage in collecting a royalty for each copy made, as distinguished from a royalty paid on the purchase price of a copier. However, recognize the fact that most prospective licensees will resist paying a royalty on throughput. Nevertheless, method claims that offer substantial savings may justify this type of arrangement.

Auzville Jackson commented on the value of a method claim versus the value of a product claim. He said, "The relative value depends on the circumstances and on the particular invention. But whenever possible, I try to obtain both types of claims. Of course, in some cases, an invention cannot be covered by both types of claims. And if the invention resides in a new product, I would prefer product claims."

The term "machine" includes mechanical devices that perform a useful function. A bicycle, roller skates, hydraulic press, spectrophotometer, engine, gear box, differential, and animal feeding apparatus are all examples of machines. And what you need to obtain a patent is an operable machine that is new, useful, and nonobvious to a person who is skilled in the art.

"Manufacture" as used in the patent statute is a catch-all term. For example, articles of clothing, clamps, a dental handpiece, marking devices, fish lures, and toys can be defined as articles of manufacture.

A "composition of matter" relates to a new product such as those produced by a chemical reaction. In other words, any mixture of two or more ingredients that produces a product that has properties that are different from the original and that is useful can be patented. However, mixing alcohol and water would not be a new composition of matter, since it is merely a more dilute solution. This is true even though the dilute solution will no longer burn. By contrast, mixing silicon carbide particles with doping agents to produce a sinterable powder would constitute a new composition of matter and would be patentable.

Now when you patent a new composition of matter, you can probably obtain claims on the method of producing it. And you might be able to obtain claims on the method of using it. In addition, you can probably obtain claims on the product itself since some ingenious chemist may synthesize your new product by using a different process.

There are two other patentable areas that are covered in a cursory manner. These relate to ornamental designs and plants. Design patents cover the appearance of an ornamental design and are frequently easy to avoid. Nevertheless, "Design patents are important," according to Auzville Jackson. He said, "They are particularly important if you are trying to protect the aesthetic value of your product. They are also important in those cases where you do not have an opportunity to get a utility patent." Actually, Auzi believes that, "A design patent can be valuable as long as you have a good product. For example, design patents have real merit where you don't want the competition to sell a look-alike."

Unfortunately, design patents don't give you much protection and are difficult to license on a profitable basis. In essence, they may prevent someone from making an exact copy of your device or a colorable imitation thereof. An advantage is that they are relatively inexpensive to obtain.

Plant patents can be obtained on asexually reproduced plants, that is, those that are produced without sexual action, but not on tuber-propagated plants. But since interest in this area is so limited and the practice so specialized, it is not covered in detail here. Those of you with an interest in this area should look for a patent attorney with experience in this field.

6.3 TESTS FOR DETERMINING PATENTABILITY

To be patentable, your invention must pass two tests. First, your invention must be "new" and second it must be "useful." The term "new" means that it is something that has not been done before. Then, if your invention has not been described in a printed publication, offered for sale, or used for more than one year, you can probably obtain a patent on your invention.

The second test for patentability relates to "useful." In other words, is there a practical application for your invention? Does it amount to something more than a scientific curiosity? And as an entrepreneur, if you find your invention is not useful, you should have no interest in pursuing it.

At times, a chemist may have difficulty in defining utility for a new composition of matter. For example, one case held that the use of a material to induce cancer in mice did not meet the criteria for utility. Therefore, if you are developing new compositions of matter, find a use for the material before investing in a patent application. Actually you should consider usefulness as part of your market evaluation.

6.4 NONOBVIOUSNESS

Section 103 of the patent statute provides, "A patent may not be obtained . . . if the differences between the subject matter sought to be patented and the prior art are such that the subject matter as a whole *would have been obvious at the time the invention was made to a person having ordinary skill in the art* to which the subject matter pertains" [emphasis added]. Actually, the statement is quoted from Graham *v.* John Deere 148 USPQ 465.

Nevertheless, Auzville Jackson suggested, "Don't get hung up on obviousness." Auzville said this because he knows that many inventors misconstrue the meaning of obviousness. Don't make this mistake. Don't assume that the criteria for obviousness is analogous to the authors of scientific text books who preceed their conclusions with "From the above it is obvious that . . . "

Actually, Graham *v.* John Deere defines the tests for obviousness. In that case Justice Clark wrote: "Under section 103, the scope and content of the prior art are to be determined; differences between the prior art and the claims at issue are to be ascertained; and the level of ordinary skill in the pertinent art resolved. Against this background, the obviousness or nonobviousness of the subject matter is determined. Such secondary considerations as commercial success, long felt need, failure of others, etc., might be utilized to give light to the circumstances surrounding the origin of the subject matter sought to be patented. As indicia of obviousness or nonobviousness, these inquires may have relevancy."

Justice Clark, speaking for the court, went on to say:

"This is not to say, however, that there will not be difficulties in applying the nonobviousness test. What is obvious is not a question upon which there is likely to be uniformity of thought in every given factual context. The difficulties, however, are comparable to those encountered daily by the courts in such frames of reference as negligence and science, and should be amenable to a case by case development."

Notwithstanding any of the above, a patent examiner may reject your patent application as being obvious to a person of ordinary skill in the art. For example, during the prosecution of the Ferris and Meltzer application on an optical cryptographic device (now U.S. Patent No. 3,178,993) an examiner devoted four typewritten pages to explaining why it was impossible for the device to work. Then the examiner went on to say that if the device did work, it would be obvious to combine the elements from several prior art references to obtain the same result. And on that basis, he rejected the claims. However, those arguments were later overcome with respect to a majority of the claims. This apparent inconsistancy by a patent examiner is mentioned so that you will not be discouraged if some of your claims are initially rejected as obvious. Just remember that, in many cases, the only problem may be one of semantics. In other words, what the patent examiner is trying to tell you is that you have not defined your invention in the clear and precise language required to distinguish it from the prior art references.

Now, in considering the question of obviousness, you will also have to decide who is a person of ordinary skill in the art at the time the invention was made. For example, the Patent Office and the courts have had difficulty in defining a person of ordinary skill. And in the case of Ex parte Marga Faulstick (138 USPQ 287), Judge Jackson said that Dr. Norbert Kreidl, a Director of Research at Bausch & Lomb, was a person of extraordinary skill. How then can you decide whether or not your idea would be obvious to a person of ordinary skill?

"A logical way to make a determination as to obviousness is to review the history of the particular art to which the invention pertains as it existed before and after the invention was made, to see what someone associated with that art actually did or failed to do when confronted with the same problem that the inventor confronted," according to Talivaldis Cepuritis, a partner in Dressler, Goldsmith, Shore, Sutker and Milnamow, Ltd., a Chicago law firm.

Mr. Cepuritis went on to quote Judge Learned Hand, who wrote:

> To judge on our own that this or that was an assemblage of old factors, was or was not "obvious" is to substitute our ignorance for the acquaintance with the subject of those who were familiar with it. There are indeed some sign posts: e.g., how long did the need exist; how many tried to find a way; how long did the surrounding and accessory arts disclose the means; how immediately was the invention recognized as an answer by those who used the new varient.

However, from a practical standpoint, what may seem relatively simple to you in retrospect may represent a significant departure from the normal approaches applied by a skilled scientist. For example, Leslie O. Vargady is one of the most creative inventors whom I have ever met and has obtained numberous patents on his inventions. And in many cases he borrowed elements from other systems and rearranged them in a manner that produced improved results. Leslie obtained patents because he is a person of extraordinary skill.

Dr. Robert Meltzer is another example of a prolific inventor. He told me that had he really applied his technical knowledge, he would have convinced himself that his optical cryptographic device wouldn't work. Fortunately, he believed in the idea and with the help of John Ferris succeeded in developing a useful device. Then, after making a working device, they analyzed why it worked. Based on hindsight, it was easy to explain. However, it would not have been obvious to a person of ordinary skill in the art at the time that the invention was made.

In considering who is a person of ordinary skill in the art, Brian Poissant, a partner in the hundred year old law firm of Pennie & Edmonds, cited the recent case of Shelcone, Inc. v. Durham Industries, Inc. (221 USPQ 891, 1984.) Brian said, "In that case, which involved a toy invention, the district court found that one of ordinary skill in the art was a person with a college or art school background and several years experience in designing toys. This finding was confirmed by the Court of Appeals for the Federal Circuit." But, the definition of a person of ordinary skill may vary from profession to profession.

When you think about one of your ideas, ask yourself if your device differs in its structure, operation, or results from those devices disclosed in the prior art. Remember that almost every invention incorporates known elements. Ask yourself: Do the elements when put together in the manner suggested produce an unusual result? If the answer is yes, assume that it would not have been obvious to a person of ordinary skill at the time that you made the invention.

6.5 SYNERGISM AND AGGREGATION

In 1976 the Supreme Court of the United States in the case of Sakraida v. Ag Pro, Inc. held that U.S. Patent No. 3,223,070, which covered a water flush system to remove cow manure from the floor of a dairy barn, was invalid. The court concluded that "While the combination of old elements may have performed a useful function, it added nothing to the nature and quality of dairy barns theretofore used." (See Vol. 189, U.S. *Patent Quarterly,* p. 449.)

In holding the patent invalid, the court concluded that the combination of old elements to produce an abrupt release of water on the barn floor can't properly be characterized as synergism, resulting in an effect greater than the sum of the several effects taken separately. And in view of subsequent decisions, it appears that the concept of synergism should be applied sparingly if at all. Thus you will need more than an aggregation or simple compilation of elements for patentability.

6.6 SUBSTITUTION AND ADDITION

If you substitute one element for another in a combination of elements, you may have made an invention. For example, one court held that the use of a laterally moving transfer car in place of a turntable did constitute an invention, even though both devices were effective in transferring a furnace car from one point to another. In that case, the invention amounted to a combination of old elements, and yet the inventors obtained a patent that was held valid by the court. However, the court did hold that the claims must be narrowly construed and that there was no infringement by the defendents, who had incorporated a turntable in their plant (187 USPQ 466).

If you add an element to a known combination of elements, you may have made an invention. For example, the patent of William Holt, U.S. Patent No. 4,115,271 is based on the addition of a baffle plate in a rotary screen filter. The rotary screen filter had been disclosed in the earlier U.S. Patent No. 3,876,548. However, in his patent, Holt stated that the additional baffle improved the cleaning action and overcame a problem that was inherent in the earlier device. Nevertheless, addition of an element that does not modify the function of a device would not usually constitute a patentable invention.

6.7 SUBSTITUTION OF MATERIALS

In general, the mere substitution of one material for another would not be patentable. For example, substituting stainless steel linings for cast iron because of its greater corrosion resistance would be a matter of design choice as distinguished from an inventive act. However, there are times when you can obtain meaningful patent coverage on a material substitution.

For example, The Carborundum Company obtained a patent on a suction box cover that was made of silicon carbide instead of edge grained maple. The silicon carbide suction box cover was used in papermaking machines as a replacement for wooden covers, and overcame a serious problem in the industry. Quite surprisingly, these diamond polished silicon carbide surfaces substantially reduced wear on a bronze screen that rubbed against the suction box cover. In fact, it was economical to replace the wood cover costing several hundred dollars with a product costing thousands. It was economical because the bronze screens were very expensive.

6.8 ABANDONED INVENTIONS

An inventor may be entitled to an invention unless it "has been abandoned." This means that, even though your invention is patentable, you can lose your right to obtain a patent unless you take steps to establish your rights. In fact, the right to patent an invention can be lost when an inventor fails to pursue it for a period of time. An invention can also be abandoned by inadvertence.

For example, if you offer a product based on your invention for sale and fail to file a patent application within one year, you may have lost your right to a patent. The same would be true if you published an article describing your invention, and failed to file the application within the one year statutory period.

Another example of lost rights is illustrated by an interference proceeding. An interference determines which of several inventors is entitled to a patent. Sometimes the first inventor loses his or her rights because that inventor abandoned the invention. This may happen if the inventor has an early conception based on an experiement, but fails to diligently pursue the invention. In other words, your failure to work on an invention can cost you your right to a patent. However, diligence in developing your invention and a properly witnessed engineering notebook will help to protect your rights.

6.9 STATUTORY BAR: PUBLIC USE OR SALE

The patent statute (U.S. Code, Title 35, Sec. 102) provides that you may lose your right to obtain a patent if your invention was placed on sale, was described in a printed publication anywhere in the world, or if it was in public use in this country more than one year prior to the filing date of your patent application. This is referred to as a statutory bar.

A statutory bar is absolute, and will prevent you from obtaining a patent.

In the United States you have one year from the date of publication, public use, or offer for sale to file an application. However, a year passes quickly. Why run a risk of losing your rights since it is far better to file your application before disclosing your invention to the public? This is particularly true if you want foreign protection.

Don't be misled by the idea that an experimental use does not act as a statutory bar. What constitutes an experimental use probably requires a legal opinion. And if you sell a product and want to treat the use as experimental, you will have to provide a number of safeguards.

In one case, an inventor submitted an affidavit to prove that he had made his invention before another inventor and included two invoices as evidence of a complete reduction to practice. The invoices showed that products encompassing the invention had been made and delivered to a customer more than a year prior to his filing date.

The inventor argued that the devices were for experimental use and did not, therefore, create a statutory bar. However, the inventor was unsuccessful, since there was no evidence of control over the use. Therefore, the court concluded that the inventor was not entitled to a patent. And they rejected his arguments because, to qualify as an experimental use, there must be full unequivocal and convincing evidence of the experimental nature of the sale.

It is true that you may want to test a new product in actual use to determine if it is suitable for the commercial market. And in a number of cases, you might ask a customer to share in the cost of a test by paying for your product even though it is for an experimental use. You can do this without losing your rights under certain circumstances. Therefore, ask your counsel for advice before you offer your product for sale. And if it's feasible, file your patent application before you offer to sell a product that encompasses your invention.

You should also be concerned about protecting your rights to obtain patents in foreign countries. Don't be confused by the difference between a statutory bar and the one year convention period for foreign filing. The statutory bar relates to your right to obtain a U.S. patent. The convention period refers to a period of one year after you file your U.S. application, and during which you can file foreign applications with the same effect as though you filed them on the same day as your original U.S. application.

Some years ago, a young attorney (now deceased) filed an extremely important patent application eleven months after a publication by the inventor. Actually, the attorney did a monumental job in a short time, and ultimately obtained broad basic protection in an emerging field of technology.

However, a problem developed when the client decided that he wanted to seek patent protection in seventeen foreign countries. There was a problem because the inventor had published an article about his invention ten months before he had disclosed it to his patent attorney. The publication fully disclosed the invention. And the laws of most foreign countries do not provide any grace period for prior disclosure. So in those countries, the public disclosure prior to the U.S. filing date was a bar to patentability. The young attorney advised his client against foreign filing even though the foreign applications would have been entitled to the U.S. filing date. He made this recommendation because the early disclosure was fatal to patent protection in foreign countries. The point to remember is that if you want foreign patents, file your U.S. patent application before any disclosure about your invention, and then file your foreign applications within the convention period.

In another case, an inventor lost his foreign patent rights without knowing it, because an employee of another company stood up at a professional meeting and told the audience about an experimental device that his company was testing. Then the professional society published this dialogue before the inventor filed a U.S. patent application. Fortunately, the U.S. application was filed within a year of the publication. However, the foreign rights were lost.

Auzville Jackson, said, "One of the leading venture capitalists told me that he had two criteria for investing in technology. His criteria were based on a broad-based emerging market and a proprietary edge. That edge was not limited to patents." However, if your invention is patentable, don't disregard your rights. Don't lose your rights through an act of carelessness.

PART 2

PROTECTING YOUR INVESTMENT IN THE FUTURE

7

The Anatomy of
a Patent

7.1   GENERAL CONCEPTS

In Part 1 you considered whether or not your idea is patentable, whether it is new, whether it meets the statutory requirements, and even more important, whether or not a patent application is cost justifiable. Now assuming that your invention has commercial potential, you will want the best patent possible. Therefore, take the time to analyze the structure of a patent and to recognize the importance of each part of a patent application.

William Marshall Lee, of Lee, Smith and Zickert in Chicago, is a former president of the Licensing Executives Society (United States and Canada) and is the chairman-elect of the Patent, Trademark and Copyright section of the American Bar Association. According to Bill, "A good patent application should include two things. First, it should include a discussion of what the inventor knows about the prior art. And second, it should include a clear description of your improvement over the prior art."

This chapter includes an introduction to the structure of a patent application, and may seem a bit detailed. Nevertheless, if you are serious about developing your invention or are considering working on your own patent application, you should read this chapter carefully and purchase a copy of the Code of Federal Regulations, Patents and Trademarks from the U.S. Department of Commerce. Make certain that you purchase the latest copy of the rules. The cost is nominal.

7.2   STATUTORY REQUIREMENTS

In addition to what Bill Lee said, an application for a patent must contain a specification, including a claim or claims, an oath or declaration, and a drawing when necessary. The law requires:

The specification shall contain a written description of the invention, and the manner and process of making and using it, in such full, clear, concise and exact terms as to enable any person skilled in the art to which it pertains, or with which it is most nearly connected, to make and use the same, and shall set forth the best mode contemplated by the inventor for carrying out his invention.

The specification shall conclude with one or more claims which particularly point out and distinctly claim the subject which the applicant regards as his invention.

7.3 THE SPECIFICATION

When you review someone else's patent you can save yourself considerable time by limiting your analysis to the most pertinent portions of the specification. You can do this for an initial evaluation. For example, William Marshall Lee said, "When you have a concept and want to review the prior art, look at the drawings and at the written description of the invention. Initially, the claims of the prior art are not that important unless you are concerned about possible infringement. Or to be more accurate, rely on your patent lawyer to review the claims. Rely on him to help you to interpret the nuances of the claims and the infringement question. All that you should do during this initial evaluation is to determine how does your improvement fit in with the prior art."

Bill Lee went on to say, "An inventor must make a candid analysis of what he has and how it differs from the prior art. But don't get fooled by some general disclosure of a broad idea. Look at the differences between your idea and what is disclosed in the prior art. And, above all else, find out what is important from a commercial standpoint." He said, "If it is not commercially important, forget it."

Now there are times when it is important to read each word in a patent. For example, you should read each word in your own patent application and make certain that it is absolutely correct. And, as Bill Lee said, "Above all else, you have to deal with complete candor." And then, as another leading patent lawyer suggested, "Have someone else read it to see if he can understand it, to see if it is complete."

Finally, when your patent is ready to issue, that is, when the claims have been allowed, reread it. Make certain that there are no errors. You, or more likely one of the secretaries in your attorney's office, will also read your issued patent carefully, word by word, to see that there are no errors in printing.

But when you read someone else's patent, limit your reading to the pertinent parts of the patents. For example, if you are concerned about infringement, start out by reading the abstract and then go to the claims.

In general, you can do what experienced patent attorneys do. They skim a patent quickly and focus their attention on the particular areas of interest. For example, begin with the drawings and if they aren't pertinent, discard the reference without looking further. After all, you should not waste time reading irrelevant patents.

The patent title may be vague and at times might be misleading. In the past, some attorneys used a broad or very vague title such as "An Optical System," which told you very little about the invention. But in today's practice, the same application might be entitled "A Linear Compensated Zoom Optical System."

Experienced attorneys frequently focus their initial attention on the drawings. For example, if you are searching for a rearview mirror that is attached to a pair of spectacles, you can see if the idea is shown by simply looking at the drawings. You can do this because the law requires an inventor to illustrate every claimed feature in the drawings. Nevertheless, you have to be careful because some features may be illustrated in the form of a graphical drawing, symbol, or a labeled box. See, for example, Figure 7.1 from U.S. Patent No. 4,124,667.

Some patents, particularly in the chemical field, do not include drawings. But don't be discouraged by patents with vague titles and no drawings. In those cases you can read the abstract of the disclosure. Or, at times, you can read the initial paragraph to see if you are interested in reading further. For example, if you were interested in powdered carbon for treating gases, and if the patent related to granular activated carbon for treating water, you might disregard the reference and go on to another patent.

Almost all unexpired patents include an abstract of the disclosure. "An abstract," according to Bill Lee, "should include a succinct summary of your contribution. It is the kernel of what is in your application." Bill went on to say, "The abstract is an important part of your patent application. It is important because a lot of patent searchers will rely on it to tell them what is in your patent specification." It does not include all of the variations of an invention, but an initial review of the abstract should help you to determine if that patent warrants further study. Examples of typical abstracts taken from the two patents illustrated in Figures 7.1 and 7.2 are as follows:

Pressureless sintering of silicon carbide to produce ceramic bodies having 75% and greater theoretical densities, can be accomplished by firing shaped bodies, containing finely divided silicon carbide, boron source such as boron carbide, carbon source such as phenolic resin and a temporary binder, at a sintering temperature of from about 1900 to about 2500 degrees centigrade.

A window assembly which is for mounting in a four-sided vehicle body opening and which includes a rigidifying frame having open ends receiving

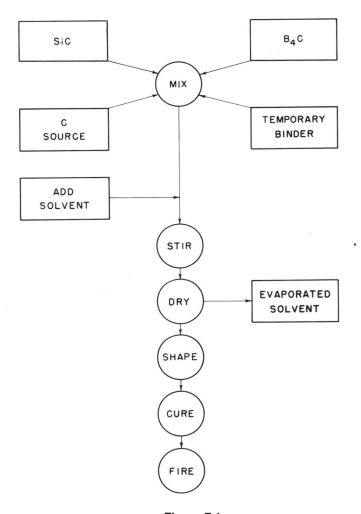

Figure 7.1

glass end panels. A glass center panel is carried by the assembly frame and is shiftable over a center opening formed between the two glass end panels.

After reading an abstract of the disclosure, consider the next section of a patent, which is usually entitled "Background of the Invention." This section typically includes one or two paragraphs on the general background or history of the development. In some cases, the background

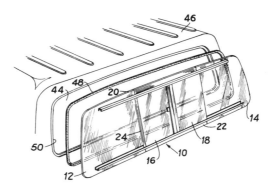

Figure 7.2

section includes information on the general problems that have been overcome by the invention. The section frequently includes useful information about prior art and should be reviewed when you are evaluating the patentability of your idea.

The section entitled "Background of the Invention" in U.S. Patent No. 4,124,667 serves as an example. It reads as follows:

PROCESS FOR PRODUCING SINTERED SILICON CARBIDE CERAMIC BODY

Background of the Invention

The chemical and physical properties of silicon carbide made it an excellent material for high temperature structural applications. These properties include good oxidation resistance and corrosion behavior, good heat transfer coefficients, low expansion coefficient, high thermal shock resistance and high strength at elevated temperatures. It is in particular desirable to produce silicon carbide bodies having high density and suitable for engineering material uses such as for example high temperature gas turbine applications. Silicon carbide is a preferred material for such use, because it can withstand greater temperature differential than conventional materials, and can therefore lead to greater efficiency in the transformation of energy.

Methods of producing high density silicon carbide bodies have heretofore included reaction bonding (also known as reaction sintering), chemical vapor deposition and hot pressing. Reaction sintering involves the use of silicon impregnants to upgrade the density of the silicon carbide and is useful for many applications, but is undesirable where excess silicon exuding from the silicon carbide body would be detrimental. Silicon carbide deposition is impractical for producing complex shapes, and hot pressing (the production of high density silicon carbide bodies by simultaneous application of heat and pressure) is impractical for some shapes, since the pressure required during the hot pressing operation deforms the silicon carbide body and requires that only relatively simple shapes can be produced by this method.

A second example of the background of an invention is taken from U.S. Patent No. 4,124,054 (see Figure 7.2). In this example the attorney defines a number of difficulties that had been associated with the prior art assemblies and points out how those shortcomings will be overcome by the new invention.

WINDOW ASSEMBLY FOR A VEHICLE

Background of the Invention

This invention relates to a window assembly for a vehicle and will have specific but not limited application to a replacement window having sliding glass panels for use in vans, trucks, and truck caps.

Heretofore window assemblies having sliding glass panels for vans, trucks and similar vehicles have been enclosed in a continuous channel-shaped frame. The ends of the frame are generally rounded which requires the frame to be formed by multiple dies. This type construction results in variations in the size and angle of the frame which in turn cause difficulty when the window assembly must be replaced, such as due to a broken or cracked glass panel or a malfunction in the window slide. Additionally, the round ends of such prior art window assembly frames narrow the glass area at the end portions of the assemblies which can cause a wedging of the sliding glass panels when they are fully opened.

In the following described invention the window assembly is designed with a minimum of frame members so as to reduce manufacturing costs and to consistently standardize the size of the assembly, thereby making installation of the assembly in a truck, van or similar vehicle possible with only a minimum of effort.

Some attorneys refer to specific patents in this section and then go on to explain why their client's invention represents an improvement over those patents. This approach has the advantage of distinguishing your invention from the most pertinent prior art patents. However, you should avoid any criticism of someone else's patent in your specification.

Don't try to put too much in this section since a mistatement might form a basis for invalidating your patent. For example, if you state that a problem is overcome by your invention and it isn't, someone could argue that you used fraud to obtain your patent. For example, do not say that all of the prior art devices are expensive if, in fact, lower cost devices are available.

William Marshall Lee said, "The summary of the invention is one of the most important parts of a patent specification." He cautioned, "Don't leave this section out. Don't rely on some group of objects, i.e., objectives addressed by an invention, to portray your invention." In general, the summary of the invention follows the background of the invention. And this section is required by the U.S. Code of Federal Regulations, Title 37, Section 1.73, which states:

> A brief summary of the invention indicating its nature and substance, which may include a statement of the object of the invention, should precede the detailed description. Such summary should, when set forth, be commensurate with the invention as claimed and any object recited should be that of the invention as claimed.

Some inventors and their attorneys misconstrue this rule. They include a number of paragraphs on the objects of the invention, paragraphs which amount to little more than stock phrases, and then go on to a detailed description of the invention. Don't make this mistake.

The rule requires a brief summary of your invention and says that you *may* include a statement of the objects. Therefore, what you want is a summary of your broadest claims. By writing a well written, carefully thought out summary of your invention, you will also avoid a rejection of your application on the basis that the claims are not supported by the specification.

The following examples of summaries are taken from the previously mentioned patents.

PROCESS FOR PRODUCING A SINTERED SILICON CARBIDE CERAMIC BODY

Summary of the Invention

According to the first aspect of the present invention, there is provided a sintered ceramic body consisting essentially of from about 91 to about 99.35% by weight silicon carbide, from about 0.5 to about 5.0% carbonized organic material, from about 0.15 to about 3.0% boron, and up to about 1.0% additional carbon; and having a density of at least about 2.40 g/cc. According to a second aspect of the present invention, there is provided a raw batch for producing a sintered ceramic body, comprising from about 91 to about 99.35 parts by weight silicon carbide having a surface area of from about 1 to about 100 m^2l/g; from about 0.67 to about 20 parts by weight of a carbonizable, organic solvent soluble, organic material having a yield of from about 25 to about 75% by weight; from about 0.15 to about 5 parts by weight of a boron source containing from about 0.15 to about 3.0 parts by weight boron; and from about 5 to about 15 parts by weight of temporary binder. According to a further aspect of this invention, there is provided a process for producing a sintered ceramic body, comprising the steps of mixing together the ingredients of the above described raw batch; adding to the raw batch from about 25 to about 100% by weight of the raw batch of an organic solvent in which the carbonizable, organic solvent soluble, organic material is soluble; stirring the raw batch and organic solvent in such a way as to disperse the carbonizable, organic solvent soluble, organic material about the silicon carbide of the raw batch; frying the stirred mixture in such a way as to evaporate the organic solvent from the mixture, shaping the dried mixture in such a way as to produce a shaped body having a density of at least about 1.60 g/cc; curing the temporary binder within the shaped body; and firing the shaped body for such time, such temperature and in such environment as to produce a density of at least about 2.40 g/cc.

The second example is taken from U.S. Patent No. 4,124,054 entitled:

WINDOW ASSEMBLY FOR A VEHICLE

Summary of the Invention

The frame of the window assembly of this invention includes an upper horizontal member and a spaced lower horizontal member interconnected by a pair or vertical members which are inwardly set from the ends of the upper and lower horizontal frame members. Each vertical frame member cooperates with the upper and lower frame members to form a C-shaped frame part at each of the end portions of the assembly frame. A glass end panel is carried by each C-shaped frame part with the end panel extending to a vertical frame member. The vertical frame members are spaced apart to form an opening therebetween. A glass center panel is supported for lateral shiftable movement over the center opening between the vertical frame members.

The outer perimeter of the assembly is defined by the upper and lower horizontal frame members and the outer edges of the glass end panels which form the curved ends of the assembly. The upper and lower horizontal frame members need not be formed by bending dies, thus enabling the assembly to be economically produced. Each sliding glass center panel of the assembly is retained between straight guide portions of the upper and lower horizontal frame members and can be slid between opened and closed positions in a non-wedging manner.

Accordingly, it is an object of this invention to provide a window assembly for a vehicle which is of economical construction.

Another object of this invention is to provide a window assembly of simplified operation for a van, truck or truck cap. Still another object of this invention is to provide a window assembly for a vehicle, such as a truck or van, which has sliding window panels and which can be simply mounted to the vehicle.

Other objects of this invention will become apparent upon a reading of the invention's description.

Clarence M. Fisher (deceased) did not include the objects of the invention in patent applications he wrote. Mr. Fisher, an outstanding patent lawyer, was a perfectionist, and in my opinion, had few equals in the profession. He recognized that the rules of practice provided that "Any object recited should be that of the invention as claimed." In other words, a poorly defined object could be the basis for holding your patent invalid. Besides, you can describe the advantages of your invention without using "objects," and at the same time overcome a stereotyped appearance. In the words of Bill Lee, "Objects of an invention don't mean a lot, but you still find a lot of them in patent specifications."

The next section in a patent application relates to a brief description of the drawings. Section 1.74 of the Rules of Patent Practice provides that when there are drawings, a brief description shall be included. Therefore, in order to comply with the rules, you will want to describe each figure briefly along the following lines.

Fig. 1 is a side elevational view of a widget according to the invention.

Fig. 2 is a perspective view of widget according to a second embodiment of the invention.

This brings you to the detailed description of the preferred embodiment of your invention. It is in this section that you describe your invention with reference to the drawings.

And when you describe your invention in this section, your description should refer to the different figures and parts by reference numerals. Consider, for example, the following:

The preferred embodiments illustrated are not intended to be exhaustive or to limit the invention to the precise forms disclosed. They are chosen and described in order to best explain the principles of the invention and its application and practical use to thereby enable others skilled in the art to best utilize the invention.

The embodiment of the window assembly illustrated in Figs. 1-6 [see Fig. 7.2] includes a frame 10 and a plurality of glass panels namely, end panels 12 and 14, and sliding center panels 16 and 18. Frame 10, which may be of a metallic or plastic, includes an upper horizontal member 20 and a generally parallel lower horizontal member 22.

The purpose of the detailed description is to fully explain an invention in such clear and concise language that a person of ordinary skill in the art will understand it. However, there are other legal requirements that must be met. For example, your detailed description must include a basis for each of the elements in each of the claims in your application.

In addition to describing your invention and the various embodiments, the specification must also include a description of how your invention works. The structural details should be described with reference to the drawing and then followed by a description of how the invention works. And if your invention is a composition of matter, include a method for manufacturing the product and a description of its application.

7.4 THE CLAIMS

A patent specification must conclude with one or more claims. These claims must be written in a formal manner and may be difficult for a layperson to understand. In fact, there are times when experienced patent lawyers have difficulty in interpreting claims. However, with practice you can learn to write and interpret claims.

The claims are probably the most important part of a patent. It is true that the terms used in the claims must find proper and adequate support in the specification. However, the claims constitute the actual descriptions of what a patent covers, and define it in much the same manner as the metes and bounds define the boundries of a piece of real estate in a deed. And in drafting claims, you must comply with a number of rules and yet define your invention and its scope as broadly as possible.

For example, claims must include each of the essential elements of your invention. However, make certain that minor variations of those elements will not avoid infringement. In many cases you can draft broader claims by using the phrase "means for" followed by a functional statement. For example, you could claim "a means for applying heat" instead of "an electrical heating element." In the latter case, someone could avoid infringement by using a gas heating element.

Another example of means in a claim is illustrated by the first claim in a patent on wheeled skateboards, U.S. Patent No. 4,120,510. See, for example, Figure 7.3.

(1) Apparatus, which comprises:

a first substantially planar support member adapted to support a rider on the upper surface thereof;

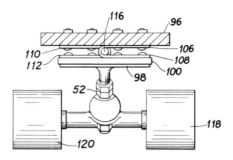

Figure 7.3

a second substantially planar support member positioned underneath said first support member;

wheeled truck means connected to the underside of said second support member for turning to the left or right in response to the tilting of said second support member respectively to the left or right about its longitudinal axis, and

means operatively connecting said first and second support members for preventing said truck from turning until said first support member is tilted a predetermined amount.

In subsequent claims, the last paragraph in claim 1 is more narrowly defined as a hinge having a pivot pin aligned with the longitudinal axis.

Your claims are the key to your protection. Don't overlook the importance of this subject since your claims could affect the amount of royalties that are paid for your invention.

7.5 SUMMARY

"A thorough analysis of an invention and of the prior art by an entreprenuer is important. In fact, you ought to conduct this type of analysis before you begin to prepare a patent application to cover your invention," Bill Lee said.

"And then," Bill continued, "in considering a patent application or an analysis of the prior art, you can always sit down and discuss it with your patent lawyer." Bill commented on this because he has encountered a number of engineers/entrepreneurs who do not want to write out an analysis of the prior art.

Now before proceeding to the next chapter, consider how you, as an entrepreneur, can determine if your attorney has done a good job in writing your patent application.

"In essence, you should determine that what you have disclosed to the attorney is in the specification," according to William Marshall Lee. "You should make certain that what he has written is understandable to you and to a person of ordinary skill in the art. And if it isn't understandable, it will have to be redone. You should also make certain that the disclosure is accurate and that everything is correct."

Bill went on to say, "It is important that you understand and agree with everything that is in the specifiction. And, finally, when you look at the claims, analyze them from a technical viewpoint. Make certain that they are clearly distinguished from the prior art and discuss any questions with your attorney."

Those of you who would like a more detailed analysis of a patent application and what goes into it are referred to *Inventions and Their Protection* by George V. Woodling (Clark Boardman/Mathew Bender, 1954)

8

Claims: The Scope of Your Protection

The claims are the most important part of your patent application because they define the boundaries of your rights.

8.1 GENERAL CONCEPTS

Business executives are motivated by profit. They seek investments that will assure them of a reasonable return with a minimum of risk. A conservative manager might accept a 10% return on a six-month money market account. In fact, some might prefer this approach to that of investing money in an unproven idea. But the fact is that with inflation of only 5% per year, a conservative financier who invests in the money market may lose money after paying taxes.

A more aggressive investor is willing to accept the risks inherent in launching a new idea in order to obtain a higher return on the investment. Such a person also knows that marketing products with a high rate of return attracts competitors. Therefore, this investor wants the protection of a patent, a patent that will prevent competitors from copying a successful product.

To find out if you have this type of protection, a prudent investor will ask: how good is your patent? In other words: How broad are your claims and are they valid? Will your patent claims provide a serious impediment to competitors? If, for example, your claims can be easily avoided, what advantage will the patented product have over a competitor's? Will your product be less expensive to produce or will it do a better job? Have you considered how long it will take a competitor to engineer around your claims and produce a similar product that avoids infringement? Have you analyzed the value of this lead time?

Answering these questions requires technical, legal, and business judgment, but begins with an understanding of patent claims.

8.2 THE PURPOSE OF CLAIMS

Your claims determine the scope of your protection. They are analagous to a land grant that tells whether you have 100 acres (approximately 40,000 square feet) or only 100 square feet. And the scope of claims can vary substantially. For example, in some patents the claims are very broad. In others, the claims are so narrow that they do not even cover the invention as practiced by the inventor.

Now, as an entrepreneur you want the broadest, valid claims that you can get. You also want to avoid an investment in a worthless patent. The problem is that your claims will be limited by what is disclosed in the prior art. For example, if one of your claims is sufficiently broad to read on a prior art device, it will be invalid. So, even though you want to obtain broad claims, you may be limited to less than you desire. Nevertheless, you can sometimes make money with relatively narrow claims. In fact, I know one inventor who received over $2 million from a licensee. His patent was very narrow and of doubtful validity.

William H. Webb is the senior partner in the firm of Webb, Burden, Robinson and Webb, P.A. Bill is acutely aware of the importance of claims because of his extensive experience in litigation. In fact, Bill litigated what may have been one of the more important inventions of this century. In that case, which involved the basic oxygen furnace invention, the actual trial (excluding years of discovery) took over one year to complete at the district court level. By comparison, a more typical patent case would be tried within a two to four week period.

William H. Webb said, "In drafting a patent application, you must be very careful to write claims that are commensurate with the scope of your invention. You must also be absolutely certain to get protection on the applicant's contribution. And, of course, you want to obtain claims of varying scope; to obtain some relatively broad claims and some narrow ones."

Bill Webb and many of his colleagues recognize a conflict when drafting claims between being definite and limiting the scope of the claims, and claiming an invention in such general terms that a claim is indefinite.

Fortunately there is an easy solution to this conflict. As Bill Webb suggested, "You are entitled to claims of varying scope." But in writing claims of varying scope, you should avoid indefiniteness. Consider, for example, the following claims, which have been rewritten in somewhat abbreviated form. The claims are directed to a filter cartridge according to the U.S. Patent No. 4,048,075 of Colvin et al.; see Figure 8.1.

> (1) A filter cartridge wherein the improvement consists essentially of an inner tubular perforated core, a pre-formed needle punched mat of nonwoven fibrous filtering material, wrapped in a continuous spiral layer around said core to form a roll of said mat; and a strand, wound in a criss cross open weave pattern around the outer periphery of the roll to form an open mesh network containing said roll.

Actually, the structure of the claimed filter is somewhat analogous to a roll of toilet paper except that the core is punched full of holes, the paper replaced by a needled fiber mat, and a mesh is provided on the outside to hold it together.

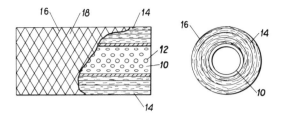

Figure 8.1

Now consider claim 2, which is narrower in scope, and reads as follows:

(2)   The filter cartridge of claim 1 wherein the fibers of said mat have a diameter range from about 0.1 microns to about 100 microns and said roll has a packing density range from about 0.06 to about 0.2.

By referring to claim 2, you can see that a competitor could avoid the claim by manufacturing a filter from fibers with a diameter of less than 0.1 micron or greater than 100 microns. The competitor could also avoid infringing the claim by manufacturing a filter with a packing density of less than 0.06 or greater than 0.2. In either of the hypothetical cases, the device would still infringe claim 1. The reason for including a narrow claim is that an infringer might, by conducting an extensive search, find a prior art reference that discloses the basic structure. But it is quite possible that the prior art would not anticipate the narrow claims.

Now consider a few words of caution from Bill Webb: "You should be very careful to make certain that you have an adequate basis in your patent specification to provide support for your broad claims; to provide support for what you hope to cover. And recognize that each of the terms which you use in your claims must have a basis in the patent specification. There must be a basis for determining what the terms mean." There is a good reason for Bill's words of caution. The reason is that your claims will be intrepreted based on what you say in the patent specification, and also by what is said during the prosecution of your patent application.

Bill Webb is acutely aware of the need for adequate support for your claim language. He is also acutely aware of the problem you may encounter if you accept a patent examiner's suggestion in amending your claims. In addition, Bill was kind enough to write the following memo on this subject for inclusion in this book.

It is elementary that there must be an adequate basis in the patent specification to fully support the claimed subject-matter, that the specific terms used in the claims must have a basis in the specification adequate to provide those skilled in the art a clear understanding of the true meaning and scope of the invention and that the claims must be limited to the invention described in the application (not just the specific embodiments set forth therein). These points should be born in mind at all times during the prosecution of an application before the Patent and Trademark Office.

Quite frequently during prosecution of an application in the Patent and Trademark Office, the Examiner will make suggestions in regard to limitations to be embodied in the claims, and in many instances, those suggestions are embodied in claims with dire results. No matter what the Examiner suggests would be acceptable to him and cause the claims to be allowable, the points mentioned above must be kept in mind and such suggestions should be carefully scrutinized with the above-mentioned factors paramount in the attorney's mind.

An example of what can happen if these precepts are not followed can be found in the litigation relating to the basic oxygen steelmaking process which revolutionized steelmaking throughout the world a few years ago. The basic Suess et al. patent No. 2,800,631 was held invalid because of the failure of the patent to comply fully with the requirements of 35 USC 112. The District Court, in the McLouth case (Kaiser Industries Corporation et al. *v.* McLouth Steel Corporation, 175 F. Supp. 743, E.D. Mich. 1959), in a lengthy opinion, extolled the virtues of the Suess et al. invention and its accomplishments in the steelmaking art and, in the last few pages, destroyed the patent protection on the ground that certain expressions utilized in the claim in issue suggested by the Examiner were not adequately supported by the specification. The main claim of the patent was addressed to the method of refining molten impure iron in the presence of a slag which comprised "discharging a stream of oxygen vertically downwardly through the slag layer onto and below the surface of the bath at the central portion thereof, to an extent to avoid material agitation of the bath by the oxygen stream . . . ". The court found that the term "material agitation" and the term "avoidance of material agitation" were not used or defined in the specification. The court also found that the limitation in the claim about the chemical reactions "producing a circulatory movement in the molten bath" was not set forth in the specification or supported thereby. It also held that the expression of blowing the oxygen onto and "below the surface" of the bath was not set forth anywhere in the specification.

These limitations in the claim were placed there in an effort to define fully the "invention," but the court held that they were not supported by the specification and, hence, the Section 112 defense, which incidentally was raised sua sponte by the District Court, destroyed one of the great inventions in steelmaking in recent generations. The Court of Appeals affirmed (40 F.2d 36).

> Thus, it is important to bear in mind the points set forth above throughout the entire prosecution of an application, and a careful check in this regard should be made immediately prior to the issuance of the patent.

Now, there are times when payments made to an inventor are more closely related to market potential than to the scope of the patent claims. Nevertheless, it is essential for you as an entrepreneur to understand the scope of your claims, the prior art, and the commercial market. An attempt to sell your invention without such knowledge would be like playing poker without looking at your cards.

8.3 FORM OF THE CLAIMS

Even though there is no statutory form for a claim, the practice of the U.S. Patent and Trademark Office requires that each claim must be the object of a sentence beginning with "What is claimed is . . . " or the equivalent. See for example, the *Manual of Patent Examining Procedures,* Section 608.01(m), which is published by the U.S. Department of Commerce. The phrase "What is claimed is" is placed at the beginning of the claims, and then each claim includes this phrase by implication. Note that each claim begins with a capital letter and ends with a period. However, you can divide various elements in paragraph form or by means of indentation to make your claims easier to read and understand.

Don't include reference numerals in your claims. It is permissible to do so if they are enclosed in parentheses, but it is not advisable. It is not advisable because there is a risk that a court might treat them as a limitation or refuse to give you the benefit of the "doctrine of equivalence." Some foreign patents include reference numerals in the claims, but it is something that just is not done in this country.

Now in preparing your patent application, you may want to arrange your claims with the broadest claim first and then follow with claims in order of descending scope to conclude with the narrowest claim. I personally prefer this approach and know a lot of patent professionals who follow this general practice. But I recognize that this approach is not always applicable and that some attorneys believe that it is better to start out with a claim that would be more acceptable to an examiner.

Generally, group your claims by type. For example, if you claim an article and a method, put all of your article claims in descending order with respect to breadth and then follow with your broadest to narrowest method claims. However, some attorneys do not follow this approach.

The problem is that, in arranging your claims in descending order with respect to breadth, you may find it is difficult to draw a clear line between what is definite and what is indefinite. For example, the use of a functional statement by itself as a claim limitation would be indefinite or insufficient to distinguish the claim from prior art. However, the proper use of a "means for" format followed by a functional statement would be definite. A review of your claims by an experienced patent professional can overcome this problem.

8.4   TYPES OF CLAIMS

In order to analyze your potential rights, consider the different types of claims. For example, a generic claim might be defined as one that covers the general concept or the broadest aspect of your invention. In effect, a generic claim covers all forms of your invention and should be distinguished from a species claim, which is directed to a specific embodiment.

An example of a generic claim together with two species claims may clarify this difference. For example, in U.S. Patent No. 3,650,102 to Economy et al., the first claim reads as follows: "An infusible cured novolac fiber." Novolac is a particular form of the chemical phenol. Claim 2, which is written in dependent form, reads "A novolac fiber according to claim 1 wherein said novolac is phenol formaldehyde."

The first claim would cover any infusible cured novolac fiber, while claim 2 would be limited to a novolac of the phenol formaldehyde type. Claim 3 of the patent is specific in a different sense in that it is directed to "A novolac fiber according to claim 1 having a diameter within the range of from about 0.1 micron to about 300 microns." Therefore, a product that falls within the range of claim 3 would still be covered by claim 1, that is, the generic claim. For comparison, a product made in accordance with claim 1 and having a diameter greater than 300 microns would be covered by the generic claim and yet would not infringe claim 3.

Since claims 2 and 3 have been written in dependent form they include all of the limitations of claim 1.

In today's practice, inventors and their attorneys are encouraged to use dependent claims because there is an additional charge for independent claims in excess of three.

However, it is sometimes desirable to include additional independent claims. So if the scope of your invention warrants additional independent claims, do not hesitate to file as many independent claims as you need to adequately cover your invention with claims of varying scope.

There is also a distinction between a product claim, such as the aforementioned claims 1−3, and a method claim, which is illustrated by referring to claim 1 of U.S. Patent No. 3,723, 588 of Economy et al. The method claim was included in the application for the earlier patent. Then the attorney filed a divisional application to comply with the patent examiner's requirement. He filed a divisional application with the method claims because the examiner argued that the method of producing the fibers was a separate invention from the fiber itself.

Claim 1 of the Economy patent reads as follows:

> A method for the production of an infusible cured novolac fiber comprising, forming a melt of a fusible novolac which is capable of polymerization with a suitable aldehyde, fiberizing said melt to form a thermoplastic uncured novolac fiber, and curing said uncured novolac fiber by heating it at a suitable temperature and for a sufficient time in a formaldehyde environment in the presence of an acid as a catalyst, and render it infusible.

A narrower method claim, or species claim, which is written in dependent form, is illustrated by claim 11 of the same patent. It reads as follows:

> A method as set forth in claim 1 wherein said uncured novolac fiber is cured by heating it in a gaseous atmosphere containing an acid and from about 10 percent to about 99 percent by volume of formaldehyde.

There is one other type of claim to consider. This type of claim is a hybrid of a product and a process claim and is referred to as a "product by process claim." Section 706.03(e) of the *Manual of Patent Examining Procedures* points out that when an article cannot be defined in any manner other than by the process of making it, it can be claimed in that manner. However, an applicant may be limited to one process by product claim, unless it can be proven that the products produced by the different claims are materially different.

An illustration of a product by process claim is taken from U.S. Patent No. 4,131,566 of Hari N. Murty and reads as follows:

Hard granular activated carbon made by the process of claim 15 and having an abrasion number of not less than about 80.

In the past, the courts have interpreted "combination" claims, that is, claims that start out with "the combination of" or "in combination" as very narrow claims. The courts held that the elimination of any element in a combination claim will avoid infringement of the claim. In the words of Justice Whittaker, "If anything is settled in patent law, it is that the combination patent covers only the totality of the elements in the claims and that no element separately viewed is within the grant." (35 U.S. 344). Some of the more recent decisions may have removed some of the onus attributed to the terms in combination. However, you should avoid using this language.

Now when you draft a claim to cover your invention, you should consider 35 U.S.C. 112, which allows for the use of "means plus function" formats in claim language. It states:

An element in a claim for a combination may be expressed as a means or step for performing a specified function without the recital of structure, material or acts in support thereof, and such claim shall be construed to cover the corresponding structure, material, or acts described in the specification and equivalents thereof.

In other words, you can claim your invention broadly by using "means for" plus a functional statement. In some cases, such as the ring toss game described in U.S. Patent No. 4,120,499, the claim will include a single means in combination with a number of other elements. For example, one of the claims calls for:

A ring toss game device comprising in combination:
  (a) a game board including a frame ...
  (b) a peg removably mounted on the board ...
  (c) support means attached to the game board for permitting the board to be variously disposed; and
  (d) a ring to be tossed at the board for retention by the peg ...

Now, "the support means" in paragraph (c) would include a hook to hold the board on a wall, a stand to position it upright, or even an airtight compartment for supporting the game board on the surface of water. The *Manual of Patent Examining Procedure* points out that a claim that recites only a single means and thus encompasses all possible means for performing a function should be rejected as functional. In other words, a mere idea is not patentable.

However, you can use more than one means in a claimed combination. For example, multiple "means plus function" statements are permissible in claims and frequently provide the broadest possible language for claiming your invention. This approach does at times result in a claim that is difficult to understand.

> An igniter for a gas burner comprising:
>
> > Ignition means and means for connecting said ignition means to a source of electrical energy and means for energizing said ignition means . . . .

A narrower claim directed to the same invention might be drafted as follows:

> An igniter for gas burners comprising a silicon carbide element, an electrical circuit connecting said element to a source of electrical energy and a switch disposed in said circuit whereby the electrical energy flows through said element when the switch is in the on position . . . .
>
> > whereby the element is heated to ignition temperature and ignites the gas.

Another type of claim frequently used in foreign applications is the Jepson claim. A Jepson claim (named after the case that first permitted this type of claim) is appropriate when you have made an improvement in an element of a known combination. In essence, all of the old elements are included in the preamble of the claim and the inventive concept is set forth as "The improvement comprising . . . ."

A typical Jepson claim taken from U.S. Patent No. 4,206,546 is written as follows:

> In a dental instrument delivery system including an instrument desk with an upper tray surface, the improvement which comprises:
>
> > providing said surface on a tray mounted on a sliding track including:
> >
> > a slide guide member mounted atop said instruments desk;
> >
> > a slide body member mounted to the bottom of said tray; and

a floating bearing assembly coupling said slide body to said slide guide;

said slide body being movable longitudinally with respect to said slide guide so that the tray may be suspended in cantilever relation over either of the side edges of said desk.

Another way to claim an invention in the chemical area is by using a "Markush" claim. But using a Markush claim, you can claim your invention by expressing a group of chemicals consisting of certain specified materials and calling for a material selected from the group. This type of claim is used where there is no commonly accepted generic expression commensurate with the scope of the invention. However, the use of a Markush claim is not permitted in mechanical cases.

8.5 NONSTATUTORY INVENTIONS

Even though a number of patentable subjects and the various approaches to claiming an invention have been reviewed, you should recognize that patents are not granted for all new and useful inventions and discoveries. For example, an arrangement of printed matter may be copyrightable but would not be patentable. A scientific principle, a method of doing business, and naturally occurring articles are not patentable. In fact, the question of protectibility of various forms of computerware has not yet been completely resolved by Congress and the courts.

8.6 CONCLUSION

In analyzing claims consider each element in the claim. Consider the fact that your claims will be interpreted in view of your specification. And ultimately, your claims will be construed in view of everything that was stated during the prosecution of your application. But for now, make certain that the language in each claim is clear. Determine whether or not the claim might be interpreted to cover a prior art device. If so, it will have to be rewritten. Make certain that you do not include any statements in your specification or claim that would limit the scope beyond that which is necessary to distinguish them over the prior art.

In the words of Bill Webb, "Include claims of varying scope, claims that clearly define your invention without undue limitations, and don't rely on the doctrine of equivalence." Use the "means plus function" format in at least some of the broader claims. And discuss your claims with your counsel until you are both satisfied that you have done the best job possible in covering your invention.

Now, in order to distinguish between broad protection and invalidity and to more fully understand the potential effect on your income, consider the fine edge between broad protection and invalidity, which is covered in the next chapter.

9

Claims: The Fine Edge Between Broad Protection and Invalidity

Proper claims are essential to maximize your return on investment.

9.1   A PRACTICAL APPROACH TO DRAFTING CLAIMS

Don't be intimidated by the legalistic language typically used in patent claims. Actually, you can learn to read and understand patent claims, and in the process may gain a better understanding of what patents are all about. You may also gain a better understanding of your own invention. However, you should not take this task lightly or overlook a need to consult with legal counsel before making any decisions based on your analysis of a patent claim.

In fact, some technical professionals may find this chapter to be a bit difficult. Some may skip over the material lightly, and relegate the job to an attorney. However, if you are willing to take the time, and refer back to the chapter when you outline your application, you can help yourself and your attorney to obtain the broadest protection for your invention. All that you have to do is follow a step by step procedure and identify the essential elements of your invention. But don't jump to conclusions.

Now, you might ask why you should worry about drafting a claim before writing a patent specification. The reason is that the value of a patent is determined by the claims. In other words, it is difficult to determine if you are justified in writing and filing a patent application without looking at the claims you hope to obtain.

This may seem like the chicken and egg syndrome, but in reality it is not. Once you have compared your idea with the prior art, you should understand the difference between your invention and those of your predecessors. And then drafting a claim first will help to quantify your thoughts and the breadth of the expected protection. It may help to explain that many, if not most, practicing patent attorneys, draft the claims before they draft the specification portion of a patent application.

So, as an entrepreneur, write down the essential elements of your invention and define each element as broadly as possible. Then ask if each element is essential for the practice of your invention. Are any of the elements patentable? If not, try to reduce the number of elements to those that are essential for an operative device. Refer to each of the elements as a "means for" and add a functional statement. But don't forget that your claim must not read on the prior art because if it covers the prior art, it will be unpatentable.

Don't get discouraged and don't hesitate to rewrite your initial claim several times. Actually, it is common practice to revise an initial claim several times.

And once you have an initial claim, or a good start on one, try to develop a claim outline. To be more specific, list all of the various modifications that you contemplate. However, don't write a claim for each minor modification. Nevertheless, you should include a sufficient number of claims to cover the practical alternatives for your invention with claims of varying scope.

Even though you may not want to draft your own application, a rudimentary knowledge of the claim drafting process can help you to determine if your application includes the best possible coverage.

9.2   FORMAL REQUIREMENTS

Within reasonable limits, you are allowed to claim your invention in language of your own choosing. However, you should select the language carefully, and recognize that there are certain formalities required if you want meaningful claims. And, if you use terms that are not fully understood by all, define them. Also, recognize that your income may depend on your claim language.

You probably remember that each claim should be written as an object of a sentence beginning with the term "What is claimed is," and that the term is written at the beginning of the claims and need not be repeated for each claim. Also, each claim begins with a capital letter and is written as a single sentence.

Don't forget that any words or phrases that you use in claiming your invention must be included in your patent specification and must be clearly defined therein, according to the Code of Federal Regulations (Title 37, Sec. 1.75). Essentially, you have to avoid ambiguity in claiming your invention.

So, if you want to claim a chair, including a seat and means for supporting said seat, make certain that you include more than one example of such means. For example, you might include a pedestal or a plurality of legs for supporting the seat in the description of your invention.

9.3   THE PREAMBLE

Your claim should include an introduction that is used to indicate the field in which the invention is applicable. This puts your claim in perspective in much the same way as the title of the invention at the beginning of the specification.

For example, if you claim an igniter for igniting gas in a furnace or stove, how would you feel if someone manufactured and sold an identical device as a miniature heating element? There are many judicial decisions that hold that the preamble of a claim does not constitute a structural limitation. Nevertheless, there are cases to the contrary, and a narrowly defined preamble opens the door to a defense in subsequent litigation. Besides, why take a chance when it would be just as easy to claim an electrical element as an igniter?

A preamble is treated as a structural limitation when the body of the claim refers back to the structure that is recited in the preamble and depends on such structure for defining an operative device. This type of claim is often referred to as a "Jepson claim." Jepson claims are used when an invention resides in an improvement in a known combination. For example, an improved grinding wheel might be claimed as follows:

> In a grinding wheel of the type having diamonds as the abrasive particles and a resin bond for bonding said particles together, the improvement comprising a metal coating on said diamonds for improving the bond between the resin and the diamond.

A claim of this type would be construed as including the limitations of diamonds and resin bond as well as the metal coating.

As a general rule, don't write a preamble for your claim that is materially broader than your invention. This may seem contrary to what has been said in the previous paragraphs, but is really a further qualification. Stop and think what it is that you have invented. It is true that you want to claim your invention as broadly as possible; however, don't try to cover something that is clearly outside of the field of your invention. After all, if your claim is too broad, it may read on the prior art and be invalid.

In the words of Tali Cepuritis, "Your best approach is to write claims of varying scope. And when you do this, also vary the preamble." For example, in the case of the linear compensated zoom optical system, the attorney could have claimed an optical system including linear compensation. Then a claim could have been added that included those elements necessary for linear compensation. A subsequent claim might then have been directed to a "zoom optical system" or even a "binocular zoom optical system."

9.4   INDISPENSABLE ELEMENTS

Your claims must include sufficient structure to define a working device. In other words, you must recite all of the elements necessary for practicing an operable form of the invention. And these elements should be tied together in a manner that shows the operation of your device. When writing claims, eliminate nonessential elements. If you don't eliminate nonessential elements, competitors will, and they will avoid infringing the claim.

Now, consider the problem of drafting a claim to cover a hand-held hair dryer. Hair dryers have been used for many years in beauty shops and have included most of the essential elements of a hand-held unit. Ask yourself what the essential elements are and how broadly you can cover the invention. How can you distinguish your hand-held unit from the old-fashioned hair-dryer that looked like a beehive on a stand?

The essential elements would certainly include a heating element and means for producing a flow of air across the heating element. So far, you have defined a device that would be anticipated by an old-fashioned electric heater having a fan behind the electrical coils.

Adding means to direct the air onto a selected portion of the hair would cover the cylindrical tube, but could still be interpreted as reading on one or more openings in the old-fashioned hair dryer. Hand supporting means and a whereby clause could then be used to distinguish the hand-held blow dryer from the prior art. Your claim might read as follows:

> What is claimed is:
> A hand-held hair dryer comprising a heating element and means for producing a flow of air across said heating element, means for directing the flow of air onto a selected portion of hair, and support means adapted to be held in the hand of an operator whereby the flow of heated air can be readily directed onto selected portions of a person's hair.

Additional structure would probably be required by a patent examiner in view of any prior art cited during the prosecution of the application. For example, the examiner might argue that a housing for supporting the electrical elements was essential and that structure for connecting the element to a source of electrical energy should also be included. Some examiners might argue that a source of electricity would be an essential element, but it is doubtful that they would persist in that rejection.

Now, if you accepted the examiner's suggestion and included a source of electricity in your claim, a competitor's device would not infringe your claims until it was plugged into an electrical receptacle. You could still sue a manufacturer for inducing infringement, but would have a better cause of action with a broader claim.

For comparison, consider the following claim taken from the U.S. Patent No. 4,167,820 of Johannes de Groot:

> An electric hair dryer including a heating source comprising a fan and a heating means, a regulating element connected to said heating means, temperature measuring means for measuring the temperature of the hair being dried and operatively connected to said regulating element in a manner effective to control the amount of power supplied to said heating means and to maintain the hair temperature at a substantially constant level, and an adjusting means connected to said regulating element for adjusting the desired hair drying temperature.

You should keep in mind that a claim defining a combination of elements will not be infringed by a device that has a lesser number of elements. For this reason, it is desirable to draft your claims with the least number of elements, but don't forget that you have to include all of the elements required for a working device according to your invention. Also, make certain that your claim does not read on the prior art.

9.5 THE PROPER USE OF FUNCTIONAL LANGUAGE

Tali Cepuritis said, "I like to include some claims which use functional language in defining the invention. But I don't like to rely on those claims during litigation except as a last resort. Claims that recite structural features are much better. Actually, Tali, like most attorneys, likes to obtain claims of varying scope. And, as a litigator for patent enforcement, he prefers to rely on the narrowest, most definite claim that covers the competitor's product.

"In my opinion," Tali went on to say, "the best way for an entrepreneur to get good claims is to work with an experienced patent attorney who knows your field. Then the attorney can guide the entrepreneur to the key features really needed. He will ask himself if any apparently key features can be eliminated. He will ask if any of these key features are patentable. He will ask about variations, and about other ways of accomplishing the same objectives. And then, he will draft the claims to cover your invention as broadly as possible."

Now as a general rule, avoid functional language except as a part of a means claim or in a whereby clause. The reason is that you cannot distinguish your invention from the prior art with functional language. However, the proper use of functional language is illustrated by the sample claim from U.S. Patent No. 4,167,820 in the previous section. In that patent the "means for measuring the temperature of the hair" is one example. Many attorneys also use functional language in a whereby clause such as the one that stated "whereby the flow of heated air can be readily directed onto selected portions of a person's hair." Such clauses are usually placed at the end of the claim, but may appear in the claim body. This type of language may avoid a rejection that your claim is merely an aggregation of unconnected elements.

Therefore, use functional language to show the inevitable result of a combination without limiting your coverage, but recognize that such language will not support patentability. And as a general rule, the use of functional language other than as a description of "means" or in a whereby clause should be avoided. Even if the functional language is overlooked by the patent examiner, it provides one more area of attack during subsequent litigation or during negotiations for a license.

9.6   GENERIC, SPECIES, AND MARKUSH CLAIMS

Generic claims are used to define your invention as broadly as possible, as compared to a species claim, which is used to define a specific embodiment of your invention. Now, in order to get broad claims and species claims, that is, claims directed to different embodiments of your invention, you will have to show that you are entitled to them. For example, if you have a number of species claims, include a number of examples in the application to support the claims of varying scope.

Patent practice in the chemical area differs somewhat from the practices in the mechanical and electrical areas. However, the following example may clarify the difference between generic and species claims and the role of Markush claims in patent practice.

Consider an invention that relates to an infrared transmitting element made from a hot pressed alkaline earth fluoride. The alkaline earth group of chemicals includes calcium, strontium, and barium. Therefore, an example of an infrared transmitting element made from each of these materials should be included in the patent specification as support for the generic claim. However, if the invention does not work with barium fluoride, you would not have a basis for claiming an alkaline earth fluoride generically.

You should also recognize that each of the individual alkaline earth fluorides, that is, barium, strontium, and calcium, would form the basis for a species claim, assuming that the element could be used to make an operative device. In fact, you would probably claim "mixtures thereof" if such mixtures could be used in the practice of your invention.

This approach leads to another question. What should you do if one of the species just won't work? In chemical cases there is an easy solution, which is to write a so-called "Markush" claim. For example, if barium fluoride would not work in the previous example, you could not claim an alkaline earth fluoride. However, you could use a Markush group and claim a material "selected from the group consisting of calcium fluoride and strontium fluoride." You could then claim each of the species. However, if you claimed each species and failed to write a generic claim, a patent examiner would argue that you had two distinct inventions and require you to elect one species and cancel the other. A divisional application could then be filed to cover the other species.

In an effort to clarify the difference between a generic claim and a species claim, consider the claim language in the optical cryptographic device invented by Ferris and Meltzer (U.S. Patent No. 3,178,903). In that patent there are two species, those relating to spherical lenses and those relating to cylindrical lenses. A generic claim was drafted to cover both and recited". . . "a planar array of lenticular elements."

9.7 PROPER WORDING AND TERMINOLOGY

The importance of using proper wording and terminology in drafting claims of varying scope cannot be overemphasized. This may seem inconsistent with the earlier statement that you can claim your invention in words of your own choice. Nevertheless, you must particularly point out and distinctly claim your invention. To do so, you should claim your invention in language that can be clearly understood by a person in the art to which it applies.

And when you start to draft your claims, don't try to write in some obtuse language that is only understood by patent lawyers. It is true that some claims are difficult to understand, but don't try to confuse what could otherwise be clearly defined. For example, if your invention resides in the use of a rack and pinion gear assembly, you might claim ". . . a gear assembly including a rack and pinion for transmitting rotational movement to linear displacement."

Write your claims in the simplest form possible, and then try to broaden each element into a means form to obtain the broadest coverage possible.

9.8 DEFINITE VERSUS INDEFINITE INTRODUCTION

The Rules of Practice before the U.S. Patent and Trademark Office require you to set forth the principal elements of your claim in a positive or direct manner. For example, in the case of the hair dryer previously referred to (U.S. Patent No. 4,167,820) the claim reads:

> A hair dryer including a heating source comprising a fan and a heating means, a regulating element connected to said heating means. . .

The fan, heating means, and regulating element are each set forth in a positive manner. It would be improper to write the claim in the following manner:

> A hair dryer including a heating source adjacent a fan in which a heating means is connected to a regulating element. . .

In the latter example, the fan and regulating element have not been introduced directly. In other words, the fan and regulating element were not set forth in a positive manner as an essential element in the invention. Accordingly, a patent examiner would probably reject the claim.

9.9 ORDER OF ELEMENTS

There is no specific rule regarding the order of elements in a claim. Nevertheless, you should incorporate the elements in a natural order so that their interaction can be readily understood. Certainly, it would not make sense to randomly list a plethora of elements in a claimed combination and thereafter explain the interaction of the elements.

Perhaps an additional example may clarify this concept. If your invention related to a steering mechanism for an automobile, you might proceed through the mechanism as follows:

> A shaft and a steering wheel fixed to one end of the shaft, a rack and pinion assembly, the pinion fixed to the opposite end of the shaft and engaging said rack whereby rotation of the wheel results in the lateral displacement of the rack, means for pivotally mounting a wheel assembly and means attached to said assembly connecting said assembly to said rack. . .

In this case, the order of elements is dictated by clarity and an endeavor to distinctly claim the invention.

9.10   ANTECEDENTS

Drafting claims requires the use of antecedents. And the use of antecedents relates to a requirement to set forth the indispensable elements in a claim positively or directly. The purpose of this requirement is to avoid ambiguity and to avoid a rejection on the basis that a particular element has no antecedent. For example, suppose you were to claim the steering assembly as: "Comprising a shaft connected to a steering wheel." There would be no antecedent basis for the steering wheel. And, if you attempted to claim the invention as: "Comprising a steering wheel connected to a shaft," there would be no antecedent basis for the shaft. However, it is easy to overcome this problem. All that you have to do is claim: "A shaft and a steering wheel connected to said shaft."

9.11   DEPENDENT CLAIMS

Tali Cepuritis doesn't think that it makes much difference if you include a number of dependent claims instead of independent claims. He knows that it will affect the filing fee but prefers to have at least one broad, one medium, and one narrow claim in independent form. "But," he said, "the litigant's job is to explain to the court what is actually covered. And, from that perspective, the form is not that important."

Nevertheless, dependent claims warrant additional attention. They are narrower than the independent claims from which they depend and include all of the elements of their associated independent claim. Therefore, you could have a problem if your independent claim is not sufficiently broad. For this reason, it is preferable, as suggested by Tali Cepuritis, to write several independent claims of varying scope and using different language in each. For example, if your invention relates to an attachment of nonmetallic articles to metallic substrates, as claimed in U.S. Patent No. 3,624,344 to L. G. Kutzer, you would disclose "a flange or shoulder" in the specification. Then, rather than claiming a flange with a number of dependent claims, you might write a second independent claim wherein you substitute the term "shoulder" for "flange."

But don't try to claim every possible permutation or combination. To do so is an invitation to a patent examiner to reject your patent for undue multiplicity of claims.

Actually, Rule 75 of the Rules of Practice before the U.S. Patent and Trademark Office provides that more than one claim may be presented, provided that each differs substantially from the others and that they are not unduly multiplied. And then the *Manual of Patent Examining Procedure* provides that "An unreasonable number of claims, that is unreasonable in view of the nature and scope of applicant's invention and the state of the art, affords a basis for a rejection on the ground of multiplicity" (Sec. 706.03).

There is one advantage to using dependent claims. The advantage is that they clearly point out each feature that you believe to be patentably distinguished from the other claims in your application. For this reason you may obtain more claims by using the dependent form than by trying to convince an examiner that the same number of independent claims was necessary to adequately claim your invention.

However, you are entitled to some latitude in claiming your invention, and to a reasonable number of claims. You are also permitted to use multiple dependent claims, that is, claims that depend on more than one claim. But it is difficult to determine a reasonable number of claims is in view of the nature and scope of your invention. It is, in fact, even difficult to develop a general rule. Nevertheless, you should be able to adequately cover most inventions with twelve to twenty claims.

Tali Ceperitis cautions inventors about taking a narrow view of their inventions and about focusing only on their basic concept. He said, "Engineers and scientists frequently focus their attention on maximum efficiency or yield. And, because of this, they may fail to consider a lot of other patentable features."

"By contrast," Tali continued, "I want to look at all of their tests. I even want to see the worst example. For example, I don't want to look only at the Cadillac Eldorado; I want to see what the Chevy Chevette looks like. I want to look at the experiments that failed so I know how far I can go in claiming the invention without including something that is inoperative."

Before adopting some general rule on the number of claims, recognize that selecting the optimum number of claims with respect to the scope and nature of your invention is an art that is developed over a number of years of patent practice. But as an entrepreneur, you can determine what the essential features of your invention are. You can probably get a pretty good idea about what the broadest claim you can obtain is. And you can probably determine which specific features you want to cover. Just ask yourself: What are the important variations? And, as a final step, try to provide claims of varying scope, so that if your broadest claims are held invalid, and your narrowest are not sufficiently broad to protect you against a competitor, you will still have some claims of intermediate scope that assure you of reasonable protection.

There are times when an inventor will include numerous claims in an application. For example, an inventor may design a new slide projector and in the course of the development work make a number of improvements over the prior art. This inventor would then file a single application to cover all the inventions. In fact, the real inventor of one slide projector included five sets of claims, which covered five different inventions. He subsequently divided the application into five divisional applications.

When more than one invention is claimed in an application, the patent examiner will normally require you to select one invention for prosecution. At that time, or at any time prior to the issuance of a patent or the abandonment of the application, you would file divisional applications to cover the other inventions. This procedure is covered in more detail in the chapter on prosecuting a patent application.

The claims in U.S. Patent No. 3,563,802 of Rupert L. Ogden relate to a fuel cell construction and provide an example of dependent claims, a Jepson-type claim, claims of varying scope, and the coverage of an invention with a limited number of claims. Ogden claims:

(1) In a fuel cell comprising a case, positive and negative porous electrodes inserted within the case and enclosing an inner space, electrolyte within said inner space, means for introducing an oxidant gas through one porous electrode and a fuel through the other, the improvement comprising having the inner space divided by a porous membrane consisting essentially of cured phenolic fibers prepared from the resin condensation product of phenols and aldehydes which can be fiberized and cured.

(2) A fuel cell according to claim 1 in which the porous membrane is a paper prepared from phenolic fibers.

(3) A fuel cell according to claim 1 in which the porous membrane is a fabric prepared from phenolic fibers.

(4) A fuel cell according to claim 2 in which the paper is self-bonded.

(5) A fuel cell according to claim 2 in which the paper is phenolic resin-bonded.

9.12   SUBCOMBINATION CLAIMS

There are cases when you may obtain an allowance of a claim on a combination of elements and recognize the desirability of obtaining a claim that is directed to only a part of a combination. For example, in the slide projector mentioned in the previous section, you might have invented a slide preheating means. Then you would want to claim that feature per se. One advantage of a claim on the subcombination is that you could assert your patent against a subcontractor who manufactured that combination.

The U.S. Patent and Trademark Office does allow claims on subcombinations in a single application. However, the subcombination must represent a functional or operable device, and constitute more than a single means claim. In reality, this goes back to identifying the key feature or the essence of your invention.

9.13   THE PROBLEM WITH PRIOR ART

There are statements throughout the patent literature referring to "reading on the prior art." This refers to the problem of distinguishing your claims from those devices that have been previously disclosed or used. There is an old axiom in patent law: If a prior art device would infringe your claim, the claim is invalid.

Now assume that your invention really is an improvement on a prior art process, and that you have found out how to eliminate an expensive step. If you draft your claim and include all of the other steps, you could argue that your invention was new, useful, and not obvious. The problem is that the prior art process would infringe your claim since the addition of the step you eliminated would not avoid infringement. For example, consider the invention relating to a method for manufacturing diamonds as disclosed and claimed in the U.S. Patent No. 3,576,602 to T. Kuratome. The claim reads:

A process for producing diamond comprising

(1) Subjecting a mixture of
  (a) nondiamond carbon,
  (b) a vanadium carbide solvent, and
  (c) a b-Zr promoter to an elevated temperature and pressure sufficient to convert nondiamond carbon to diamond;
(2) cooling the resultant product; and
(3) separating diamond therefrom.

Now assume that your invention enabled you to produce the diamond at room temperature; you might draft an almost identical claim by leaving out "to an elevated temperature" and the cooling step. Thus your claim would read as follows:

(1) Subjecting a mixture of
  (a) nondiamond carbon,
  (b) a vanadium carbide solvent, and
  (c) a b-Zr promoter to a pressure sufficient to convert nondiamond carbon to diamond carbon; and
(2) separating diamond therefrom.

You could argue that the elimination of the heating and cooling steps was nonobvious, resulted in a lower cost product, and if it were true, resulted in an increased yield. Nevertheless, the claim would still read on the prior art process. In other words, the practice of the prior art process would read on your claim, which would make your claim invalid.

There are several solutions to this type of problem. You could add a limitation such as "at room temperature" (defined as a range of temperatures) after pressure, recognizing that competitors could then elevate or reduce the temperature to avoid infringing your claim. It is true that they might infringe the earlier patent, but that is probably irrelevant to your pocketbook, unless, of course, you have found a way around a patent that is not available for licensing.

However, in most cases you will find that there is something else that is required to make your process work. If there wasn't, the earlier patentee would have claimed his or her invention in a way that covered your concept. So if a catalyst were required for your process, the proposed claim could be modified by adding the words "in the presence of a catalyst" before "to a pressure." And in this case you would have differentiated your claim from the prior art, at least as set forth in the example cited.

9.14   CLAIMING A SINGLE INVENTION WITH CLAIMS OF VARYING SCOPE

If you recall, Tali Cepuritis spoke about the advantages of claiming an invention with claims of varying scope. As a litigator, he wants to build a picket fence around an invention. He wants broad claims that will encompass all of the variations of your invention and he wants narrow claims that he can assert against any infringer that copies the features covered by that claim.

There is also the question of including more than one invention in a single application. The Code of Federal Regulations provides that two or more "independent and distinct inventions" may not be claimed in one application. The term "independent" has been construed to mean that there is no relationship between the two or more subjects. For example, you might argue that in a slide projector all of the subassemblies are related. Nevertheless, a patent examiner would be upheld for distinguishing between a slide preheater and a slide changing mechanism.

A process and apparatus for carrying out the process may be included in a single application. But you may be required to file a divisional application in order to cover both.

The reason for the rule that prohibits multiple inventions in a single application is that you pay a filing fee for a patent search and examination on a single invention. And remember, an examiner is evaluated on the number of cases handled. Therefore, the examiner does not want to do three or four times the amount of work for the same amount of credit.

In considering method claims, there is a method for making a product, and a method of using it. At times, you might want to take a different approach. For example, you might want to claim a combination of means for producing a result, and a number of steps in a process for accomplishing a similar result. And in those cases where the method can have no other result or use, you are permitted to maintain both types of claims in a single application. However, if the method is applicable to some other use, an examiner will require a restriction to a single invention.

Actually, many applications are initially rejected for claiming more than a single invention in the application. In many cases they are rejected because the broad claim that ties a number of specific inventions together is not patentable. Then the examiner argues that each of the species claims is an independent invention. On the other hand, there is a good reason for including multiple inventions in a single invention. The reason is that an examiner who requires a restriction will be unable to reject one or more of the applications on the basis of double patenting.

9.15   WORDS AND PHRASES IN CLAIM DRAFTING

According to Tali Cepuritis, "Each word that you use in a patent claim is important." So when you draft your patent claims, use care in the selection of each word and phrase and eliminate those words that are not essential. You should know that each word in a claim must be supported by the use of that same word in the specification. You should also use generic terms whenever possible. And you should list the indispensable elements that make up your invention and a number of alternative terms that can be used to define each of those elements.

This brings you to the choice of a particular word, a choice that may make the difference between a valuable patent and a worthless piece of paper. It is a choice that should be made by an experienced attorney. For example, the very first word after your preamble could unduly limit the scope of your claims. Words such as "comprising," "having," and "including" have been judicially recognized for their breadth. In contrast, phrases such as "consisting of" have been construed narrowly. The phrase "consisting essentially of" might be considered in between the two extremes, except that in chemical cases it is more closely associated with the broad terms.

So in claiming your invention, you will want to follow the general rule as set forth in the AMI Industries case, wherein Judge Jones wrote, "As a general rule the claims to a mechanical invention can be framed as broadly as possible in light of the prior art. . . " (see Vol. 204, p. 588 of the *U.S. Patent Quarterly*). Following this rule would result in selecting the term "comprising," which does not preclude the use of additional elements.

By contrast, "consisting of" should be reserved for a limited or narrow claim since it may be construed as consisting *only* of the listed elements. This term has, however, found frequent use in chemical applications for either a species claim or the introduction of a Markush group, a group of chemicals any one of which is essential for the practice of the invention.

9.16   A FINAL WORD ON DRAFTING CLAIMS

You can usually overcome the problems associated with drafting claims by having your proposed claims reviewed by a patent attorney who has had at least several years of patent experience. Nevertheless, you can learn by drafting a proposed set of claims and a complete description of your invention. Then, with the help of your attorney, you can put your claims in final form and obtain the broadest possible protection. Chapter 13 is devoted to this approach as well as to the other aspects of working with your lawyer.

For the uninitiated who persist in proceeding without counsel, there is some help, but it is fraught with risk. The *Manual of Patent Examining Procedure* has a special provision for inventor-filed applications (see Sec. 700.07i). It provides: In cases where an application is being prosecuted by an inventor without the aid of an attorney, and when an examiner believes that the application includes patentable subject matter, the examiner should draft one or more claims and suggest them to the applicant.

However, as an entrepreneur, don't take this approach. The problem is that a patent examiner's training is predicated on distinguishing claims over the prior art. It isn't the examiner's job to seek the broadest claim language allowable. That should be your job with the help of counsel.

Remember that the value of your patent is directly related to the breadth of your claims.

10

Patent Drawings

A picture is worth a thousand words.

10.1   GENERAL CONCEPTS

William Lacey has over thirty years experience as a patent draftsman. He has worked for many patent lawyers and knows how to illustrate an invention. "Making a patent drawing," according to Bill, "is a lot different than making a drawing for a skilled machinist. It is different because you can leave out a lot of details. For example, for a machinist, you may have to show four pieces with all of the tolerances. But in a patent drawing, you may be able to simplify things and illustrate the same concept with a single piece."

Bill went on to say, "When you make a patent drawing, you want to illustrate the invention as clearly as possible. You want to illustrate the invention for a judge or for an average person who is skilled in the art. You should also try to keep the drawings as simple as possible. In other words, don't confuse the invention with a complex drawing."

Now when you apply for a patent you must furnish a drawing " . . . where necessary for an understanding of the subject matter sought to be patented," according to Volume 37, Section 1.81 of the Code of Federal Regulations. You might, of course, question whether or not a drawing will be necessary to understand your invention. However, in most cases that are outside of the chemical field, you will include a drawing as part of your patent application.

As a general rule, you will include a drawing because it is the best way to illustrate your invention. Besides, you may encounter a problem if you do not include a drawing. For example, you could have your application rejected on the basis of having an insufficient disclosure. And if you do not have a drawing to rely on, you might not be able to overcome that rejection. While a drawing is not a cure-all for a poorly written disclosure, a good drawing is usually a vital part of your application.

There is a problem associated with adding drawings by amendment, that is, after the filing date of your application. You will not be able to rely on a drawing that was added by amendment as support for a broader claim than that which is supported by the original specification.

As a general rule, include a drawing as part of your original application. In many cases, you can rely on a relatively simple drawing. For example, if you had invented a new type of sandpaper, a simple drawing could easily show a backing sheet, a layer of adhesive, a layer of abrasive particles, and a sizing coating, that is, a resin coating over the top of the abrasive particles.

Now, before proceeding with the formal requirements for patent drawings, consider a few words of advice from Bill Lacey, who said, "In many cases you can simplify a drawing by taking a section. But take a section in a manner that will give you a clear illustration of the invention."

Bill also had some words of advice for inventors who want an experienced patent draftsman to prepare their drawings. Bill suggests, "If you have a working model, it is usually much easier for a draftsman to make drawings based on that model. But even if you don't have a model, let the draftsman see your pencil sketches. Hand sketches are fine, but it will help if you can keep them in proper proportion, or at least, put in the general dimensions."

Illustrate each feature of your invention (each element that you claim.) If you don't point those features out to your draftsman, they may not show in the finished drawings.

10.2   FORMAL REQUIREMENTS

When you file your patent application, you should submit your formal drawings on two or three ply white bristol board and in India ink. Occasionally, you can file an application with informal drawings. This is sometimes done to avoid a delay in filing an application, but eventually you would follow up with formal drawings. The reason for formal drawings is that they will become a permanent part of the patent record and will be reproduced and published when your patent issues. And since the drawings are part of the permanent record, the rules of practice prohibit the use of white correction fluid.

Bill Lacey commented on the use of India ink. He said, "Not many draftsmen have the skill to make drawings in ink." It is true that most skilled draftsmen can make good pencil sketches and that most attorneys work with pencil drawings before finalizing an application. But in the end, the drawings must be done in ink, and the lines have to have the proper thickness.

The lines must be of a proper thickness because they distinguish what is being shown and because the formal drawings will be reproduced and published when your patent issues. This reproduction will be done in a manner that reduces the size of the original drawing by about one-third. Also, when the Patent and Trademark Office publishes an abstract of your patent in the *Official Gazette,* one of the representative drawings will be included after a further reduction in size.

Because of these reductions, your original drawings must be submitted on either an $8\frac{1}{2} \times 14$ inch or 21.0×29.7 cm sheet. On 21.0×29.7 cm sheets the top margin should be at least 2.5 cm with a left side margin of 2.5 cm. The right side margin should be 1.5 cm and the bottom margin 1.0 cm. Shading should be used sparingly with the light coming from the upper corner at a 45% angle. "Shading should be used sparingly so that the lines do not blend together when the drawings are reduced in size," according to Bill Lacey.

The rules also require lines to be clean, sharp, and solid, In addition, you must avoid fine or crowded lines. Figures 10.1 and 10.2 are typical patent drawings from a patent on a mechanical device. Figure 10.1 is a perspective view showing the overall assembly of a teaching device according to U.S. Patent No. 4,123,852. Figure 10.2 is a side elevational view of the same device.

In making your patent drawings, identify the different views used to illustrate your invention and use consecutively numbered figures. You should also use reference numerals that are at least $\frac{1}{8}$ inch high to identify the parts. Don't crowd the reference numerals together or allow them to interfere with a clear showing of the parts. You should also make certain that your reference numerals, like the lines, are clear and absolutely black.

In some cases, you can use graphical representations or symbols with labels for conventional elements. This is one way to simplify your drawings. An example of this practice is illustrated in Figure 10.3, which was taken from U.S. Patent No. 4,124,780 on an FM/stereophonic receiver providing a test signal.

Now, when you are illustrating your invention, remember that views on the same sheet should be arranged in the same direction so that all reference figures can be read without moving the drawing to a different

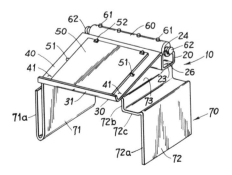

Figure 10.1

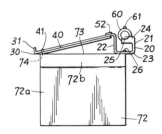

Figure 10.2

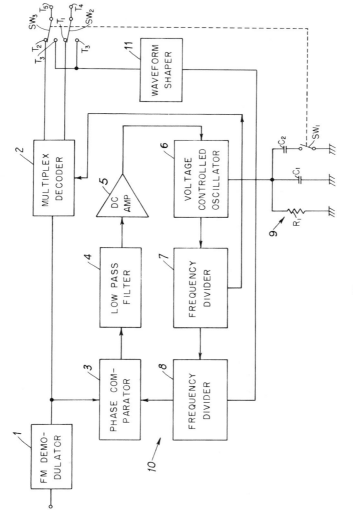

Figure 10.3

position. You should also remember that the U.S. Patent and Trademark Office rules relating to drawings will be strictly enforced. In other words, if your drawings are improper, an examiner will object to the drawings and corrections will be required.

10.3   FLOW CHARTS

Many attorneys include a flow chart as a drawing in patent applications on chemical processes. In fact, some attorneys include a flow chart for any application that includes method or process claims. It can be argued that a flow chart is not necessary for an understanding of the invention. However, from a practical standpoint this type of drawing is relatively inexpensive. Besides, the use of a flow chart may avoid an argument with an examiner, and may make it easier to draft your patent specification.

An example of a chemical flow chart or schematic diagram is shown in Figure 10.4, taken from U.S. Patent No. 4,124,693 of Shropshire et al. That invention relates to a process for recovering bromine.

10.4   DESIGN PATENTS

The rules of practice with respect to drawings in design cases have been stringently enforced since the drawing is the claim. The drawings in a design case constitute much of the disclosure for the design patent specification that includes little or no description of the ornamental design. What this means to you is that you must include a sufficient number of views to constitute a complete disclosure of the appearance of your invention, and shading and other drawing requirements must be complied with exactly.

10.5   USE OF PHOTOGRAPHS

You might argue that the answer to any problems in patent drawings could be avoided by use of a photograph. Unfortunately, photographs may be excluded from the final application. However, photographs can be used where it is virtually impossible to reproduce an illustration by drafting techniques. The *Manual of Patent Examining Procedure* provides that photographs are not acceptable unless they come within one of the following categories: "Crystalline structures, metallurgical microstructures, textile fabrics, grain structures and ornamental effects." In those cases,

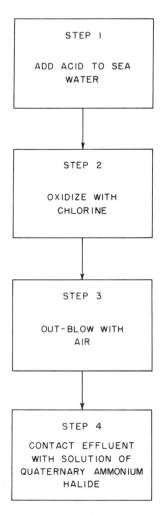

Figure 10.4

the photographs must be printed on sensitized paper, a double weight with a smooth white surface. They must also show your invention more clearly than could be done with India ink.

10.6   ELECTRICAL SYMBOLS

In some cases, you can use symbols in a drawing. Such symbols as included in the publication of the American National Standards Institute Inc.,

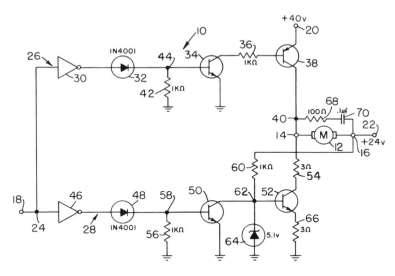

Figure 10.5

1430 Broadway, New York, New York 10018 are generally acceptable for patent drawings. An example of the use of symbols is shown in Figure 10.5, which is taken from Figure 1 of U.S. Patent No. 4,124,811 on a circuit for bi-directionally powering a moter, issued to M. J. Anderson.

10.7 CONCLUSION

It is difficult, if not impossible, to provide a rule of thumb as to how many figures or what type of figures are necessary to adequately illustrate your invention. In a way, it's like drafting the claims and determining how many claims are needed. However, if you remember the principle that each of the features in the claims must be illustrated in the drawings, and if you provide drawings in accordance with the rules of practice, your application will be complete. Just remember that if you claim an alternative form or a second embodiment, it too must be illustrated in your drawings.

11

The Patent Specification

A patent specification is an important part of a legal document. It is the foundation on which your patent rests. Your claims may define the scope of your invention, but they are interpreted in view of the specification. The purpose of this chapter is to tell you what should go into a patent application, including the specification, and to help you work with your attorney to do a better job, and at the same time, to assure yourself that you have done your part to fully protect your rights. This chapter is not intended to serve as a substitute for an experienced patent lawyer.

The main thing to remember in writing a patent specification is that the description of your invention must be sufficient to enable a person of ordinary skill in the art to make and use your invention. And, at the same time, it is essential to describe your invention in a manner which will distinguish it from the prior art. Therefore, think about why your invention works, and how it differs from the prior art.

Now as an entrepreneur/inventor, you probably have the most intimate knowledge about your invention and considerable knowledge in the field. For example, Leslie O. Vargady invented an improved optical measuring device and worked closely with his attorney in drafting a patent application. The originally drafted claims distinguished the invention from the prior art that had been disclosed by an extensive patent search. Nevertheless, Leslie pointed out that the claims were too broad, since they would cover a device that had been manufactured and sold in Germany during the 1930s. Leslie then worked with his attorney to redraft the claims. After that they revised the draft of the specification to clearly describe his invention and at the same time to distinguish it from the earlier German device.

You might also consider the approach used by a creative chemist and prolific inventor who drafted numerous applications himself. Then, after writing an application, he submitted it to his attorney for review and filing. Within a short time, this creative chemist dominated an entire field with numerous patents, the majority of which he had drafted himself. Certainly you can become more proficient in preparing an application with each case that you write. You may also, by concentrating your efforts in a single field, develop a portfolio of patents and a reputation as an expert in the field.

As an entrepreneur, you can write a draft of your own patent application. By doing so, you should learn what goes into an application, how the application is arranged, and how to do a better job in communicating with your lawyer. Besides, a carefully written disclosure will help your attorney to prepare your application in a more efficient manner.

If you do write a draft of an application, you should, like the creative chemist, ask an attorney to review your work and make any necessary revisions before the application is filed. After all, it is the attorney's job to translate your idea into precise language and to make certain that all of the legal requirements are met. It is the attorney's job to get the broadest possible protection for your invention.

In writing a patent specification, you want to get the essence of why your invention is good across to the reader and to show what modifications can be made. You want to prevent someone from designing around your claims. And one way to do this is by clearly defining your invention and a number of variations in the specification.

In essence, it is not difficult to write a detailed disclosure of your invention. This disclosure will form the basis for a patent specification. It is not difficult to write a disclosure if you start out as an attorney would, by reviewing the prior art patents that were disclosed by a patent search. Look for patents that are most similar to your idea and observe how those attorneys described their client's inventions.

Then draft an initial claim in the broadest terms possible and prepare a complete claim outline. The claim outline will point out the important features that must be described in your specification. And you will need to illustrate each of the claimed features in the patent drawings. Then your detailed description of those drawings will lead to a complete disclosure.

But before you write a detailed description, reflect for a moment on what it is that you are trying to do. Remember that in writing a detailed description, you should define the precise invention for which you seek a patent. What you want to do is describe your invention clearly since any vagueness in the description may be detrimental. And if your invention relates to an improvement, you must point out that part or parts that constitue the improvement. Try to describe your invention and the most preferred manner of using it in "full, clear, concise and exact terms" so that a person of ordinary skill will be taught how to practice the preferred embodiment of your invention. Also, remember that the rules of the U.S. Patent and Trademark Office (rule 71) require that the best mode for carrying out the invention must be set forth.

11.1   THE TITLE

You must include a title at the beginning of your application. The rules of patent practice provide that "The title of the invention, which should be as short and specific as possible, should appear as a heading on the first page of the specification . . . ." In fact, Section 606.01 of the *Manual of Patent Examining Procedure* provides that the patent examiner may require a change in the title if it isn't descriptive of the invention claimed.

If, for example, you selected the word "Furnace" for your title and claimed a method for insulating a furnace, your title would not be descriptive of your invention. In such cases, the patent examiner would probably require a change to: "A Method for Insulating a Furnace." The view of the U.S. Patent and Trademark Office as stated in the *Manual of Patent Examining Procedure* is that a slight loss in brevity will be more than offset by the gain in informative value.

Nevertheless, in selecting your title be definite and brief. Most important, keep in mind what it is that you are claiming as your invention. In other words, if you claim a process and apparatus, your title should be directed to a "Process and Apparatus for a . . . "

11.2   AN ABSTRACT OF THE DISCLOSURE

An abstract of the disclosure may either directly follow the title, or be provided on a separate page, often the last page of the application. Older patents, that is, those issued in the early 1960s or before, do not have an abstract, but in today's practice, you must include an abstract of what is disclosed in the specification.

Many lawyers leave the abstract until last. They do this because it is easier to write an abstract of a patent specification after they have written the specification. Besides, you will probably become more knowledgeable as you proceed and may include additional information in the specification as you go along. And then you can fine tune the specification before you write the abstract.

In order to prepare a patent application, It takes a long time to do the job right. And it's easier to do the job right if you start with drafts of at least some of the claims. Try to write the broadest claims first and then proceed to the narrowest ones. And once you are satisfied with the claims, consider the drawings. And after that, it's easier to write a specification that will support your claims and adequately disclose your invention.

In essence, the abstract is a short paragraph that tells a reader what is in the detailed description.

So when you prepare your abstract, write it in narrative form. In general, describe your disclosure in about 50–250 words. For example, consider the abstract from U.S. Patent No. 4,124,667, which reads as follows:

> Pressureless sintering of silicon carbide to produce ceramic bodies having 75% and greater theoretical densities, can be accomplished by firing shaped bodies, containing finely divided silicon carbide, boron source such as boron carbide, carbon source such as phenolic resin and a temporary binder, at a sintering temperature of from about 1900 to about 2200°C.

Or consider the abstract from a patent titled "Composition and Process for Injection Molding Ceramic Materials":

> Ceramic compositions that may be injection molded and subsequently sintered are described. A particular ceramic material, such as silicon carbide, is coated with a mixture of thermoplastic resin and oils or waxes, and utilized as a feed material in an injection molding process. The molded product may be subsequently sintered at 2000°C to 2200°C to produce a hard, dense article.

When you start to draft your abstract, remember that an abstract is not a summary of your invention. All that you want to do is tell a reader at a glance what your invention is about, that is, essentially what the reader can find by reading your patent specification.

An abstract represents an attempt by the U.S. Patent and Trademark Office to make it easier for technically trained personnel to use the patent literature. After all, one of the purposes of the patent system is to disseminate technical information. Therefore, when you write an abstract, remember that the purpose of an abstract is to enable technically trained individuals to quickly determine whether or not they are interested in the detailed disclosure.

Before going on to the next section, consider one more abstract, which is taken from U.S. Patent No. 4,123,804 entitled "Glove Pockets":

> A pocket for garments defined by a half glove or half mitten sewn to the exterior or interior of a pair of trousers, so as to define a hand engaging concavity. The pocket may be in the form of a regular glove with particulate finger portions or a mitten and may be sewn, as well, to garments such as a shirt, blouse or skirt.

By this time, you may feel that you already know more than you want to about an abstract of an invention. However, before writing an abstract for your own application, review the abstracts from the patents disclosed by your patent search. Compare these abstracts with the detailed specification. And consider the "Guidelines for the Preparation of Patent Abstracts" in the *Manual of Patent Examining Procedure,* Section 608.01(b), which states:

> The content of a patent abstract should be such as to enable the reader thereof, regardless of his degree of familiarity with patent documents, to ascertain quickly the character of the subject matter covered by the technical disclosure and should include *that which is new* in the art to which the invention pertains [emphasis added].

This means that if your invention represents an improvement over a prior art device, the abstract should be directed to the improvement. And when applicable, your abstract should include the identity and use of a chemical composition, the ingredients in a mixture, the steps in a process, and yet, it should not include extensive details. And in writing an abstract, avoid using legal language such as means or other claim terminology.

11.3   BACKGROUND OF THE INVENTION

The background of the invention does serve a useful purpose. In fact, this section should help to give a judge a better understanding of your invention. It should help him to understand how your improvement differs from the prior art.

If you discuss the best prior art in this section, you may defuse an argument by an infringer who alleges that your claims are invalid. In essence, this section on the background of the invention should be directed to the claimed subject matter in your application. For example, you might start this section by filling in the blanks of the following sentence:

> This invention relates to a _____ and more particularly to a _____ .

A reference to U.S. Patent No. 4,144,207 illustrates a completed paragraph. In that patent the background of the invention starts out with, "The present invention relates to injection molding of ceramic articles and, in particular, to the production of dense, hard articles having industrial uses." The application then goes on to clarify that the invention will be discussed with respect to silicon carbide, but that other metal carbides may be utilized.

Another example of the opening paragraph is taken from U.S. Patent No. 4,120,529, which is entitled "Removable Roof Panels for Vehicles":

> This invention relates to vehicle bodies and more particularly to removable panel arrangments for the roof of vehicles and the method of installing such panels in the roof portion of conventional automobiles.

After the brief intorduction, proceed with the background of your invention. In other words, describe the state of the art as it exists. Then describe how your invention overcomes any problems that have not been solved by the prior art.

Actually, it's fun to write about the background of your invention since this portion of the patent specification is less structured than the detailed description. This part of your application is where you should set out the problems of the prior art and then go on to show how your invention addresses those problems. However, don't get carried away and include a lot of material in this section. Don't miss the most pertinent prior art. In doing so, you may actually undermine your own patent.

And then there is another problem in making references to the prior art. You are prohibited from making derogatory statements about prior art patents. Nevertheless, if you know of prior art that might suggest your invention, it must be called to the examiner's attention. As a rule of thumb, refer only to the closest prior art and indicate why your invention constitutes a patentable improvement.

Some attorneys prefer to discuss the background of the invention in a general way. They do this without referring to a specific prior art reference, that is, without listing patent numbers. But then they include the specific references in an information disclosure statement, which is discussed in more detail in Chapter 12. For now consider two examples. A first is taken from U.S. Patent No. 4,144,207:

> Silicon carbide has long been known for its hardness, strength, and excellent resistance to oxidation and corrosion. Silicon carbide has a low coefficient of expansion, good heat transfer properties, and maintains high strength at elevated temperatures. In recent years, the art of producing high-density silicon carbide materials by sintering silicon carbide powders has been developed. High-density silicon carbide materials find utility in the fabrication of components for turbines, heat exchange units, pumps, and other equipment or tools that are exposed to severe corrosion or wear, especially in operations carried out at high temperatures. The present invention relates to sinterable

metal carbide compositions which may be injection molded and subsequently sintered to produce high-density products. The present invention further relates to the use of silicon carbide as the ceramic material and, in particular, to ceramic compositions containing predominantly the alpha crystalline form of silicon carbide.

A second example of the background of the invention is taken from U.S. Patent No. 4,120,529, "Removable Roof Panel for Vehicles." It reads as follows:

Removable panels have been provided of the type in which a pair of panels are disposed in association with the door openings at opposite sides of the vehicle. In such an arrangement, installation is made by cutting away openings in the roof leaving a portion of the original body disposed longitudinally of the body and between the openings which are to be covered by the panels. Such arrangements are referred to as T-tops or hatch tops and are difficult to make since they require careful positioning of templates relative to each other and complex installation and finishing of the perimeter of the roof openings. In addition, such installations weaken the vehicle body or change the characteristics of the body to withstand certain loads imposed during operation of the vehicle.

At this stage in the preparation of a patent application, you may question the difference between the practices of various attorneys. For example, some attorneys continue on with a number of objects of the invention while others include a summary of the invention. In general, it is a question of style.

The late Clarence M. Fisher, a distinguished patent attorney, deplored the use of "objects" in a patent specificiation. He argued that it was better to describe the advantages of an invention and avoid the stereotyped form relied on by so many attorneys.

Technically speaking, objects are part of the background of the invention. They do, however, follow directly from the previous section and can logically be included prior to a summary of the invention. Referring, for example, to U.S. Patent No. 4,120,529 you will see that the specification proceeds immediately after the background of the invention with "It is an object of the invention to provide a removable panel . . . " and a number of additional paragraphs on the objects of the invention.

By contrast, you will not find any objects in U.S. Patent No. 4,144,207, which proceeds from a background of the invention immediately to a general description of the invention.

11.4   THE SUMMARY OF THE INVENTION

Section 1.73 of Title 37 of the Code of Federal Regulations requires that you include "A brief summary of the invention indicating its nature and substance, which *may include a statement of the objects* of the invention, should preceed the detailed description" [emphasis added].

This rule means that you must include a summary of what your invention is. In today's practice this is a separate section of the patent specification and includes a heading such as "Brief Summary of the Invention," or "General Description of the Invention."

So when you start to write your summary, refer to your broadest claim. Then try to rewrite it and put it into a form that is more readable. And make certain that the summary of your invention is commensurate with the scope of your broadest claim. Actually, it should be easy to write the summary of your invention by breaking up your broadest claim into several sentences, and clarifying any means by an addition of "such as" with a definitive example. You may also want to include functional statements to further explain the interaction or purposes of the various components or elements in the claim.

For clarification look at the following two examples, which are taken from the two patents previously referred to. In each case the summary of the invention is a little longer than most summaries. The first example relates to an injection moldable ceramic composition and discloses a composition that is suitable for injection molding, a product, and a process for making that product.

GENERAL DESCRIPTION OF THE INVENTION

It has now been found that compositions containing a sinterable ceramic material may be injection molded. In general, the compositions of the present invention contain from about 70 to about 86 percent by weight of a ceramic material, such as silicon carbide; the remainder of the composition comprises sintering aids, a thermoplastic resin material, oil or wax having a vaporizing point less than that of the thermoplastic resin material, and, preferably, a lighter, more volatile oil. The light oil may be animal, vegetable, or mineral. The composition may also contain excess carbon or a source of excess carbon that will facilitate a subsequent sintering operation. The components are mixed and formed into an article by known injection molding techniques. The formed article is then baked at temperatures up to about 1000°C preferably in a nonoxidizing environment to remove resins, waxes, and oil, but to prevent or inhibit the removal of the residual or carbon from a carbon source material. The article is then sintered at temperatures between about 2000°C and 2200°C. The sintered product is of high density and is substantially free of internal stresses. The sintered product retains the shape originally molded but reduced in volume by known and predictable shrinkage which takes place during sintering.

The second example relates to a removable roof panel and is commensurate with the claims in that case. In this patent the inventor recognized that there were a number of prior art devices, and it was necessary for the inventor to distinguish his invention from the prior art. In doing so, he included the method of installing the panels in his summary. That summary reads as follows:

A removable roof panel arrangement and method of installation of such panels in vehicles has been provided in which the original body of the vehicle is cut transversely to remove a roof section to the rear of the windshield header. The removed roof section is replaced with forward and rearward frame members which are joined by a central longitudinal member and a reinforcing member which has portions disposed transversely of the vehicle and longitudinally of the vehicle and which is fastened to the transverse frame member and central frame member so that the beaming strength and resistance to torsional deflection is retained in the vehicle body. The roof opening defined by the forward, rearward and central frame forms a trough for accumulating and completely and rapidly draining all moisture from the vehicle roof to the sides of the vehicle when the vehicle is being driven or is parked at different altitudes. The molding acts also to retain a resilient seal which engages the roof panels closing the opening to form a weather-tight roof with the seals themselves forming an auxiliary drainage system to accumulate and drain moisture that may escape the sealing surfaces engaging the panel. The panels themselves are held detachably in position and may be formed of transparent, opaque or solid materials.

11.5   THE OBJECTS OF THE INVENTION

In the previous section you have read that the objects of the invention may be included in the brief summary. However, many of those attorneys who include objects put the objects in the specification before the summary.

One particular problem in writing objects is that many inventors like to expound on every conceivable benefit that might be derived from their invention. For example, many patents include an object that the invention can be produced at relatively low cost. In many cases this statement is indefinite, since there is no disclosure as to relative to what. A more serious problem would exist if the cost was appreciably higher than the prior art devices. It is better to avoid the use of such objects because they may restrict the interpretation of the claims.

To overcome this problem, write this section of the patent specification in a narrative form. Just write in a reader-oriented manner so that your application will be read and appreciated. And then you can be proud of your invention and your patent.

11.6   THE DESCRIPTION OF THE DRAWINGS

A description of the drawings follows the summary of your invention. You can prepare this description of the drawings by merely filling in the blanks. Your only problem is to select those views that will clearly illustrate your invention. For more information and examples, see Chapter 10.

An example of the description of the drawings can follow the simple format that follows:

> The invention will now be described in more detail in connection with the following drawings, in which Figure 1 is a (plan, sectional, or perspective) view illustrating one embodiment of the invention; Figure 2 is a (plan, sectional, or perspective) view illustrating a second embodiment of the invention; and so on.

11.7   THE DETAILED DESCRIPTION OF YOUR INVENTION

When you write the detailed description of your invention, don't overlook the technical details. Judges will go with the words; they have to go by what is written in the patent specification.

So when you are writing a patent specification, remember that you have to disclose the whole thing. Don't hold back or try to keep part of it secret.

Now, the detailed description of your invention should enable any person who is skilled in your field of technology to make and use your invention without resorting to extensive experimentation.

And when it comes to being understood, you are an expert in the field of your own invention. Even though your patent attorney has considerable expertise in writing patent applications, you can help by writing a clear technical disclosure and by clarifying any language that is peculiar to your field.

For example, a skilled ceramist was quite concerned when he moved to another company and began working with a new attorney. The new attorney had an excellent background in metallurgy, but was unfamiliar with ceramics. The ceramist was frustrated by a lack of understanding. What this means to you is that you have the ultimate responsibility for preparing a technically correct description of your invention.

Your detailed description also serves as a dictionary for the terms used in your claims. In other words, the terms used in the description provide support, or an antecedent basis, for all of the terms used in the claims. Just make certain that those terms are clearly defined.

The first two paragraphs in U.S. Patent No. 4,120,529 illustrate the use of reference characters in the detailed description of your invention. Referring now to the specification of that patent:

> The removable roof panel arrangement of the present invention is incorporated in an automotive vehicle body 10 having a roof portion 12 extending rearwardly from the windshield 13. The roof portion 12 is provided with a pair of openings 14 and 16 which are best seen in Fig. 3 and are an extension of the window openings 18 and 20 disposed at opposite sides of a longitudinal center line 22 of the vehicle as best seen in Fig. 2. The openings 14 and 16 are closed with detachable panels 24 and 26, respectively, which may be removed if desired and when in place as seen in Fig. 2, form a weather-tight roof assembly.
>
> In general the openings 14 and 16 are formed by portions of a forward frame member 28, a rearward frame member 30 and a central frame member 32. The frame members act to form three sides of each of the openings 14 and 16. The fourth side of the openings merges with the window openings 18 and 20. When panels 24 and 26 are in place as seen in Fig. 2 the sill or edge portions 34 of the panels form the fourth side and act to engage the upper edge of the windows 36 which close the window openings 18 and 20.

In some cases you may want to use subheadings such as those used in U.S. Patent No. 4,144,207, wherein each of the component parts of the composition are described in detail under an appropriate heading such as A. Ceramic Material; B. Sintering Aids; C. Carbon; and D. Injection Molding Additives.

11.8 THE BEST EMBODIMENT

In writing your patent specification, show your preferred embodiment. And then show those things that add inventiveness to it. Show those alternatives which will form the basis for your species claims. And remember, if you don't disclose it, you can't claim it. However, you don't need numerous alternatives which are obvious. Just put the emphasis on your preferred embodiments.

Section 1.171(b) of the Code of Federal Regulations provides that "The best mode contemplated by the inventor for carrying out his invention must be set forth." This means that if your invention is related to an acid treatment of coal, you would have to disclose which acid worked best and within what range of concentration. You should also indicate that this is your preferred embodiment.

The current practice in the U.S. Patent and Trademark Office is to accept an operative example as sufficient to meet this requirement. This means that the U.S. Patent and Trademark Office will accept an application with a disclosure of a single embodiment. Nevertheless, you should disclose more than a single embodiment if you want the best coverage possible. In addition, point out which is your preferred embodiment that is, which variation you consider to be the best way of using or applying your invention at the time of filing your patent application.

It is surprising that a number of entrepreneurs and inventors want to obtain a patent and yet resist disclosing their invention. Perhaps they would be better off relying on a trade secret. But if you have this problem, you can defer making a decision. You can do this because the U.S. Patent and Trademark Office will hold your application in confidence until you pay the final fee and the patent issues. So if at the time your patent application is allowed, you are not satisfied with the breadth of your claims, you can abandon the application and rely on the law of trade secrets for your protection.

Before going further, consider what happens if you find it difficult to determine which is your preferred embodiment. For example, consider a patent application on a glass composition of the type used in manufacturing sunglasses. In this case, the client company desired to commercialize two compositions, one of which would transmit 31% of the light and the other 19%. In effect there were two preferred embodiments. So they disclosed two preferred embodiments, but also disclosed the conditions under which each was preferred.

11.9 DESCRIPTION OF THE ALTERNATIVES

As an entrepreneur, you should disclose more than one form of your invention. You should disclose more than one form as an aid to providing the basis that is needed to support claims of broad, medium, and narrow scope. If you are filing a patent application on an invention in the chemical area you should include enough examples to support a number of claims of varying scope. Therefore, if you claim a composition having from 90 to 99% silicon carbide, you should have an example showing each extreme as well as something in between.

11.10   THE OPERATION OF YOUR INVENTION

In dealing with inventions in the chemical field, a complete disclosure should include a statement of utility. In other words, you must teach a person of ordinary skill in the art how to use your invention. And in chemical cases, you must also teach a person how to make the compound.

For example, some years ago, an inventor in Germany filed a patent application on a glass composition and his application was rejected because there was no explanation of how to make the glass.

Judge Jackson, sitting in the U.S. District Court in Washington, D.C., listened to an independent glass technician tell how he had made the glass based on reading the disclosure and based on his general knowledge. The judge then ruled that the application was deficient and that even though the new glass compositon could be made by standard glassmaking practice, the specification failed to disclose that fact.

One other problem you should consider relates to the completeness of your disclosure. For example, some applicants have referred to components by the improper use of a trademark and failed to include a proper description of an ingredient. Don't make this mistake. For example, don't refer to silicon carbide as "Carborundum" (a registered trademark of the Carborundum Company), since a trademark may be used on more than one product.

However, you can identify a product by its chemical name, and then refer to a commercially available product such as one sold under a particular trademark. Just remember to accurately identify any chemical characteristics of the material used in practicing your invention. For example, if you refer to coating a substrate with Kodak photo resist, hardening portions of the resistant material by exposure to light, and removing the unpolymerized material, you will need a more definite description of Kodak's photosensitive material.

At times you may not be able to identify a material and may have to rely on a trademark. For example, in the early days of using photo resist for chemical etching, the formulations of the materials marketed by the

Eastman Kodak Company were considered a trade secret. In such cases, the only disclosure possible was, "An organic photo resist material such as those marketed by Eastman Kodak and described in specific product brochures." However, as a general rule, do not use a trademark to describe an essential element in your application.

11.11 CONCLUSIONS

I can't give you a rule of thumb for the length of a patent application. It just depends on the complexity of the invention. But I can say that if you write it well, there is no need to beat it to death. And if your invention is simple, keep it simple. Focus on what the invention is. Look at the closest prior art and show how your invention differs from the prior art. Just remember, you must disclose everything that is necessary to teach a person skilled in the art to use your invention.

Now, your patent application is unique, and at the same time, it is a complicated legal document. Take the time to write a clear description of your invention and model your specification after what others have done. Write it in good English, use terms of the art with care, and avoid legalistic language. You can probably write an adequate disclosure and with a little help from an experienced patent attorney, obtain a good patent.

As a last word of caution with respect to your patent specification, make certain that you have defined each of the claimed features, revise your description, and revise it again.

11.12 THE OATH OR DECLARATION

Now before proceeding to the chapter on patent prosecution, consider the oath or declaration. The oath or declaration is a vital part of your patent application and should be prepared and carefully considered at the time of filing your application. A form for the oath is printed in the rules of practice.

Just make certain that the facts stated in your oath or declaration are true.

12

How to File
and Prosecute Your
Patent Application

Donald J. Quigg is an assistant secretary of Commerce and the commissioner of the U.S. Patent and Trademark Office. Before that, he was the deputy assistant secretary and deputy commissioner. And, before moving to the U.S. Patent and Trademark Office, Don was chief patent counsel for Philips Petroleum.

In a speech before a group of inventors on February 8, 1985, Commissioner Quigg said, "I can't urge you too strongly to get professional help in preparing and prosecuting your patent applications. I urge inventors to use a registered patent attorney or agent because if you do not, you stand to lose all of your rights." In other words, filing and prosecuting your own application without the assistance of a patent lawyer is a little like buying a house without having the title searched.

Now as an entrepreneur, you should be concerned about protecting your rights. And before going further, you should recognize that what you and your attorney do during the prosecution of your patent application will affect your patent coverage. You should also understand the procedures for obtaining a patent, and what is going to happen to your patent application.

12.1 FORMALITIES

Before you submit your patent application to the U.S. Patent and Trademark Office, make certain that it is complete and that you have complied with the requirements of the U.S. Patent and Trademark Office. For example, your application must include:

1. A complete specification, including one or more claims.
2. An oath or a declaration.
3. Drawings when necessary.
4. The prescribed fee.

The application must be written in English, and must be legibly written or printed in permanent ink. From a practical point of view, your application should be typed on a single side of good quality paper. Don't use easy-to-erase paper since it is not acceptable to the U.S. Patent and Trademark Office. Use legal size paper 8 to $8\frac{1}{2}$ by $12\frac{1}{2}$ to $13\frac{1}{2}$ inches with a margin of at least 1 inch on the left-hand side of the page. The top of each page should have a margin of at least $\frac{3}{4}$ inch. Cases filed in accordance with the international Patent Cooperation Treaty should be filed on $8\frac{1}{4}$ by

$11\frac{3}{4}$ inch paper. In the latter case, $1\frac{1}{2}$ line spacing is used instead of the double spacing on the legal sized paper. In either case, the pages of the specification should be numbered sequentially.

If after typing your application you include any interlineation, insert, or change, indicate that the change was made before signing the oath or declaration. You do this by signing your name and the date in the margin next to the change. But after you sign the declaration, don't make any changes except by a formal amendment filed in the U.S. Patent and Trademark Office.

Then mail your application, specification, claims, drawings, oath or declaration, and proper fee to The Honorable Commissioner of Patents and Trademarks, Washington, D.C. 20231.

Don't forget that your patent application must be signed. The rules of patent practice provide that the signature to the oath or declaration will suffice provided that it is attached to the specification and refers to the application. And when you sign your application, do so in front of a witness or a notary and use at least one full given name.

The present filing fee for an independent inventor or small business entity for an original application is $170 plus $17 for each independent claim in excess of three and an additional $6 for each claim in excess of twenty. These figures are subject to change and may be increased before this book is published. You should also note that there is a different fee for design patents. If you are filing an application for a design, the fee is $125.

If you send your application by Express Mail and include a proper certification to that effect, you can obtain a filing date according to the certificate date, unless it happens to fall on a Saturday or Sunday. However, any paper filed by Express Mail must have the number of the Express Mail mailing label placed thereon prior to mailing.

12.2 FILING RECEIPTS

After you mail your application to the U.S. Patent and Trademark Office, the Application Division will conduct a preliminary examination to determine if it is complete. If it is, they will send you a filing receipt. The filing receipt shows the official filing date, that is, the date that your application was received in the U.S. Patent and Trademark Office, the serial number assigned to your application, the name of the applicant, title of the application, and the division or group to which the case has been assigned. The receipt should be checked for accuracy and a revised receipt requested if vital errors are found. This filing receipt should be maintained in your patent file and kept in a safe place. If, for example, your application is lost in the Patent Office, your filing receipt will help to prove that you are entitled to the original filing date.

This acknowledgment is also your official notice that your application has been given a filing date, and that it has met the prerequisites for filing. Note the serial number assigned to your application, and refer to the serial number, date of filing, name of applicant, and title whenever you inquire about the application or respond to an office action. Note also whether a license to file abroad has been granted with the issuance of the filing receipt.

12.3 CLASSIFICATION

After the U.S. Patent and Trademark Office has determined that your application is complete, they send the application to the classification division, which is responsible for assigning applications to the proper group of patent examiners for examination. The examiner in the classification group will look at your claims to determine which group of examiners is responsible for the area of technology in which your invention resides.

You may recall the *Manual of Patent Classification*, referred to in an earlier chapter on patent searches. That manual, which is published by the U.S. Department of Commerce, lists the classes and subclasses in which patents are classified, the responsibilities of each group of examiners, and additional information on classification.

Some patent applications contain claims that are directed to different inventions. In those cases, the different claims should be examined by various examiners. For example, one application included claims for a composition of matter and claims for a process for sintering the same. This case was assigned to the examiner responsible for compositions of matter. Then that examiner required the attorney to elect one set of claims to prosecute. If you are requested to make an election, you must do so, even if you disagree with the examiner. However, you should reserve your rights in the nonelected claims, and may want to file a divisional application to cover those claims at a later date.

Any reader interested in more details about the classification of patents is referred to the "Development and Use of Patent Classification Systems," which is available from the U.S. Patent and Trademark Office.

12.4 THE INFORMATION DISCLOSURE

The rules of practice before the U.S. Patent and Trademark Office encourage an applicant for a patent to file an information disclosure statement at the time of filing the patent application or within a period of three months thereafter. I talked with Lawrence A. Hymo about this practice. Lawrence Hymo is a partner in Cushman, Darby and Cushman, a well-known Washington, D.C. law firm that I have relied on for a number of years.

Larry Hymo said, "The practice we follow is to disclose whatever art we know of as early as possible. And we provide copies of the prior art as required by the rules. We also point out the most pertinent portions of the prior art and explain how the claims are distinguished from the cited art. We do this to make certain that the U.S. Patent and Trademark Office considers the best art we know about. Besides, it creates a presumption that any claims we get are valid. And it avoids future problems if your patent is involved in litigation."

Section 1.98 of Title 37 of the Code of Federal Regulations provides that "Any disclosure statement . . . shall include (1) a listing of patents, publications or other information; and (2) a concise explanation of the relevance of each listed item. The disclosure statement shall be accompanied by a copy of each listed patent, or publication or other item . . . ."

12.5 AN OFFICIAL ACTION

After your application is assigned to an examiner, nothing usually happens for several months. Then the patent examiner to whom the case has been assigned reviews the application. The examiner reads your claims and the specification to make certain that there are no serious omissions. The examiner will also make certain that the features you claim are adaquately supported by the specification.

Next, the examiner will conduct a search to determine if your claims are patentable. Actually, the examiner goes through files of patents and picks out the most pertinent references that might anticipate your claims, that is, those references that might anticipate your claims as they are presently written. Usually the examiner is not concerned with anything that is not defined by the claims.

The present practice in the U.S. Patent and Trademark Office calls for a thorough search, so that hopefully it will not be necessary to conduct a second search after you file a response to the first office action. This concept may be more correct in theory than in actual practice, since it is often difficult to anticipate how you or your attorney will amend the claims.

Now, in evaluating your claims the patent examiner will ask, "Do these claims read on the prior art?" If the answer is yes, your claims will be rejected. If the answer is no, the examiner will next ask, "Is the claim obvious to a person of ordinary skill in the art by combining two or more references to produce the claimed invention?"

If either question's answer is yes, the examiner will send you an office action that includes the bases for rejecting your claims. In some cases, the examiner may cite additional references as being of interest. Your job is to study all of the references cited and decide how to distinguish your claims from the cited art.

First office actions frequently include rejections of the claims based on Sections 102, 103, and 112 of the patent statute. Just remember that the examiner usually deals with attorneys and assumes that you are familiar with the terms of the patent art. An examiner may, for example, merely reject your application under Section 102 and list one or more references.

Now, if you recall, Section 102 of the patent statute provides that a person is entitled to a patent unless the invention was described in a printed publication before it was invented by the applicant. Essentially, a rejection based on Section 102 means that the examiner's has found that your invention is really anticipated by the prior art.

A rejection based on Section 103 says that your idea would have been obvious to a person of ordinary skill in view of one or more references. And at times an examiner may clarify such a rejection by stating that it would be obvious to combine the elements shown in one reference with those shown in another.

Now, when you come to a 112 rejection, recognize that Section 112 of the patent statute requires you to include a written description of your invention and the manner of using it in such full, clear, concise, and exact terms that someone else would be enabled to use your invention; the description must also set forth the best mode contemplated for carrying out the invention. In addition the statute requires that your claims particularly point out and distinctly claim your invention. Therefore, an examiner who rejects an application under Section 112 may be telling you to rewrite your claims to clarify what it is that you claim as your invention.

It is possible to encounter a serious problem with a 112 rejection if you do a poor job writing your application and leave out some essential feature. When this happens, you may have to rewrite your application and refile it as a continuation-in-part. A continuation-in-part application will require another filing fee. However, you could be precluded from filing a continuation-in-part application if, for example, you offered to sell a product encompassing your invention more than a year ago. In that case, you would have lost your rights because the patent rules do not permit you to insert new matter. But if you have carefully prepared your application, a 112 rejection may amount to a mere formality that can easily be overcome. And if that is the case, you may be close to obtaining an allowance.

Larry Hymo said, "Think carefully about what you are doing before you amend a patent application." Larry said this because he knows that amending an application can result in "file wrapper estoppel." And file wrapper estoppel means that you will be prevented from having your claims interpreted in a manner that is inconsistent with what you have done, that is, what you have argued to distinguish your claims from the prior art.

If you argue that your invention is distinguished from the prior art because you operate at an ambient temperature while the prior art discloses an elevated temperature, you will be prohibited from interpreting your claims to cover an elevated temperature even though that express limitation has not been included in your claims. Please note that this is a simplified example and that the question of file wrapper estoppel is often complex. Nevertheless, it does illustrate the need for an experienced counsel for prosecuting your application.

A few years ago, one of my associates was asked to evaluate a patent belonging to an entrepreneur. The original patent was well written and had been carefully prosecuted. But later the entrepreneur had learned of a more pertinent reference and decided to prosecute an application to reissue the patent himself. As a result, the reissue patent was basically worthless. Later, my associate met with the entrepreneur to discuss another one of his inventions. The inventor insisted that he would file and prosecute an application on the new invention. He pointed out that he had his own copy of the patent statute and rules of practice. The problem was that his copies were over five years old. They did not include changes that had been made during that period. My associate did not pursue the further development of the invention. But if he had, he would have insisted that this application be prepared and prosecuted by a registered patent attorney at our expense.

Now in order to have your application reconsidered after an office action, you must respond to the office action in writing, within the period of time set by the examiner (usually three months), or within a duly obtained extension of time. And in responding to an official action, you must distinctly and specifically point out any new information and arguments the examiner should consider, as well as the examiner's errors, in a professional and diplomatic manner. You must also point out why your claims as amended overcome the examiner's rejection.

An abstract of an amendment, illustrating the proper form, follows:

IN THE UNITED STATES PATENT AND TRADEMARK OFFICE

Applicant:
Serial No.: 123,456
Filed 6/01/1981
Examiner:
Group Art Unit: 345
For: GAS IGNITION CONTROL

AMENDMENT

Honorable Commissioner of Patents and Trademarks
Washington, D.C. 20231

Dear Sir:
Responsive to the Official Action dated . . . , please amend the above identified patent application as follows:

IN THE SPECIFICATION

In line 1, page 9, please delete the word "The" and substitute —the—.
On page 9, line 1, please delete the comma at the end of the line and substitute a period.

IN THE CLAIMS

In line 3 of claim 1 in subparagraph (a), please delete "an" and substitute—A resistance type—.
In line 1 of subparagraph (h) of claim 1, please delete "an" and substitute—said—.
In line 1 of subparagraph (h) of claim 1, after "means" please insert—being—.
In line 3 of claim 2 in subparagraph (a), after "A," please insert—resistance type—.
In line 25 of claim 2 in subparagraph (d), after "said," please insert—first—.

REMARKS

Claims 1 through 7 have been rejected under 35 USC 112 as being vague and indefinite. The amendments suggested by the Examiner to overcome the rejection have been made. Reconsideration and withdrawal of the 35 USC 112 rejection are respectfully requested.

Claim 1 has been rejected under 35 USC 103 as being obvious over U.S. Patent No. 4,150,938 to Renshaw et al. in view of U.S. Patent 3,060,997 to Maney and U.S. Patent No. 4,125,355 to Rozzi. Claim 1 has also been rejected under 35 USC 103 as being obvious over U.S. Patent No. 3,196,923 to Selinder in view of the patent to Rozzi.

Claims 2 through 7 have also been rejected under 35 USC 103 as being obvious over Renshaw et al. in view of Rozzi and Maney.

The combination of Renshaw et al. with Rozzi and Maney is also ineffective against claims 2 through 7 for the same reasons that this combination of references is ineffective against claim 1.

It is clear that the Examiner has tried to find individual components of the applicant's claimed circuit and combine them piecemeal to obtain the claimed invention. The combinations must fail since. . . .

The applicant notes that U.S. Patents Nos. 3,026,932 to Algino, 3,144,898 to Queever, and 2,331,712 to Miller have been cited to show control systems with pull-in and hold circuits. The circuits described in these patents are clearly unrelated to the applicant's circuit, and it is clear that combining the additional references with the references previously discussed would add nothing which would result in the suggestion of the applicant's claimed apparatus. No further comments concerning these references will therefore be made.

In view of the foregoing remarks and amendments, the applicant respectfully submits that the applicant's claimed novel apparatus for automatic fuel ignition is unobvious to one skilled in the art in view of any of the cited references whether they are considered alone or in any combination. The applicant, therefore, respectfully submits that all claims are now in condition for allowance, which action is requested.

Dated: _____

Respectfully submitted,
Attorney for Applicant

Now, when amending your claims, it is frequently desirable to rewrite them instead of adding or deleting material. And if you amend a claim substantially, it is preferable to present the claim in rewritten form with the additional words are *underlined* and the deleted material enclosed by brackets.

12.6 AN INTERVIEW WITH A U.S. PATENT EXAMINER

At times it may be difficult to convince an examiner that your claims should be allowed. In some cases, you can call the examiner on the telephone and suggest a telephone interview. Ask when it would be convenient to discuss the application and then call back at the agreed time. These telephone interviews can be very effective; however, they are not always as effective as a personal interview.

In the words of Larry Hymo, "A personal interview with the patent examiner frequently helps in obtaining an allowance of claims which are commensurate with your invention." However, before you or your attorney attempt to interview a patent examiner, have your attorney prepare a proposed amendment. In fact, it may be desirable to send the proposed amendment to the examiner before the interview.

Typically, an interview with a patent examiner takes about thirty to forty-five minutes. And after the interview, the examiner and your attorney will prepare and sign a short summary of their discussion. Then your attorney may be required, or decide, to file an amendment to put the case in condition for an allowance, or in better condition for an appeal.

During a personal interview, your attorney "Should respond to each of the examiner's bases for rejection," according to Larry Hymo. "Your attorney should point out what it is in your claims that distinguishes them from the prior art. Show how they differ from the prior art, and then explain why your invention is better. What he will do is to identify the difference between what is in your claims and what is disclosed or suggested by the prior art."

There is also a question whether or not you as the inventor should participate in an interview with the patent examiner. Lawrence Hymo said, "An inventor's participation depends on circumstances, particularly the kind of issues to be discussed. When the issues involve technology, and the inventor communicates well he can be very helpful."

12.7 A FINAL REJECTION

In many cases, a second official action is made "final." In other words, it says that the examiner will not consider further arguments. However, as a practical matter, you can usually obtain consideration of one more amendment. The reason is that most examiners will accept an amendment after finalization if it places the case in condition for allowance, or in better condition for appeal. But don't count on making extensive changes that would require the examiner to make an additional search. Nevertheless, most examiners are reasonable in considering these amendments. And if it appears that there is a patentable invention, the examiner will continue to work with the applicant or the applicant's attorney to define the invention in a manner that will be allowable.

But an examiner who believes that there is no patentable invention disclosed may enter the amendment only for the purposes of appeal.

At this time you still have a few alternatives. Nevertheless, what you do next could adversely affect your rights. Therefore, if you have not interviewed the patent examiner, perhaps it is time to do so. And you may want to make use of an affidavit by an expert to overcome the rejection. It may also be time to file a divisional or continuation application.

12.8   FILING A DIVISIONAL OR CONTINUATION APPLICATION

A divisional application is a patent application claiming an invention that was disclosed in an earlier application. The divisional must be filed before the original application issues as a patent or before it is abandoned, and should include that portion of the disclosure that relates to the invention now being claimed. However, in practice, many attorneys refile the same specification, but limit the claims to those that were not elected for earlier prosecution.

Just remember, if you plan to file a divisional application, you must do so before the parent application is issued as a patent or abandoned. Either you file a copy of the original application as filed, together with a proposed amendment canceling the claims that were prosecuted in the original application, or the amendment should also add, "This is a division of application Serial No. . . . filed. . . . "

Note: Divisional applications are limited to nonelected inventions as a result of a restriction requirement.

A continuation application is similar to a divisional, but is directed to an invention that was claimed and prosecuted in the original application. And a continuation application must be filed before the issuance or abandonment of its parent application. Now one reason for filing a continuation application is to overcome an examiner's allegation that you are now claiming something different from what was originally claimed. Another reason for filing a continuation application would be if, after receiving a Notice of Allowance, you learned of a more pertinent reference than those cited by the examiner. Then by filing a continuation you can have the new references reviewed by the Patent Office, avoiding the likelihood of obtaining an invalid patent or of later being accused of fraud for failing to call the reference to the examiner's attention.

12.9   INTERFERENCES

As strange as it may seem, there are times when two or more people make the same invention at approximately the same time. Certainly, changes in our environment, technological advances and other factors trigger more than one individual's mind to seek a solution to the same problem. Besides, there are many scientists in different laboratories who are working on similar problems.

The U.S. Patent and Trademark Office has a procedure for determining under law which of two or more applicants for a patent on the same invention should receive the patent. This procedure, which is referred to as a patent interference, is different from the practice in most foreign countries. In most foreign countries, the first inventor to file a patent application is awarded a patent.

Interferences are complicated legal proceedings and should not be handled by a novice. Books that go well beyond the scope of the present treatise have been written on the subject. However, there are a few basic concepts you should keep in mind. First, there are a number of advantages associated with an earlier filing date. Therefore, whenever feasible, you should file your application promptly.

Also, detailed records that are properly witnessed are important in establishing your rights because it may be necessary for you to show by documentary evidence when you first conceived of your invention. And a properly witnessed engineering notebook may mean the difference between obtaining a valuable patent or having that same patent issued to someone else.

There is one other concept to consider in interferences, the "reduction to practice." A reduction to practice is the first time you practice your invention. In other words, when did you make a device according to your invention? When did you first use the process? Now when you talk about a reduction to practice, you are talking about the invention that is defined by the claim or claims involved in the interference. For example, if a single element in a claim involved in the interference was missing in your experiment, you would probably be precluded from using that experiment to show a "reduction to practice."

If you can establish your date of conception and a reduction to practice by a witnessed notebook, and if you were the first to make the invention and reduce it to practice you should be awarded priority. Even if you were not the first to reduce your invention to practice, you might still be awarded a patent if you worked diligently toward that goal. And if you did not diligently pursue your invention, you might still win an interference proceeding if you filed your application before the other party reduced the invention to practice. So keep good records on your progress in working on your inventions.

Now as an entrepreneur, there is another aspect of interference proceedings you should consider. Interferences are expensive and may cost more than a patent's potential value. Therefore, many corporations try to resolve these conflicts by an agreement under which the winner will grant the loser a royalty-free paid up license to practice the invention.

However, as an entrepreneur you may not want a royalty-free cross license. For example, if you believe that your invention will result in a valuable patent, you may want to invest in the interference proceeding. On the other hand, this might be an appropriate time to offer your rights to the other party.

Interferences can be costly, but in some cases, you can minimize these costs by agreeing to an exchange of evidence without resorting to depositions or other courtlike procedures. Even so, don't underestimate the complexity or costs of an interference and consider the advice of your attorney.

12.10   THE NOTICE OF ALLOWANCE

Good news comes in small envelopes containing an official Notice of Allowance of your application. Congratulations are in order because you are about to be awarded a U.S. Letters Patent. Quite probably, you will have seen an informal Notice of Allowance, but if not, the Notice of Allowance advises you of the number of claims allowed, the issued fee due, and the time in which you will have to pay the fee.

This is good news because most of your work in obtaining a patent is now complete. However, you should review your application once more to assure yourself that the claims are of the broadest scope possible, that there are no uncorrected errors in the specification and, most important, that the examiner has considered the closest prior art that you know about.

If, for example, an action from a foreign patent office cited a closer reference than those relied on by the U.S. examiner, you should call this fact to the examiner's attention.

12.11   THE FINAL FEE

The Notice of Allowance includes a statement of the final fee due and payable to the U.S. Patent and Trademark Office. The issue fee for a patent is $280 for a small entity or $560 for other than a small entity. The fees are payable to the U.S. Commissioner of Patents and Trademarks. However, these fees are subject to change, so you should refer to the latest set of the Rules of Practice.

12.12   ISSUANCE OF YOUR PATENT

Approximately five months after paying your final fee, you will receive your U.S. Letters Patent. However, your work is still not finished. You should read the patent carefully to make certain that there are no errors in printing. And if an error has been made, you should request a Certificate of Correction from the Patent Office. Then put your patent in a safe place. In a way, it is like the title to your car and may be needed in the future.

12.13   THE EFFECT OF FRAUD

Fraud in obtaining a patent has been mentioned earlier. However, it is covered here in slightly more detail. Generally, the basis for fraud is when an applicant and/or the applicant's attorney may learn about prior art that is more pertinent than that found by an examiner. For example, when an applicant files patent applications all over the world, it is likely that one of the foreign examiners may find a more pertinent reference than the U.S. examiner. There is also the fact that it is expensive to litigate a patent. And a defendant, or alleged infringer, should not be put to this expense if some prior art has been withheld from the examiner. Therefore, an applicant is responsible for calling the reference to the examiner's attention.

Now, if you sue someone for infringing your patents, the defendant's lawyer will attempt to show that any statement made during the prosecution of a patent application, any statement in the application itself, or any knowledge of prior art that was not called to the examiner's attention constitutes fraud.

However, if you have been absolutely candid in dealings with the patent examiner, you will not have a problem. Just remember that you have a duty to advise the examiner of the best prior art that you know about and to be absolutely honest in what you say to get your patent allowed. In other words, absolute integrity is essential in all dealings with the U.S. Patent and Trademark Office. Applying this fundamental rule will assure you of the best patent obtainable and avoid future grief.

12.14   POST ISSUANCE FEES U.S.

Your U.S. patent gives you the right to prevent others from making, using, or selling any process or product that is covered by your claims for a period of seventeen years. However, to maintain that period of exclusivity, you are required to pay the following maintenance fees.

For maintaining an original or reissue patent, except a design or plant patent, that is based on applications filed on or after August 27, 1982 in force:

Beyond four years, a fee of $225 for a small entity or $450 for other than a small entity is due by three years, six months after the original grant:

Beyond eight years, a fee of $445 for a small entity or $890 for other than a small entity is due by seven years, six months after the original grant:

Beyond twelve years, a fee of $670 for a small entity or $1340 for other than a small entity is due eleven years, six months after the original grant.

If you fail to pay the fee on time, you can still pay it within a six-month grace period. However, such payments will require an additional $100 fee for a small entity or $200 for other than a small entity.

12.15   REEXAMINATION AND REISSUES

There may be times when, through no fault of your own, you obtain a patent that is defective. The claims may be too broad or even too narrow. If, for example, your claims read on the prior art, they are invalid. And if they do not cover a competitor's device, they are too narrow.

Now assume that after your patent issues, you learn of some prior art that might invalidate one or more of your claims. In this case, you would probably want to file for a reissue patent. You can do this because the patent law provides;

Whenever any patent is, through error without any deceptive intention, deemed wholly or partly inoperative or invalid, by reason of a defective specification or drawings, or by reason of the patentee claiming more or less than he had a right to claim in the patent, the Commissioner shall, on the surrender of such patent and the payment of the fee required by law, reissue that patent for the invention disclosed in the original patent, and in accordance with a new and amended application, for the unexpired part of the term of the original patent. No new matter shall be introduced into the application for reissue.

Recognize that a reissue application is not a cure-all for defective patents, but a remedy with limitations. One limitation relates to a "doctrine of intervening rights." That doctrine provides that a manufacturer who commences to manufacture or use your invention before the issue date on the reissue patent *may* be permitted to continue those operations irrespective of your patent rights. However, the doctrine of intervening rights is an equitable defense and as such, is subject to a court's discretion.

You could also ask to have your patent reexamined if you learn of some prior art that was not considered by the patent examiner. Actually, this is a useful procedure for a patent owner who wants to clearly establish a presumption of validity before filing a suit for infringement. It is less expensive than litigation and may remove a cloud on the validity of your claims. In fact, the attorneys for Cheesebrough, owner of the Howard Head patent on an oversize tennis racquet, followed this procedure. They asked the U.S. Patent and Trademak Office to reexamine their patent in view of the prior art that was called to their attention by an alleged infringer.

12.16   FOREIGN FILING

Many, if not all, entrepreneurs should consider the benefits and costs for obtaining foreign patents. You should also realize that after filing your U.S. patent application, you have one year to file foreign applications if you want to obtain the benefit of your U.S. filing date. Filing within this period will give you priority over some other inventor who files a foreign application after your U.S. filing date, but before your foreign filing date. This is important since most foreign countries apply the "first to file" rule, which means that whoever files first gets the patent.

But many foreign countries do not allow an inventor to obtain a patent if there has been a public use and/or disclosure of the invention before the filing date. Therefore, you can avoid problems and take advantage of the convention period by filing your U.S. patent application before publishing an article about your invention and before offering a product covering your invention for sale.

Many corporate attorneys agree that corporations waste more money on foreign filing and on the maintenance of foreign patents than on all other aspects of proprietary property put together. For example, as a rule of thumb, estimate your cost at about $1200 per case per country to file foreign patents. So, if you want patent coverage in 10 foreign countries, it will cost an extra $12,000 to file the applications. And then you can expect additional costs for prosecuting the applications. However, some countries, such as Canada, the United Kingdom, and Australia, cost less, since translations can be avoided. It is also possible to reduce these costs slightly by filing in the European Patent Office.

Don't overlook the fact that foreign countries also impose a tax or maintainance fee on patents. Such fees, which in West Germany amount to 3300 DM for the final year of your patent's life, require a substantial investment over the life of the patent.

What this means to you is that it is difficult to justify foreign filing unless you license your invention to a company that agrees to pay the costs. However, it is frequently difficult to license an invention within one year of the filing date, and at the same time allow the purchaser time to file within the Convention period. As an alternative, you might want to avoid publication or public use, and plan on filing non-Convention cases in foreign countries. It is true that you will lose the benefit of your earlier filing date. However, you may be able to convince a licensee to pay for the foreign filing.

Now consider the advantages of working with an attorney and what you can do to obtain the maximum benefits from legal counseling at a minimal cost.

13

Working with Your Attorney

Lawyers who represent themselves have fools for clients. Clients who buy more services than they need are merely foolish.

A few years ago, John, a brilliant chemist, made a significant breakthrough in organic chemistry. He studied the patent literature, and with considerable effort, prepared and filed a U.S. patent application. The patent examiner rejected his application and suggested that he engage a patent attorney.

The inventor then hired an attorney, but continued to write his own applications and amendments. Before John filed them, however, he consulted with his attorney. His attorney reviewed the work and listed himself as the attorney of record. John obtained numerous patents and worked effectively with his attorney. He worked effectively because he was not only a creative chemist, but a person who had developed an ability to do his own patent work. Nevertheless, he used counsel when he needed assistance.

John's approach may be appropriate for a few entrepreneurs. However, the majority of entrepreneurs would do far better if they hired a patent professional and then concentrated on the business of making money. Those of you who would like to work on your own application should consider the advice of Alan Rose, a partner in the Los Angeles law firm of Poms, Smith, Lande and Rose. Before joining that firm, Alan was director of patents and licensing for Litton Industries. He also served as treasurer, secretary, and president of the Patent Law Association of Los Angeles. He wrote Chapter 9, "Industrial Property Rights" in a text, *U.S./U.S.S.R. Technology and Licensing* (Licensing Executive Society, 1974), and has written articles such as: "Protection of Intellectual Property Rights in Computers and Computer Programs" and "Territorial Limitations in Licensing Agreements."

Alan Rose said, "There are a number of things that an entrepreneur can do to protect his inventions. For example, I find it helpful to have regular contacts with an inventor. And at times, it is easier if an entrepreneur fills me in on the details of his invention in his own terms. It's easier if he tells me what he has actually done, and what he thinks is his invention. I find this approach far better than one short meeting during which an inventor tries to dump everything out of his mind at one sitting."

As Alan Rose and many other experienced attorneys know, there are some inventors who describe their ideas in vague terms and expect the attorney to get them a patent and make them rich. Generally, this approach doesn't work. But there are times when an attorney can work from a meager description, prepare and prosecute an application, and obtain a patent. Frequently, however, the attorney needs additional information.

13.1 DEVELOPING A TEAM EFFORT

As a general rule, make certain that you have a commercially viable idea before you hire a patent lawyer. Don't spend hours conducting laboratory experiments. However, do learn what others are doing in the field, and review the development of your own idea before meeting with a lawyer.

Stan Lieberstein suggested "To obtain the best patent for the least amount of money, read several books on patents, and if possible, take a course on drafting patent applications." There are several such courses, such as the ones offered by the Practicing Law Institute in New York City. Mr. Lieberstein continued: "I have one client who follows this approach. And he consistently writes a draft of the patent specification." Then Stan reviews the draft with the inventor and suggests changes. Stan added, "The savings for the inventor can be substantial."

Certainly, a patent attorney has knowledge that you need. Your attorney's role may be analogous to that of the place kicker on a professional football team. You use the place kicker to attempt a field goal. However, you would not ask the place kicker to run with the ball a dozen times to get the ball in position for an attempted field goal. So if you follow the example of a football coach, you won't waste your money by asking your attorney to do a part of the job that you can do more efficiently.

As an entrepreneur, try to establish a team effort wherein you let your attorney concentrate on what the attorney does best. Then use your knowledge to provide information the attorney needs to obtain the broadest coverage on your invention.

13.2 COST EFFECTIVENESS

Don't be overly concerned about the cost of using a patent lawyer. The alternative may be much more expensive. Besides, you can get the help of an experienced lawyer without wasting money as long as you don't waste your lawyer's time. For example, Alan Rose suggested, "You can avoid unnecessary costs by providing good drawings and complete examples and technical specifications, as well as a listing of advantages and special results achieved by your invention. Do this before your attorney starts to draft the application."

And if you are like other creative people, you probably have more than one good idea. So learn to work with your attorney on one thing at a time, beginning with your first invention. Try to become more efficient in working with your counsel on subsequent developments.

13.3 THE PRELIMINARY SEARCH AND OPINION

Alan Rose said, "A preliminary search is usually done in Washington. However, sometimes a search is not undertaken because the inventor knows what has been done in the field." He also said, "A preliminary search may cost approximately $400 to $700 with an opinion, but search costs may vary considerably, depending on the complexity of your inventions."

Now, as an entrepreneur, you should consider the results of a patent search before you decide to file a patent application. Ask your lawyer for advice.

And when you authorize a search, ask your attorney to request five to six, or perhaps ten to twelve, references that are indicative of the prior art. By reading these references, you will obtain a better grasp of the prior art, and perhaps, a better understanding of what you need for your own application.

After studying the prior art, your attorney will give you an opinion. This opinion should include a brief analysis of the prior art and should point out one or more features that appear patentable. However, there is one approach that may help you to get a better opinion. Ask your lawyer to draft a suggested claim to give you an idea of what type of coverage can be expected in view of the prior art.

But be prepared to pay for the time your attorney spends in outlining an initial claim. You should also recognize that this approach may provide more detail than you want. However, as an entrepreneur, you should consider the scope of your expected coverage and how easy it will be for a competitor to avoid your patent. Probably the best way to do this is in a discussion with a patent lawyer.

13.4 THE PREPARATION OF YOUR PATENT APPLICATION

Alan Rose said, "Don't try to write your own claims. Just tell me what your invention is and what you know about it. Try to give me a good disclosure. Think in terms of teaching someone else how to use your invention."

Now, assuming that you have reviewed the results of a search with your attorney, consider your next step. Alan said, "I like an inventor to give me a detailed description of his invention. I want this so that I can draft claims of varying scope. I want to write some broad claims and also some narrow ones."

Alan went on to point out, "I need two types of information. For example, I need a detailed description of the preferred embodiment, and a statement of alternative arrangements as a basis for the broadest possible claims which may be available."

So when you plan to meet with your attorney, be prepared with the type of information that Alan Rose suggested.

13.5   THE PROSECUTION OF THE APPLICATION

A U.S. patent examiner will review your patent application and prepare an office action. Then this office action will be sent to the attorney of record. Your attorney should forward a copy of the action to you for your comments. In some cases, your attorney will suggest changes to put the application in condition for allowance.

And there are times when your attorney can take care of procedural matters and place your application in condition for allowance. However, any changes should be carefully considered. No changes should be made without your agreement.

Occasionally, a U. S. patent examiner will call the attorney of record and suggest changes that would place the application in condition for allowance before issuing an action. The examiner may call and request an election of certain claims for further prosecution. In either case, your attorney should keep you fully advised.

13.6   PARTICIPATION IN THE SALE OF YOUR INVENTION

Patent attorneys are not always the best sales people. Nevertheless, they are skilled in their field of law and frequently have valuable contacts, and can suggest ways to sell your invention.

So if you want to license or sell your invention, ask your lawyer for recommendations. Find out what terms the lawyer would consider reasonable, and if the lawyer has any suggestions as to the companies or individuals whom you might contact. Actually, you should have considered these questions before deciding to file your application.

And if you want to sell an invention, don't be misled by the worthless services offered by numerous invention marketing organizations. These organizations offer to market your invention for the payment of a fee and they make most, if not all, of their income from collecting fees from inventors.

Remember that the world will not beat a path to your door to buy your invention. Nevertheless, after reading Chapters 15 and 16, you should be prepared to sell your invention.

13.7 CONTRACTUAL NEGOTIATIONS

Never sign a contract until it has been reviewed by your lawyer. And if you enter into negotiations without your attorney, make it clear that any agreement is subject to review by your attorney. Actually, you should consider your attorney's advice before you start any negotiations. And, in many cases, you should take your attorney with you and consider any legal advice before you make a commitment.

One advantage to working with a lawyer like Alan Rose is that he has worked for large corporations and has corporate clients. Alan knows what goes on inside large and small corporations and how to negotiate effectively.

So before discussing a contract with a potential licensee, review the critical points with your attorney. And whatever else you do, don't call and ask your attorney to participate in a telephone conference with the other party without some previous understanding about the ground rules for the negotiation.

Now, to be more effective in a negotiation, you and your lawyer should function as a team. You should prepare for the negotiation together, but it is up to you alone to make the final decision to accept or refuse an offer. You must also decide which points to concede. Use your lawyer as counsel, so that you can make the most intelligent decision.

Finally, by working with your lawyer you can become more successful and, at the same time, develop a friendship based on mutual respect and appreciation for each other's talents.

14

Trademarks

Trademarks are symbols used by manufacturers or merchants to identify their goods and distinguish them from those of competitors.

As a corporate lawyer, I have had the good fortune to work on various trademarks in different fields. For example, I've worked on trademarks like Head skis, Paragon timers, Hatteras yachts, Carborundum abrasives, Tuboscope inspection services, Harley Davidson motorcycles, and many more.

I learned that the value of a mark depends on the mark itself, the commercial marketplace, and on the practices of its owner. I learned that some of the practices of well-meaning advertising agencies, and even the inadvertence of a trademark owner, can destroy a valuable mark. I also learned a trademark can be enormously valuable for an entrepreneur. In fact, it can play a significant role in the development and licensing of an invention. However, a trademark is much different from a patent and will in many cases be less important than a patent for an individual inventor.

If you recall, you read in an earlier chapter about Betty Graham, a Dallas executive secretary who invented a new product for correcting typographical errors. She painted over the error with a thin coating of white paint, using a fine brush. A patent attorney told her that the idea wasn't patentable.

Nevertheless, this incredible woman had perseverance. She called her product Liquid Paper® Correction Fluid and advertised it in a secretarial magazine. She received thousands of orders. The product was an immediate success, and yet she received a number of complaints. But by modifying the formula so that it dried more rapidly, she formed the basis for a successful company. And her trademark became one of their most valuable assets.

A similar product was introduced by Litho Arts, a Chicago corporation, under the name of Snopake®. It, too, became a success and within a few years, a number of similar products were also introduced into the marketplace. However, the original two products maintained a large share of the business. Fred Poper, president of Litho Arts, commented that when he was approached by a major corporation about the sale of his company, they considered the Snopake® trademark to be one of his most valuable assets.

Now, as an entrepreneur, recognize the role of a trademark in the development of your business. To do this you will need to consider a few of the basic principles about the selection and use of a trademark. Consider the advice of Richard H. Compere. Mr. Compere is a partner in the Chicago law firm of Willian, Brinks, Olds, Hofer, Gilson & Lione Lt. and is my idea of a trademark expert because he takes a practical approach and has helped my company avoid costly mistakes. Actually, Dick has represented two companies for whom I have worked and has litigated several matters on their behalf.

Dick tells entrepreneurs, "In considering trademarks, you should decide whether you want to use your company name as a trademark or to select a separate trademark for your products."

14.1   WHAT IS A TRADEMARK?

A trademark is any word, name, symbol, device, or any combination thereof adapted and used by a manufacturer or merchant to identify their goods and distinguish them from those manufactured or sold by others.

As an entrepreneur, you should realize that the primary function of a trademark is to distinguish your goods from those of your competitors, to serve as a guarantee of consistency of quality to your customers, and to serve in an advertising capacity to help in the sale of your products. In essence, your trademark is your brand name. And as such, it represents your reputation. It will also enable your customers to recognize your product as a result of your reputation for quality.

You should also know that certain characteristics must be present to establish a valuable trademark. For example, in the United States, you develop your rights in a trademark by actually using it to identify your goods. In fact, you begin to establish your rights with the first use of your mark. And when you file an application to register a trademark in the U.S. Patent and Trademark Office, it is the first use in interstate commerce, that is, the first sale to someone in another state, that establishes your right to a federal registration.

Now, as an entrepreneur, you should select a distinctive mark. You should select a distinctive mark because you will not be able to protect a mark that is merely descriptive. For example, "steel belted radial tires" is descriptive of a type of automotive tire and would not be registerable. You should also avoid using someone else's mark, and don't select a mark that might be confusingly similar to another trademark. For example, if a company is selling Country Time lemonade mix, you should not try to adopt Country Prize as a trademark for the same product.

14.2   SELECTING A TRADEMARK

When you select a name for your product, you may be making one of your most important decisions as an entrepreneur. And when you make this decision, you should base it on marketing and legal considerations. For example, Dick Compere said, "Advertising agencies frequently recommend a descriptive mark, one that is difficult, if not impossible, to protect. On the other hand, I would recommend a distinctive mark so that you can establish a strong trademark, so that you can build a big corral around your mark."

At this stage, forget technical considerations and assume the role of a vice president of marketing. Think in terms of a nondescriptive brand name that will help you in selling a product. Try to select a name that will clearly distinguish your product from those of a competitor. Try to select a name that will appeal to a customer. Select a name that may be suggestive of a desired result, but not descriptive or misdescriptive of the product. Consider the characteristics of marks like Liquid Paper® and Snopake® for typewriter correction fluid.

A few years ago, a client developed a system for purifying water and wanted to adopt a trademark incorporating "aqua". After learning that there were hundreds of trademarks that included "aqua", Bruno Miccioli, the project manager, suggested the word "Aquella," which was the Italian word for little storm. The term was adopted and subsequently used and registered.

So when you select your trademark, consider a few basic rules. First, choose an arbitrary or coined word, rather than a descriptive phrase. You should select an arbitrary word since it will form the basis for a strong proprietary position. By doing so, you can avoid a common mistake made by marketing executives who promote their products with a descriptive phrase and then are disappointed when a competitor uses a similar description. For example, the people at The General Tire Company of Akron, Ohio, tried register "Super Steel Belted Radials" but were unable to convince the U.S. Patent and Trademark Office that the term was not descriptive. On the other hand, it is possible to obtain a good trademark if the name is suggestive, or if it describes a vague characteristic or a fanciful allusion of the product. London Fog® is an example of a suggestive mark that has become a valuable trademark for rainwear.

Unfortunately, there is no master list of words that are descriptive or suggestive. In fact, you can't even rely on dictionaries. Dictionaries aren't much help since they fail to record the exaggerations and distortions of words used in advertising. Nevertheless, it may help to remember that a trademark examiner, in deciding if your mark is registerable, will examine the word's meaning based on its use with a particular product.

For example, Samuel Moore & Co., of Aurora, Ohio, failed to obtain a trademark for "superhose" since the term was simply descriptive of the product—a normal combination of words used to denote a hose of superior quality.

Now, as an entrepreneur, consider some additional thoughts for selecting a trademark. For example, a short and simple mark is easier to remember. And a mark should be capable of reproduction in any size or color and usable in ethnic neighborhoods and probably in foreign markets.

14.3 AVOID CONFLICTS WITH ESTABLISHED COMPETITORS

Dick Compere said, "A number of businessmen make a common mistake when they select a name for their product. They rely on a corporate name clearance, and then assume that they have a right to use that name on a product. Then at a later time, these businessmen learn that they are infringing someone's trademark and have to change the name on their product." Dick went on to say, "Make certain that you have trademark clearance before you start to promote your selected name."

Fortunately, it is easy to avoid trademark infringement. All that is required is to request a trademark search. A trademark search is inexpensive, costing \$200–\$250. Then, assuming that there are no conflicting marks disclosed by the search, you can begin to develop your rights in your trademark.

But there is one more caveat. Your trademark rights will be limited to the class of goods on which they are used. Nevertheless, there are times when you may be prevented from using a mark on a product that is quite dissimilar to that of the registered user.

For example, one court prohibited the showing of an X-rated film which included a scene with a cheerleader. The cheerleader was wearing a uniform identical to those worn by the Dallas Cowgirls. The court held that the use of the uniform was an infringement on the rights of the Dallas Cowgirls and was disparaging of their trademark rights associated with the uniform.

Now, as an entrepreneur, would you use Scott for a liquid furniture polish? Certainly, you should recognize the preeminence of Scott Paper in the household market. However, back in the 1930s, when Lee Scott of Denver, Colorado, developed his furniture polish, he was probably unaware of any claim of exclusivity claimed by a Philadelphia manufacturer of toilet tissue. He named his product Scott's Liquid Gold.

After two years, Lee Scott sold his business to John and Rose Hartmann, who continued to sell the product. The Hartmanns sold about 15,000 bottles of Scott's Liquid Gold in the Denver area and in 1951 sold the business to Jerome Goldstein for $350. The Goldsteins gradually increased the business until sales exceeded $16 million annually.

At this point, Scott paper complained about the use of the Scott name. The attorneys for Scott's Liquid Gold argued that their client was the first to use Scott on furniture polish and accordingly should be permitted to continue to use the Scott name.

The court ruled against them. The rationale behind extending a mark's protection in areas in which it has not been used was explained by Judge Stapleton. One merchant should not direct customers from another by representing what the first merchant sells as emanating from the second. It has been recognized that a merchant has an economic interest in the use of a trademark even in another field. Therefore, the law provides that unless the borrower's use is so foreign to that of the owner as to insure against any identification of the two, the borrower's use is unlawful.

In the above case, the manufacturers of Scott's Liquid Gold were probably not severely damaged, since the term Liquid Gold was recognized as the major part of their mark.

The standard for determining trademark infringement is "likelihood of confusion." However, the following factors, which are used to evaluate the facts, were pointed out by Judge Stapleton in the Scott case. They are:

1. The strength of a mark.
2. The degree of similarity.
3. The expense of the goods.
4. The channels of marketing.
5. The promotional target.
6. The relatedness of the goods in the mind of a purchaser.

Keeping these factors in mind should help you to select and use your mark in a manner that will not conflict with others.

14.4 USING YOUR TRADEMARK PROPERLY

In order to protect your rights, you must use your mark properly. For example, it is not sufficient to use a mark in advertisements or brochures because the law provides that a mark must be placed on the product or the package containing the product. Your mark will increase in value as long as you use it properly and don't let it be destroyed by careless or improper usage.

Dick Compere said, "If you are starting a new business with an unusual product, you must also get a generic name for the product. For example, when the people at Windsurfing International started to promote a surfboard with a sail on it, they called it a Windsurfer and obtained a federal trademark registration for that term. Over 10 years later, they began to emphasize the term sailboard as a generic term for the product. However, the court held that windsurfer was generic." By contrast, the Xerox Corporation has for many years emphasized that Xerox is a trademark, a brand name for copy machines and other products.

As an entrepreneur, you can avoid problems if you use your trademark as an adjective modifying the common name of the product. Don't use it as a noun or allow it to be used as the name of the product. Don't use the plural or possesive forms. And make certain that your trademark is spelled correctly and in the same manner in which it is registered. You should also recognize that a trademark can be enhanced by using a typographical distinction between the mark and the product name. For example, the trademark might be all capital letters. Or, at the very least, capitalize the first letter of the trademark and follow the mark by an ® or ™. The ® should be used only after a trademark that is federally registered.

Always use your trademark correctly, not only on the product, but also in articles, advertising, and in correspondence, because your misuse can result in the loss of a valuable asset.

14.5 THE STRENGTH OF A TRADEMARK

As previously mentioned, your trademark may become an invaluable asset. However, its value will depend on its distinctiveness or on its tendency to identify your goods as coming from a particular source.

In the words of District Court Judge Lavel, "Trademarks are divided into four categories forming the spectrum of trademark strength, ranging from those trademarks so inherently weak as to receive no legal protection, to those so strong as to command broad protection" (see Proctor & Gamble Co. *v.* Johnson & Johnson, Inc. 205 USPQ 697 at p. 707).

Judge Lavel went on to say, "At the weakest end of the spectrum are the generic marks, which cannot be registered and receive no protection.

At the strongest end are the arbitrary or fanciful marks. In between are descriptive marks on the weaker side, and suggestive marks on the stronger side."

He said, "Descriptive terms are those which forthwith convey an immediate idea of the ingredients, qualities, or characteristics of the goods. They are entitled to registration only upon proof that they have acquired secondary meaning, or in other words, have become associated in the public mind with the product or its source."

And then, the Judge said, "Suggestive terms are those which require imagination, thought and perception to reach a conclusion as to the nature of goods. They can be registered without proof of secondary meaning."

Thus even though Proctor and Gamble had sold over 300 million units of Sure deodorant in seven years, and spent over $100,000,000 promoting the name, the judge held that the Sure mark was not very distinctive. In fact, he said, "Sure lacks originality and uniqueness." And, he indicated that Sure was a common adjective that had been used to convey a quality. He went on to say, "The Sure mark shares the features of laudatory marks, like best, outstanding, or supreme, which are entitled to little or no protection."

Therefore, as an entrepreneur, follow the advice of Dick Compere, who said, "Select a mark that you can protect, not a descriptive mark. And then, as your mark becomes more famous, your rights will get broader and broader."

However, if you insist on a descriptive mark, your rights will be relatively narrow. In other words, you will not be able to extend your rights to cover goods that fall into some other classification. You will not be able to extend your rights because the public will not assume that you have any sponsorship or control over the product.

Now, once you have selected a mark and obtained clearance to use it, place it on the product or on the product's package, and make your first sale in interstate commerce. Then you will be ready to register your trademark.

14.6 REGISTERING A TRADEMARK

Don't represent yourself in trademark matters. Select a trademark specialist or a patent lawyer to register your mark.

And before you register a trademark, talk to your lawyer about selecting the class or classes of goods that are applicable. Be prepared to submit the following to the U.S. Patent and Trademark Office:

1. The name of the applicant.
2. A name and address to which communications can be directed.
3. A drawing or other identification of the mark sought to be registered.
4. An identification of goods or services.
5. Five identical specimens or facsimiles of the mark as actually used.
6. A date of first use of the mark in commerce, or a certified copy of a foreign registration if the application is based on such foreign registration to Section 44(e) of the Act, or a claim of the benefit of a prior foreign application in accordance with Section 44(d) of the Act.
7. The required filing fee for at least one class of goods or services.

Your costs for obtaining a trademark will be relatively modest; in most cases they will not exceed several hundred dollars.

14.7 TRADEMARK PROSECUTION, OPPOSITION, AND AFFIDAVITS UNDER SECTIONS 8 AND 15

A U.S. trademark examiner will examine your application to determine if it meets the legal requirements for registration. For example, the examiner may conclude that your mark is confusingly similar to a registered mark and reject your application. Actually, your application might be rejected on a number of grounds such as being deceptive, immoral, or scandalous, as disparaging or falsely suggestive, and so on.

But if your application is rejected, you usually have two to six months to file a reply. Then the examiner will reexamine your application. At times, you may interview the examiner in an effort to convince him or her that your mark is entitled to registration. At other times, you may appeal the examiner's final rejection.

Now, assuming that you have convinced an examiner that your mark is registerable, it will be published in the *Official Gazette*. Then any parties who believe they might be damaged by your registration may file an opposition.

An opposition is a proceeding before the Trademark Trial and Appeal Board of the U.S. Patent and Trademark Office. In this proceeding, one party tries to prevent the other from obtaining a trademark registration. In many ways, the proceeding is similar to litigation, since it provides for discovery by both parties, filing of motions, and a final interparty hearing.

But assuming that no one opposes your mark, or that you are successful in overcoming an opposition, you will receive your registration. However, your trademark rights still depend on your actual use of the mark. And if you fail to use your mark properly, you can lose your trademark.

Therefore, you will want to continue to use your mark and to file affidavits under Sections 8 and 15 of the Trademark Act. An affidavit, or declaration under Section 8, must be filed between the fifth and sixth year of registration. This affidavit must show that your mark "Is still in use or that its non-use is due to special circumstances." If you fail to file this affidavit, your registration will be cancelled.

Now, as an owner of a registered trademark, you will also want to file an affidavit under Section 15 in order to obtain the benefits of incontestability. This affidavit may be combined with your Section 8 affidavit or may be filed separately at any time after five years of registration. In this affidavit you must list the goods or services stated in your registration on which the mark has been in continuous use in commerce for a five year period. And this five year period has to be subsequent to your date of registration. The affidavit must also show that the mark is still in use, that there has been no final decision that is adverse to the owner's rights, and there are no pending proceedings involving the mark in the U.S. Patent and Trademark Office or in the courts.

Care must be exercised in preparing this affidavit. For example, you must limit the affidavit to those goods on which you are using the mark. And if your registration includes other goods on which you have not continuously used the mark, you must exclude them.

Incontestability means that an infringer can no longer dispute your rights in the mark. However, there might be other defenses to a charge of infringement.

14.8 CANCELLATION AND OTHER PROCEEDINGS

A cancellation proceeding is very similar to an opposition, except that it involves a registered trademark. For example, suppose that you find that someone has a trademark registration for a mark that is confusingly similar or identical to your mark. And then you discover that your rights are paramount to that registrant's. For example, you learn that you have actual and continuous use of your mark before that of the registered user.

Your recourse would be to file a petition to cancel the earlier registration. But in this case, you would have to overcome a presumption that the owner of the registration is entitled to the exclusive use of the mark.

There are two other proceedings related to confusingly similar or identical marks. The first relates to a concurrent proceeding that involves the same or similar marks, but under conditions where no confusion is likely. The second relates to an interference where confusion is likely. And, in the case of an interference, the Trademark Trial and Appeal Board would determine which of two applicants is entitled to the registration.

14.9 OTHER CONSIDERATIONS

Before leaving the subject of trademarks, there are a few points that may interest an entrepreneur. For example, there are questions concerning the degrees of similarity that are permissible between marks. Or, in other words, how can you tell if you would be entitled to register your proposed mark in view of someone else's prior use of a similar term?

Dick Compere said, "The real test is: Will the consumer assume that the manufacturer of both products is the same? And if the natural assumption is that they are, you will probably be precluded from registering your mark."

However, Dick went on to say, "Don't overlook the reaction by the prior user. If, for example, they find out about your use, most likely they will not sit back and allow you to infringe on their rights." And as an entrepreneur, you should try to avoid litigation whenever possible.

There are other tests that are used to determine if two marks are likely to cause confusion in the marketplace. For example, in the Proctor & Gamble *v.* Johnson & Johnson Inc. case, Judge Leval wrote: First of all, the characters of the mark must be considered. When arbitrary or fanciful marks are involved, the distinctiveness of the marks will make the public more conscious of similarities than differences." He went on to say that "Sure and Natural" is significantly and noticeably different from "Sure" and that "Whatever similarities exist between the marks is thoroughly undermined by the differences in visual presentation."

Another test that is applied by the courts to determine if a mark infringes on the rights of another relates to the proximity of the products, that is, are they sold in the same stores or the same areas of a store? Nevertheless, the question still boils down to the likelihood of confusion. And evidence of actual confusion is most persuasive.

The courts also consider the sophistication of the buyer as a contributing factor in considering confusion between two marks. Essentially, a sophisticated buyer, for example, a technical professional, will be more careful in selecting a precision instrument than an average buyer would be expected to use in selecting a product from the supermarket. Therefore, the sophisticated buyer is assumed more likely to know whose product is whose.

Now, there is one further caveat in considering the similarity of two marks. If there is evidence that the subsequent user is attempting to palm off the new products as those of the prior user, the subsequent user will not receive the benefit of any doubt. In fact, the subsequent user will probably be enjoined from using the mark and may be forced to pay a large sum of money to the prior user.

Before proceeding to the next chapter, consider the question of a nominal or token use of your mark. For example, Proctor and Gamble adopted a minor program under which they shipped small amounts of products in interstate commerce to maintain their rights in certain trademarks that were not otherwise used. However, Judge Leval concluded that token use did not maintain a protectable interest in a mark. He cited Judge Friendly's landmark opinion in La Societe Anonume des Parfubrs Le Galicon v. Jean Patou, Inc. 181 USPQ 545 (2nd Circuit, 1974) to the effect that "Usage which is sporadic, nominal and intended solely for trademark maintenance is insufficient to establish and maintain trademark rights."

What this all boils down to is that "There is no such thing as property in a trademark, except as a right appurtenant to an established business or trade in connection with which mark is employed" (Hanover Star Milling Co. v. Metcalf 240 US 403, 1916).

Finally, for those of you who have a further interest in the law of trademarks, there is one comprehensive treatise on the subject. That excellent reference is *Trademark Protection and Practice* by Jerome Gilson (Matthew Bender, 1983).

PART 3

SELLING YOUR IDEAS

15

Selling Your Inventions

Edgar D. Young, of Trilon Discovery Corporation in Columbus, Ohio, believes in developing new businesses based on inventions. But then, Ed is an inventor, an innovator, journalist, author, and former advertising executive. He said. "It's up to you to sell your inventions and it frequently takes five or six years before you make any money."

Ed has been successful in selling inventions because he recognizes the importance of selling in bringing a new product to the market. In fact, he believes "Many creative people often need assistance in selling their ideas."

Ed Young recognized this problem and took an idea to the City Council of Columbus, Ohio. He convinced them to invest in a program to create new businesses, to invest in new ideas. He said, "Now, I look at four to five inventions a day and probably have 200 inventions available for licensing in my office."

And, in Ed's opinion, one key to success in selling your invention is "You need a good salesman. You need someone who will create excitement, someone who will sell *you*. After all, an inventor can't usually sell himself. What he needs is a professional salesman."

In fact, Ed has advised some inventors to "Forget the patent attorney and find a good salesman." He said this because, "If you can't sell a product, nothing else matters." And as a result of Ed's enthusiasm for inventions, his office has created 186 new jobs in Ohio and resulted in over $3,200,000 changing hands.

Now as an entrepreneur, put yourself in the position of vice president of marketing. You may choose to handle your own sales or to follow the advice of Ed Young and hire a professional. But before you decide, consider the case of a new cereal product.

In the early 1960s the Kellogg Company introduced a new cereal containing freeze-dried ice cream. The addition of milk was supposed to reconstitute the ice cream. And when the new product was introduced at the company's sales meeting, it was well received. Many of the sales staff were ecstatic.

But when the product was introduced into two test markets, it didn't sell. Was the price too high? Or was the product, which tasted like a lump of sugar saturated with milk, insufficiently developed? The fact is that many product failures can be attributed to inadequate marketing. Also, many new products never even reach test markets because someone failed to convince management they had sales appeal and profit potential.

Every new product needs a mentor who will promote the product within a company.

At the start, you must serve as your product's on mentor. You alone are responsible for selling a group of people on your product's profit potential. You are responsible for imparting sufficient enthusiasm so that a licensee will do an adequate job of marketing your product.

But before proceeding, think for a moment about your role as vice president of marketing. Many executives in this position have had years of experience in sales. They have successfully sold products, have worked directly with customers, and have risen to an administrative position.

However, even if you don't have the background, you can be effective as the vice president of marketing if you believe in and are enthusiastic about your invention. In fact, you can learn to enjoy this role and to promote your own invention. But you have to be realistic.

Now, as an entrepreneur, recognize that selling is a craft. Good sales people are not born. They are ordinary men and women who have worked hard and learned how to sell. And there is no reason why a creative individual cannot do the same. After all, if you want to sell a business opportunity, you only need a single customer. Therefore, you can be selective in approaching a customer, and you will deal with individuals who are interested in business opportunities.

Consider, for example, the experience of H. Gordon Howe, Director, Technology Transfer Program at Research Corporation in Tucson, Arizona. Research Corporation works primarily with universities and then licenses the universities' inventions to established companies. In Gordon Howe's words, "We look for technically sophisticated inventions, file for patent protection, and then look for a corporation with the ability to develop the invention and market products that embody the invention."

Gordon Howe advises individuals, "Your first step is to file for a patent application because most major companies won't look at or seriously consider ideas unless you have filed for patent protection. And even after filing, it is difficult to convince many companies to seriously consider an outside submission."

Nevertheless, there are advantages in licensing inventions to companies that have a strong marketing organization and channels for distribution. So one of your first steps in licensing your invention is to select the most promising candidate.

15.1   SELECTING YOUR TARGET

A trip to your public library and a review of *Thomas's Register* will help you identify companies that sell products compatible with your invention. You should also look at other sources, such as *Standard & Poor's Directory to Corporations* and *Moody's International Index*. Then select a candidate with an established marketing organization.

But Ed Young cautions, "Don't take your invention to the wrong company. Don't take it to a company with a product that will be displaced by your invention." For example, if you have an improved spray gun for spraying insecticide onto rose bushes which reduces the amount of insecticide used, don't take it to a company that manufactures insecticides. In that case, you should probably go to the consumer or to a company with complementary products.

In the early 1960s, a client who had developed a freeze-dried soup in Europe was seeking a licensee to manufacture and sell the product in the United States. He identified those companies that were marketing soups at the time. Then he went on to identify other companies in the food industry that might expand into the soup field. For example, a manufacturer of a powdered beverage such as a Kool Aid drink mix might be interested in expanding into other products. Rich Products of Buffalo, New York, manufacturer of Coffee Mate, a nondairy creamer, was another possible candidate, and subsequently announced plans to enter the freeze-dried food field. Lipton, who at the time marketed a powdered onion soup, was considered a better candidate than Campbell, who seemed committed to canned products. But none of the companies was willing to invest in this inventor's product. And then, a number of years later, a similar product became popular. The client's product was developed before there was a commercial market for it. And his patent did not cover the process eventually used by the manufacturers of the similar products.

But in identifying candidates for developing your invention, keep track of the activities of companies in a particular field by reading periodicals. For example, if your invention relates to plastics, subscribe to *Modern Plastics*, or at least read a number of back issues at your local library. And when you review technical literature, note those companies announcing new products that would be compatible with products according to your invention. Go to the library and identify those companies that should be interested in your development.

Next, consider your list of candidates and note carefully each company's marketing emphasis. Generally, you will find that a company that emphasizes industrial sales will be relatively unsuccessful in selling products at the consumer level and vice versa. Therefore, if your product is designed for the average consumer, select a company with a strong consumer sales organization.

Consider, for example, a hypothetical inventor who has developed an improved friction material, who has discovered a replacement for asbestos. The new material will produce better gaskets and improve the friction in brake and clutch linings. Such an inventor would certainly want to consider companies such as the Manville Corporation and Raymark as potential licensees, since they are leading manufacturers of these materials. And, even more important, these companies have the ability to sell in the automotive field. They would both appear to be far better candidates than Ford or General Motors, which are concerned with selling the final product.

You should also consider a company's size when selecting a licensee. For example, if your product has a limited market and profit potential, it would probably not be of interest to a General Electric or DuPont. However, a smaller company would be more enthusiastic about a small market or less profit potential than one of the billion dollar multinational companies. As an executive in the development department of a major oil company said, "We would not consider any new project unless it had potential revenues in excess of 100 million dollars."

Therefore, focus your attention on a few companies. Then separate them into three groups: (1) those that are in a related business, (2) those likely to enter a related business, and (3) those that might not fit into the other two categories and yet for some reason might be interested in your invention.

Now, many successful sales people talk about "qualifying a prospect." They have learned not to waste their time trying to sell to the wrong customer. For example, someone who sells power boats will not spend a lot of time trying to sell that product to a "sailor" who refers to all power boats as "stink pots." And, as an entrepreneur, you should not waste your time with a company that has little interest in your invention.

Consider the advice of Gordon Howe, who said, "At Research Corporation, we have an advantage in obtaining a serious evaluation of our inventions since we have an established track record. Besides, the companies know that we have already screened out those inventions that have limited potential."

Gordon went on to say, "It is also important to have a contact within the company [the potential licensee], someone that you know and can talk to." In other words, don't base your effort on sending letters to an unknown officer in the companies that you select as potential licensees.

One former associate suggested making your initial approach to your second or even third choice. He suggested this because your second or third presentation will be more polished, and you will have learned to answer the difficult questions in earlier presentations. After all, if you listen, you can obtain marketing information from each presentation. Then you can be more effective when you talk with your best prospect. But if the first company wants to buy your proposal, sell it and assume that they are the best prospect.

However, if you are unable to sell your invention to one of your first three choices, review your presentation and reevaluate your selection of potential partners. And remember, a number of major companies rejected Chester Carlson's xerography invention.

Some entrepreneurs suggest a shotgun approach to marketing. They suggest that you write the same letter to a number of companies, and the one that gets there first with the most is the best licensee. This approach has been successful, but is not recommended. The shotgun method should probably be used only by someone who has substantial experience in licensing inventions.

15.2 DON'T PAY SOMETHING FOR NOTHING

There are many organizations that offer to market inventions and then do not perform any meaningful services. These so-called invention promoters are usually characterized by the fee they charge for their services. There is nothing wrong with charging for one's services, but these individuals earn their living from these fees. A number of them have little or no marketing ability. For example, one company circulates a ditto copy listing numerous inventions to a large number of the Fortune 500 companies. Most, if not all, of the recipients file these copies in the wast basket without consideration.

15.3 CONSIDER THE USE OF A CONSULTANT

If you are concerned about packaging your invention, consider the use of a consultant. Consider using a recently retired executive, sales manager, advertising manager, or the like, who can put together an effective presentation. You might also consider a professor at one of the local universities. At times, an initial lunch, at your expense, will tell you whether or not a consultant is qualified, and if that consultant can provide valuable marketing information. Your initial consultation may also identify a number of areas that need further study, and may add credibility to your presentations.

15.4 HOW TO PREPARE FOR AN INITIAL PRESENTATION

Before approaching a potential partner, learn as much as you can about their business. Review their annual report, advertising brochures, and any published articles about the company. Then focus on how your invention can help their business.

Many inventors forget to sell their services in their zeal to sell an invention. However, your time is valuable and you should be paid for your services. But be reasonable. For example, you might suggest a consulting contract at $200 or more per day, with a provision that half of the consulting fee would be treated as an advance on royalties that are in excess of any minimums.

But before you try to sell your services, consider how, why, where, and when your services will be needed. Consider what you can do to produce an early return on an investment. Consider what you can do better than your partner.

There are cases where an invention is sufficiently developed so that the licensee does not need your services of a consultant. Nevertheless, it is advisable to provide for at least one day of consulting services per month for a review of their progress in commercializing your invention. This review will also assure your participation in commercializing your invention. Besides, it will help you to maintain a continuing dialogue with your partner. And it is often up to you to maintain a high level of enthusiasm for your invention.

Selecting the right individual within a company is sometimes more difficult than selecting the right company as a partner. And the importance of selecting the right individual cannot be overemphasized. It is important because the right individual can make things happen. And the right individual can obtain the human and financial resources to commercialize your invention.

Fortunately, there are several approaches for selecting this individual. For example, consider a division or operating unit with annual sales or less than $50 million. You can approach the division general manager of the vice president of marketing. Either of these managers should be receptive to outside ventures and have the ability to launch new products.

The names of division managers or marketing managers can be found in a Dun & Broadstreet report or in other sources. You can also talk to a company's customers and learn who would be your best potential contact.

And when you talk to a customer, ask for an introduction. An introduction by a good customer can go a long way in obtaining a receptive audience.

Gordon Howe suggested, "Try to establish a contact through your lawyer to find someone within the company to get an introduction, since going in cold is very difficult." And when you select an individual, make certain that person has the authority to make a decision to enter into agreements. In larger companies it may be more difficult to reach the actual decision makers. Nevertheless, find out who is responsible for making decisions.

There are times when you should approach a larger company. For example, there are times when the level of investment or size of the market will exceed the human and financial resources of the smaller organization. But before approaching a larger corporation, reflect for a minute on what you can do to sell effectively. Think about what you can do to help them and at the same time to help yourself.

For now, focus on the problems of a venture with several years of research and development, a prototype, and nominal sales, that is a company still in the early entrepreneurial stage. This type of company will probably encounter resistance when they approach the large corporation. Nevertheless, you can succeed if you recognize the problem associated with a large corporation and follow a few suggestions.

The nub of the problem is that the large corporation normally has a plethora of investment opportunities and limited resources. In fact, their executives are bombarded with requests for human and financial resources. Their sales department wants another sales person, distribution wants a new warehouse, production wants more efficient machines, finance wants another accountant, and so on.

Furthermore, you face a reluctance to change, the not-invented-here (NIH) syndrome, a reluctance to invest in technology, and a lack of entrepreneurial spirit, as pointed out in *Intrapreneuring* by Gifford Pinchot (Harper and Row, 1985).

You can overcome these problems if you select a company that has good distribution within your area of interest. The reason is that few companies are successful in marketing in more than one area. For example, in the early 1960s, Bausch and Lomb was effective in selling to ophthamologists and optometrists, but with the exception of sunglasses, did not do well with consumer products. Consider what happened when they tried to market a slide projector. It was a good product, but a commercial disaster.

Now, when you approach a corporation, you need more than an idea, more than an invention, more than a patent application. What you need is a prototype and a well thought out and carefully documented business plan. This business plan should include marketing, financial, and production requirements. You should also include technical considerations, information on your proprietary position, and a statement that you know of no patent or trademark infringement problems.

Now, for those of you who want to sell a venture to a corporation, there is one secret for success. This secret is amazingly simple. The secret is actual sales. For example, if you can show that you have sold ten, twenty, or one hundred units, that is a lot more impressive than a patent application. And if you can show sales plus profits, a proprietary position, and freedom from infringement problems, you probably have a winner.

15.5 STRUCTURING A PRESENTATION

If you hope to sell effectively, organize your presentation. Your time is valuable and so is the time of each member of your audience. So don't try to save time by inadequate preparation. You may have only one chance to sell your invention. You may have only twenty or thirty minutes, perhaps an hour, in which to sell your proposal.

Therefore, organize your presentation and prepare an outline such as the following:

1. Market identification.
2. Profit potential.
3. Product description.
4. Competitive analysis including proprietary rights.
5. Financial requirements.
6. Technical analysis.
7. Business proposal.

When you follow your outline, keep the emphasis on the potential market and profit potential. After all, business executives are often preoccupied with profit and are not always patient. It's your job to generate enthusiasm for your proposal. Don't turn your listeners off by a vague or technically oriented presentation.

Business managers are also impressed by facts. In other words, don't exaggerate the potential market. Focus on that segment of the market that will be served by your invention. Point out the advantages your invention offers within this market segment. And then point out the profit potential.

In those cases where your invention relates to a process for a company's in-house use, a different approach may be appropriate. In this case, seek out the manufacturing personnel and emphasize cost savings and manufacturing efficiencies. But before you approach the manufacturing management of your target corporation, consider the advantages of a nonexclusive license or an exclusive license that is limited to a particular field.

And be realistic whenever you discuss your project with a potential licensee. Determine what gross margins are typical in an industry. Then show how your product fits into that industry, and its advantages over the competition. For example, some years ago a client company licensed a product to a food industry in which gross margins were quite low. The new product was applicable to a very small portion of the market, but it offered an exceptionally large margin. Therefore, the profit potential was sufficient to attract a number of licensees and the patented products generated many thousands of dollars for the patent owner.

So, when you prepare your presentation, draft a proposed pricing structure and an estimate of the manufacturing costs. And, if your pricing structure and profit margins are not consistent with industrial norms, be prepared to explain any deviations. Technical problems and suggested solutions should also be identified.

When you are preparing a presentation, recognize the fact that successful products attract competition. Therefore, if you have a strong patent position, you can assure a corporate manager of a protected market. However, even if you have a strong patent, be realistic about price elasticity. Price elasticity indicates a customer's sensitivity to price or willingness to buy at a higher price. You should also consider what action the competition will take when business is lost because of your new product. Will your competitors lower their prices, introduce improved products, or copy your development?

Now, today's business management is concerned about the cost of capital. They need to know how much it will cost to commercialize your invention. Are there large capital costs for new or specialized machinery? Will additional sales staff be required? Can your product be handled by their present sales staff, manufactured in their present plant on existing equipment? In other words, can they add significant profits to their earnings with a minor investment?

So when you prepare your presentation, think in terms of what your customers want and what you can do to help them reach their goals.

15.6   HOW TO MAKE AN INITIAL APPROACH

One of the best ways to contact a potential licensee is with a personal introduction. You might think that it is difficult to get a personal introduction. It isn't, if you are willing to work for it. For example, talk to several customers of your potential licensee, find one who will introduce you to your target's sales manager. After all, an introduction by a customer can lead to a receptive audience.

You could ask your patent attorney to call a corporate patent counsel. However, corporate patent counsels handle hundreds of outside submissions each year, which makes it difficult to get special treatment for each one. Besides, it is usually up to the operating divisions to consider new ventures. And it is your job to sell that division on the merits of your invention.

Consider the case of Gilbert S., an entrepreneur who had developed and patented a new product. Gil contacted the corporate secretary, explained that he was a stockholder and a successful businessman. He told his contact he had developed a new product that could be marketed by one of the corporation's divisions.

Gil had sold a number of these products at a profit and had a video tape illustrating the product. The corporate secretary viewed the tape and then introduced Gil to the division general manager. Then Gil entered into a consulting agreement with the company and participated in the further evaluation of his invention.

Now consider what you can do if you can't obtain a personal introduction. Write a brief letter to the individual who will have an interest in your invention. For example, if your product was appropriate for the Insulation Division of the Carborundum Company (now owned by SOHIO), you would not write to the president of SOHIO. However, you could pick up the phone, call the division, and ask the operator for the name of the division general manager or for the manager of new products.

Then write a brief letter along the lines suggested in Appendix A. Don't go into too much detail, but include enough information to suggest why your proposal should interest this company. All you want to do is get an appointment for your initial presentation.

Suggest that you will telephone in a week or ten days to follow up on the company's interest. Don't write a letter and wait for something to happen. Chances are that your letter may have been forwarded to someone else, or may be lost. But if you state that you will call within a week or ten days, an alert secretary will keep track of the letter.

15.7 GETTING AN APPOINTMENT

When you call for an appointment, don't try to sell your proposal over the phone. The sole purpose of your call is to get an appointment. Therefore, identify yourself and the name of your company. Refer to your letter and suggest alternate dates for an appointment.

Assume that your invention relates to ceramic fibers and that you have written to Mr. Alex Golden, Vice President and General Manager of Carbon Company's Insulation Division. Place a call to Mr. Golden and tell his secretary that you are calling to set up an appointment. She may tell you that the letter has been referred to Mr. Halpin, the division's New Products Manager, and transfer your call to Mr. Halpin.

Then, on reaching Mr. Halpin, you might say, "Mr. Halpin, my name is Jane Doe. I represent a small company in Elmira, New York, and I'm calling to follow up on my letter. In that letter, I mentioned that our company has developed a new application for your ceramic fibers. I plan to be in Buffalo within the next two weeks and wondered which week might be convenient for you. I would suggest an initial meeting of about thirty to forty-five minutes."

Now, if your product is highly technical, you might suggest that the application will involve some technical problems and that your contact might want to have a product engineer available.

One fault common to inexperienced sales people is that they fail to listen. They don't pick up valuable information about a prospective customer. For example, if you suggested having a product engineer participate in the meeting and were told by Mr. Halpin that he was a chemical engineer, make a note of that fact. And then, in some subsequent meeting you might mention that, "If I remember correctly, you have a chemical engineering background." A statement of this type suggests your interest in an individual and helps to sell your proposal. In addition this information can help you to prepare a presentation that will appeal to the customer.

Before scheduling a meeting, your customer might ask for additional information. Just remember you do not want to go into the details of your presentation, but do want to add to your contact's interest. Therefore, an appropriate answer might be "It is difficult to discuss the details of the application over the phone, but the new product will require from one to five million pounds of fiber per year, and will compete favorably with vacuum cast products." Remember, be candid. In other words, the above example would only be used if the facts stated were true to the best of your knowledge.

Now, there is one caveat. Don't identify yourself as an independent inventor. This phrase may set off an alarm. Then the recipient will forward your inquiry to the corporate patent department and you will receive a form letter stating the policy for submitting unsolicited ideas. And your job will become more difficult.

15.8   THE INITIAL INTERVIEW

An initial interview with a potential licensee will probably determine if you will succeed in selling your invention to that company. And if you don't do things right, you might not get another chance. Therefore, the planning and organization of your presentation are vitally important. You should also recognize the importance of the first few minutes. Remember, it is your job to sell your proposal and yourself. So, after the introductions, don't waste time on idle conversation.

If the company's representative asks if you had a good trip, you might answer, "Yes, thank you, and I might add that your directions to the office were excellent." Then, you might go on to say, "Mr. Halpin, I recognize the importance of your time, and would like to show you how you can participate in a multimillion dollar business. Let me take just a few minutes to tell you about our organization and a new product that incorporates your high temperature fiber . . . ."

Confidence is important in selling. Therefore, practice your initial presentation before you leave for the meeting. Have rehearsals. You can also use 3 × 5 cards to review the key points of your presentation while waiting for your appointment. A small flip chart with key points indicated is an excellent visual aid and will help you make an organized presentation.

Don't be upset by the thought of a formal or an informal presentation. It is normal to feel uneasy. Besides, uneasiness usually goes away once you start. And confidence will come with practice. Recognize that you are well prepared, that you have a good invention, and that the potential licensee is interested in hearing about it. And even if this company doesn't buy your proposal, you will learn more about the business, and how to sell the next prospect. As one salesman said "Customers are like streetcars. If you miss one, there is always another coming along the line."

It may seem unnecessary to discuss dress. However, proper dress is important. Your clothes should be neat, slightly conservative, and suitable for a business environment. In other words, don't go to a business meeting in a rumpled suit, white socks, and scuffed shoes.

Remember that your appearance and your attitude are important. You want to appear confident and gain the respect of your audience. However, don't be arrogant or talk too much or too rapidly. And don't be upset if someone plays the devil's advocate. Just be courteous and answer all questions to the best of your ability.

Above all, be sensitive during your presentation. Listen to comments from your audience and ask questions. After all, you can learn about their business and then use that information to sell your invention. If you are asked a question and don't have the answer, say so. Nobody has all the answers all of the time. Just say, "That's a difficult question to answer at this time, but I will get back to you." This is an obvious lead for a follow-up meeting.

Successful sales people recommend the use of "how, what, why, and when," together with "you." For example, "Let me show you how this product will fit in with your marketing program." The purpose is to keep the audience's interest, and, at the same time, get them to associate themselves with your proposal.

Don't overlook the importance of timing. For example, you might want to schedule the initial meeting for 11:30. Then, you can offer to take the prospective licensee to lunch. Lunch is a good time for social discussion. And by taking a prospective licensee to lunch, you can learn more about the company's needs. At the same time, you can verify information about the individuals whom you will meet at the next meeting, about the organization, and about the industry.

For example, you might say "I'm very impressed by your company. Could you tell me a bit more about your marketing organization?" Most managers are proud of their organization and will provide considerable information. And then additional questions, such as "Why are you more successful than your principal competitor," may lead to a wealth of information.

During your initial presentation, try to schedule a second meeting. If, for example, you have been unable to answer all of the audience's questions, you might say, "John, you have been very helpful in providing information and I need some time to answer some of your questions. I suggest another meeting in about two to three weeks. I would also like to make another presentation, tailored to your company's technical needs. Do you have any other questions or suggestions for another meeting?"

In selling a business opportunity to a larger corporation, it is almost impossible to complete a sale by talking to a single individual. Therefore, you should anticipate a larger group for your next meeting. Ask if others will attend and, if so, who are they? Learn as much as possible about their backgrounds. You might also suggest meeting at your facilities. After all, meeting at your facilities might be an effective way to show what you have accomplished and what type of resources you can bring to the venture. This assumes that you have something to show.

Now, before leaving the initial meeting, emphasize the importance of time. Mention that you are not presently talking with other companies and that you want to proceed without delay. And then, if the company does have an interest in your proposal but needs a little time to complete their evaluation, suggest a *reasonable* option period.

As a general rule, a second meeting should take place within two to six weeks. Then, if you have been successful, you will make a second presentation to a number of the company's personnel. Therefore, prepare new flip charts and show how your product fits into the company's plans. Have the answers to any questions that were previously asked, and incorporate meaningful information you have obtained during the first meeting into your second presentation.

And if your prospect expressed some concern during the initial presentation, be prepared to discuss that concern.

15.9   THE DEBRIEFING

During the initial meeting you should have written down any questions that you were unable to answer, and noted important points. Then, after leaving the meeting, write down as much as you can remember about the meeting. Carefully review your presentation. What areas were troublesome? If more than one person attended the meeting, who seemed to be the decision maker? Make certain that you remember everyone's name. Did you follow your plan? If you didn't, why not? Did you cover your key points?

Next, ask yourself what you learned about the operation of the target company. Were any of your assumptions about market size, estimates of the candidate's strengths, and assumptions about their competition confirmed? Start to think about how you can use this information in your second meeting, or if you were unsuccessful, think about incorporating the additional information in a presentation for another company.

15.10   THE SECOND PRESENTATION

Those of you who reach this stage have a prospect with a bona fide interest in your project. But don't stop selling. You can't stop selling even after a contract is signed. Nevertheless, you have passed a substantial hurdle. In fact, you have reached another difficult stage. You have come to the time when you want to "close the sale."

Consider, for example, that a second presentation will probably involve a number of people. For example, a typical meeting might include someone from marketing, an engineer or two, a financial manager, and perhaps a corporate lawyer. Don't be intimidated. Just remember that all these people are at the presentation because they are interested in your proposal.

Remember that not everyone will have heard your initial presentation and may have only a sketchy outline of your proposal. Even those who did hear your earlier presentation may have forgotten some of your salient points. Therefore, review your previous discussion. Mention points that were agreed to and proceed to answer any earlier questions. Explain how you would overcome any objections that were raised at your last meeting.

One other approach that might prove helpful is to list any previous objections alongside statements that overcome the objections. Include the points your first audience agreed to. You should also recognize that it is helpful to get your customers to participate. Some sales people suggest the use of "we" in discussing the results from the previous meeting, and recommend that you include your customer in the presentation. In other words, create an image that you are working together.

And don't overlook the importance of visual aids. Visuals are important, but should be simple. For example, use pictures, graphs, or diagrams whenever possible. And as you proceed with a presentation, stop frequently to ask questions. Stop and make certain that your prospects are with you. Stop and ask questions such as: "Do you see the opportunity for synergism in sales?" OR "Would this help your other sales?" Ask questions that will lead to a "yes" answer.

It may be too early to close a deal, but it is a good time to try. For example, as you discuss the business proposal, emphasize that "time is of the essence," and that it is important to close the deal and to get on with the important task of making money.

As a general rule, the larger the company, the longer it takes to make a final decision. However, you might suggest an option. Recognize that it may take from four to six months or longer from the time of an initial contact to a fully executed contract. In the interim, try to sell the prospective licensee on the advantage of a consulting contract, or suggest that they pay an option fee as an advance against future royalties.

Many companies will accept a reasonable option agreement or consulting contract. For example, you might ask for $1000 or $2000 per month and provide for two or three days per month of consulting effort. And recognize that a consulting arrangement is particularly advantageous, since it allows you to work with your customer in selling your proposal to their top management. A typical consulting agreement is set forth in Appendix J.

Now, when you make your sales presentation, remember to sell yourself. Remember to focus your attention on the customer's problems and demonstrate your ability to help solve them. Show your desire to help the customer and to successfully market your product at the earliest possible time.

Remember that what you are really selling is an invention and that invention is an intangible. Besides, your customer will probably compare your business opportunities to others available. To do this their management may construct mathematical models or computer scenarios before making a final decision. But when you participate in this type of analysis, you can often influence the decision, and even if unsuccessful, will have obtained a wealth of information while collecting some money. At the very least, you will have enhanced the package you have to sell to the next candidate.

However, if your customer terminates the option, follow up by calling the person who was most supportive of your project. Ask if that individual could be more specific as to why the project was rejected. You should also ask if he or she would be so kind as to tell you of any shortcomings in your presentation or materials. This type of information might not be what you want to hear, but if candidly given, is invaluable.

In working as a consultant, you will probably be asked to sign a secrecy agreement, which states that you will not disclose any of the company's confidential information. You must honor this agreement. And use extra care in talking with a second prospect, so that you do not disclose confidential information of your previous contact. Furthermore, consult your lawyer before signing any agreement.

15.11   CONTINUED BUSINESS NEGOTIATIONS

By and large, the biggest mistake that small entrepreneurs make in dealing with a large corporation is that they ask for too much. Many of them want instant riches and an unrealistic share of future income.

You can avoid this mistake if you are realistic. Recognize the corporation's risk in launching a new product and make certain that they have plenty of incentive to promote your venture.

As a rule of thumb in licensing, you should get no more than 20% to 25% of their pretax profit. And, as a general rule, large corporations will not pay more than 5% royalty based on net sales. In fact, in some highly competitive, high volume industries, a $1\frac{1}{4}$% royalty is considered high. It is also customary to provide a declining royalty, so that when annual sales reach a given level, the royalties on additional sales will be at a lower rate.

When you are negotiating a agreement, keep selling. Ask questions like: How long do you think it will take to reach sales of a certain level? Then use a portion of that figure, perhaps half, as a proposed basis for minimum royalties.

Now, since it frequently takes four to ten months to reach a final agreement, you will probably have a number of discussions regarding contractual terms. These business negotiations are covered in more detail in Chapter 17.

15.12 THE KEY ELEMENTS FOR SUCCESS

For those of you who want to license your inventions to a large corporation, who want to use the corporation's marketing expertise, established channels of distribution, and adequate financing, there are seven keys for success.

First, select a partner with a strong marketing organization, with established distribution, and with expertise in your field of interest.

Second, deal directly with the appropriate division general manager or that division's vice president of marketing.

Third, obtain a personal introduction to the division general manager or to the vice president of marketing. And, if possible, obtain an introduction from an important customer.

Fourth, sell your venture as a business opportunity, not on the basis of technology. In other words, put the emphasis on market size and profit.

Fifth, use evidence of actual sales whenever possible.

Sixth, be reasonable when you structure a working relationship with your partner.

Seventh, even after the agreement is signed, continue to work with your partner to make your venture a success.

16

Environmental Influence and the Role of Strategic Planning

As an entrepreneur, you are probably sole proprietor of your own company. You are chairman of the board, chief operating officer, chief financial officer, sales manager, corporate scientist, lab technician, labor force, chief cook and bottle washer. And in this role you will make major decisions that affect the success or failure of your business. In other words, it is up to you to generate vast profits through the development of good ideas or to lose your investment.

Now, if you want to succeed, look beyond technological problems and solutions. Look at the potential market, distribution, financial, and production requirements.

Don't be intimidated by the role of chief executive. In most cases you can rely on good common sense. You can also avoid the complexity of multinational decisions as well as the plethora of conflicting views with which a senior executive must cope. Nevertheless, it is important to consider the problems of your counterpart and to understand the decision making process in order to compete with a corporation or to convince its subordinates to invest their time and money in your invention.

16.1 THE ENVIRONMENT FOR SMALL BUSINESS

On March 10, 1982, *Business Week* reported that, "For the first time in American history, small businessmen and women throughout the land are about to become the most powerful political lobby in the country." Arthur Levitt, Jr., who wrote the report, went on to say, "My own feeling is that the greatest impact of this new program may turn out to be the reawakening of respect for, as well as the self-respect of entrepreneurship in American life."

Think for a moment about the previous quotes.What are the implications? How will these implications affect you as an entrepreneur?

Consider also that inflation provides a powerful impetus for small businesses. It is true that inflation has been reduced during the past few years. Nevertheless, it has continued for over forty years and will probably be with us for quite a few years. It is also true that inflation will increase your costs. However, you are investing time, and can at the same time improve your own productivity. Besides, you will not have to cope with a lack of effort associated with a large work force and should sell your time at an inflated value. For example, if you invest ten hours of time in developing your invention and value your time at $25 per hour, you will have invested $250. And then, if you sell your invention one year later, and inflation was 5%, you would expect to sell that investment for $262.50.

As an entrepreneur you can increase your rate of productivity and increase the number of hours worked without having to worry about a lot of legal constraints, union contracts, local political considerations, and a plethora of other problems that adversely affect a large corporation.

You also have one advantage over your biggest competitor. You can do development work far more cheaply than a large corporation. For example, in a large company a relatively modest program will cost $75,000 or more. That is the approximate cost for one year for a one-person effort, including overhead. In fact many companies estimate that the cost of overhead is equal to 100% of the cost of salary including fringes.

So by applying yourself, avoiding the frustrations of bureaucratic approvals, program reviews, accounting controls, and other nonproductive procedures, you may accomplish far more in a given period of time at a small fraction of the costs for a large corporation.

A lawsuit between Drew Chemical Corporation and Star Chemical illustrates the advantages of a small company. Drew Chemical produced a beaded combination stablilizer-emulsified product by means of a special tower. This special tower cost Drew approximately $250,000 to build. Two former employees of Drew formed Star Chemical Company and built a nonsophisticated tower. Their tower was a concave affair made from plywood, 2×4s, and a polyethylene liner. Star's approximate cost for their tower was $600. And Star's tower worked effectively.

Nevertheless, a large corporation can do some things better than a small company. They can frequently handle national marketing, distribution, and large-scale manufacturing more effectively than an individual. And there are times when a development program will require the financial resources of a large company. However, don't underestimate your own capabilities or your ability to make a meaningful contribution to a development program.

16.2 THE ENVIRONMENT AND THE LARGE CORPORATION

Your counterpart, the chief executive officer of a major corporation, is probably concerned about a declining rate of growth. This executive is concerned because performance is measured by profits and profit growth. The problem is to obtain growth without relying on an expanding market. Fortunately, you may have the answer to this problem. You may have the solution for this individual and an opportunity to obtain an adequate return on your investment.

Actually, the problems of a chief executive officer of a major corporation are complex. For example, the growth rate of the gross national product in a major industrial nation such as the United States has declined. And with the strength of the U.S. dollar, major corporations are facing increased competition from imports. For example, Japanese cars, tv sets, cameras, and electronic calculators, as well as Brazilian shoes and boots and other foreign products, have a major impact on the U.S. economy.

Even those companies that are not directly affected by such imports often experience a ripple effect. For example, a supplier of components and materials to a U.S. manufacturer will have their market diminished as their customer loses market share. Besides, many U.S. manufacturers are buying foreign components. So even small businesses will be affected by the loss of jobs and earnings attributed to the purchase of foreign products.

And if things weren't bad enough, the U.S. government intervention has made matters worse. Your counterpart, the head of a large corporation, is concerned about the monumental amounts of paperwork required by the various agencies of the U.S. government. Our corporations are being forced to comply with innumerable regulations imposed by the Environmental Protection Agency, OSHA, and other government agencies.

Consider the problems confronting Frederick J. Ross, Chief Executive Officer of Raymark, Inc., as that company faced the 1980s. One of their major product lines was based on friction materials for use as brake linings, clutch facings, and the like. Many of the products included asbestos. And the U.S. government environmentalists had decreed that asbestos be replaced. On top of this, there was a decline in automotive sales.

Mr. Ross in his earlier career at Carborundum established a mandate. He challenged himself and his management with "no dips in earnings." You might well ask how an executive confronted with such monumental problems can meet that challenge. You might ask what you can do to help these companies meet the challenges of the 1980s. You should also recognize that creative managers need new products.

And then there is another factor that affects you as an entrepreneur. The United States has been traditionally recognized for its leadership in technical innovation. However, other countries such as Japan have now taken the lead in technical innovation. This has come about because more and more companies are directing their technical efforts toward compliance with government regulations. Therefore, these companies will have to depend on creative individuals and will be more receptive to business proposals with profit potential.

So before you proceed, recognize that many corporations have adopted a concept advanced by their financial executives, the concept of acquiring small companies with growth potential rather than trying to develop their own new products. As more large corporations follow this approach, however, the number of successful small companies diminishes. Therefore, the large corporations will be forced to move back into the developing cycle, and to invest in developments at an earlier stage. What this means to you is that the time may have arrived for you to sell your invention to a large company.

This description of the environment for large corporations should not be intimidating. In general, you are taking the role of a general who must reconnoiter the terrain before formulating tactics. Remember, your goal is to maximize your profit from the sale of inventions. And you may be able to maximize your return by forming a partnership with a corporation.

16.3 STRATEGIC PLANNING IN A LARGE CORPORATION

Essentially, strategic planning is the process for developing a strategy that will assure management that the company's policies and actions are directed toward a common goal. It involves an analysis of an industry, of one's own company and the competition.

Strategic planning is usually applied to long-range planning. However, strategic planners recognize that today's activities will have a significant impact on plans for tomorrow.

Strategic planners must also consider the effect of decentralized operations, which put more demands on the division general manager. Decentralization also deprives corporate management of the "hands on" feel for what's happening in the marketplace.

One approach that was popular with strategic planners a few years ago was to break down a company's business into categories, such as stars, cash cows, dogs, and problem areas. The dogs are sold off, but cash cows and problem areas need new products, something that will enable them to gain an advantage in the marketplace. This is because their companies have deprived them of the necessary funds to generate their own ideas. Therefore, they need your help.

In general, management invests their resources in the star performers, and expects the star performers to grow. For this reason, the stars are also interested in new opportunities. Remember that they are in competition with other stars. On the other hand, the so-called dogs are really desperate. They need your ideas for survival. Besides, the value added by your invention may enable the parent company to sell that division (the so-called dog) at a better price. The problem children also need your help since they are also fighting for their existence.

The Haloid Company of Rochester, New York, was an example of a company with a faltering product line. But their management had the foresight to recognize an opportunity in electrostatic printing. The company grew and became very successful as the Xerox Corporation on the basis of an untried invention. Some other company could do the same with your invention, if you show them how your invention fits into their business. Show the corporate management how your invention will use their strengths, and/or meet their needs.

Remember that successful companies usually focus their strategy on reinforcing attractive businesses. Therefore, if you can show them how your invention supports their business, you just might convince them to invest in your technology.

16.4 USING STRATEGIC INFORMATION TO SELL YOUR IDEAS

The high degree of secrecy associated with strategic planning within some corporations approaches paranoia. For example, lawyers who work with corporate managers recognize the sensitivity of this type of information, and take steps to prevent any disclosure of this sensitive information. And yet much of this information is available to the public by "reverse engineering." All you have to do is study the company's press releases. Read the information in their annual reports and proxy statements, and the information supplied to the S.E.C. Talk to the company's customers and to competitors and put the pieces together.

As an individual, you should study your prospective partner, the industry, and the major competitors. Read annual reports, business and industrial periodicals, product brochures, and any other published information you can find. Don't limit yourself to one company. Study several companies in an industry and learn why some are more successful than others.

Remember that your goal is to capitalize on your inventions. To do this effectively, you must demonstrate that your invention offers a business opportunity, a new product, an expanded market, manufacturing efficiency, or other competitive advantages. You must present your invention as an opportunity that fits within a target company's strategic plans.

Management allocates human and financial resources to those businesses that will maximize the long-term benefits for the company. Therefore your job is to convince management to allocate resources to commercialize your invention. And you can do this by showing them that your invention offers a greater rate of return than their internally generated programs.

Think about strategic planning and how your invention fits into a company's strategic plans. Consider what effect your invention will have on present operations. By considering these matters, you can sell an operating manager on your proposal, and help that manager to convince the rest of management to provide adequate human and financial resources.

In a way it's a lot like selling technology to the Soviet Union. The U.S.S.R. has a controlled economy, based on a five-year plan. If there is no provision in the five-year plan for the purchase of your technology, you will not be able to sell it to a Soviet organization. If, however, your technology will enable that organization to meet their goals under the plan, you will find a receptive market.

As a result of inflation and the competitive nature of the business environment, many corporations have reduced their technical efforts. And yet many of these same companies need new products. They need your help. Their alternative is to copy a competitor's product and risk the high costs of patent litigation. Hopefully, you have a better alternative.

16.5 CORPORATE STRATEGY FOR R&D

Corporate research and development plays a major role in a new product development at many major companies. However, the role of the R&D group, as well as its structure, does vary. For example, in some companies the R&D groups may be confined to relatively basic research, while in other companies such groups are directed to finding new business opportunities. Because of these differences, it would be relatively impossible, and certainly beyond the scope of this treatise, to describe the many approaches to corporate research. Nevertheless, you should consider corporate strategy as it relates to a company's research and development activities.

One problem associated with the separation of a central research laboratory from the operating divisions is that the scientist in a laboratory tends to become more academic and less in tune with the needs of the marketplace. And in companies with a central lab, a divisional researcher tends to focus on short-range projects, minor product improvements, and cost reduction. This establishes an opportunity for you to provide the intermediate developments in the form of products that will reach the marketplace within a two to five year period.

However, you may encounter a conflict between operational and strategic direction. For example, top management may be more concerned with longer term projects, while the division manager is primarily concerned about the present year. Your job is to convince both groups on the merits of your proposal.

An example taken from the Carborundum Company a few years ago illustrates an effective approach to the management of a research and development program. At that time, top management had recognized a business opportunity in the water treatment field. Legislation had provided for more stringent standards, and there appeared to be an inadequate capacity for producing granular activated carbon on a worldwide basis.

Thus Ted Welton was charged with the responsibility of putting Carborundum into the water business. Welton assembled a task force of technical, marketing, and legal personnel and launched a major program. He utilized outside consultants, evaluated a number of technologies that were available for license, and at the same time funded an internal program to explore the feasibility of developing an improved process for producing this material.

An extensive patent search was conducted, and over 350 U.S. patents were reviewed by the lawyers and discussed with the technical personnel.

Negotiations for the purchase of technology were initiated and an evaluation of other projects in the water area were conducted until an internally developed process was proven to be superior to other alternatives. Financial and marketing analysis were also completed and approval obtained for building a semi-works plant.

Throughout this period, Carborundum had been devoting a major effort in financial and human resources to the water project. Nevertheless, Welton's research organization continued to be receptive to new technology related to the water business.

You can see from this approach that it would be difficult to sell a project that would divert a company's efforts from a commitment of this kind. You should also realize that a company is reluctant to go into a new business until it can develop a competitive advantage.

Other research and development projects were also continuing during this same period. In fact, a second program was initiated and continued to grow to an equal or even greater importance than the water project.

As an entrepreneur, your prospects for selling an unrelated project to a large research organization is relatively small, unless you can convince management that your proposal fits into one of their programs.

16.6 TACTICS AND RECONNAISSANCE— VALUABLE AIDS IN SELLING YOUR IDEA

Your goal is to convince a corporate executive that your proposal will give that corporation a competitive advantage, in other words, to convince the executive that your invention will lead to greater profits.

Now, in selling an invention, be sensitive to the needs and feelings of your customers. Remember that they have expertise in a given field and know about their competitor's strengths and weaknesses. Remember that many of them do have sensitive egos. A few of them will even resent an outsider who suggests an opportunity that perhaps they should have come up with themselves.

Some years ago, the executives of a medium-sized welding company refused to consider a new welding system on the basis that they had previously lost money on one. They were only interested in selling components. This introverted approach failed to take into account what their competitors were doing, where the technology was going, and might be referred to as a "buggy whip mentality." Nevertheless, there are numerous people of this type throughout major corporations. And some of these ultraconservative managers even reach high positions. When they do reach a high position, they continue to frustrate more progressive managers. Nevertheless, if you are confronted by negatively oriented individuals listen to their arguments, answer their questions, and hope that they are merely playing the devil's advocate. On the other hand, the negative reception may be a clear signal to seek another candidate.

A division general manager evaluating a competitor is looking for the market in which that competitor is most vulnerable. You will be able to sell your idea more effectively if you have this type of information and can show that your product can be utilized to take advantage of the competitor's vulnerability in order to dislodge the competitor from a segment of the market.

You can obtain this type of information from one or more conversations with someone who has worked in the field. In the words of a prominent lawyer, "There is nothing more dangerous than a salesman with a martini in his hand." Therefore, try to attend one or more of the industry's trade shows or a technical conference. Talk to the people at these conventions and obtain a wealth of competitive information.

As an example, let's assume that your invention relates to a dairy product. You have researched the industry and a number of the leading companies in the field by spending a day or two at the library. A trip to the state university and an appointment with one of the professors can also produce useful information. An initial conference, or even a lunch, will help to determine whether a few hours of a professor's time as a consultant may provide you with answers, and a credibility factor in introducing your product to the market.

Each year the dairy industry, like most others, has a large annual convention. Attendance for a few days can provide you with product information, market research, and competitive intelligence. Besides, there is really no substitute for talking to people who are knowledgeable in the field. You will find that the sales people and technical representatives at these conventions have a substantial amount of information and will disclose that information to you. If you have a friendly outgoing personality, and express an interest in their products, you'll probably be introduced to one of their executives. An introduction of this type may be the key to a successful sale.

Those of you who choose to work on the forefront of technology should recognize that changes in the environment will affect your products. Consider what effect pollution controls, limitations on exhaust emissions, noise controls, oil shortages, and such, will have on your business.

Remember that major corporations, and even small ones, invest in growth opportunities. Therefore, they are all seeking businesses that are likely to produce a return in excess of the rate of inflation. They all allocate resources, financial as well as human, and probably need strong entrepreneurial managers to develop growth opportunities. Perhaps you should sell yourself along with your inventions.

Larry Little of St. Louis, Missouri, took this approach after inventing a new process for making sour cream. He went to work for Meyer Blanke Company of St. Louis and continued the technical development of his process, as well as helping his new employer with the sale of his process to dairies.

16.7 THE UNITED STATES, ITS ENVIRONMENT
AND TERRAIN

The United States has for a number of years occupied a position of prominence in the world economy. That position was obtained because of our leadership in technology. Note, for example, the dominant position in computers, electrostatic copiers, photographic film, commercial aircraft, semiconductors, and many other areas.

More recently, we have seen advances by Japan and others in the electronics industry, chemicals, and even in manufacturing automobiles. Today it seems that other countries are devoting more effort to developing technology and will continue to overtake the United States in innovation.

At the same time, corporate researchers in some U.S. companies are becoming more frustrated by an increase in planning, increased paper-work, and a preoccupation with financial analysis. And even though the politicians have voiced alarm over the loss of leadership in innovation, little is being done to provide incentive for the scientists in research organizations. One bill has been introduced in the Senate to provide payment to corporate inventors modeled after the German system. How-ever, it is doubtful that the proposed bill, even if adopted, would help.

Notwithstanding the problem, our country's future economic health does depend on technology. This economic dependence on technology, coupled with the fact that many corporate researchers are either frus-trated by or preoccupied with making their products comply with govern-ment regulations, places a tremendous burden on you and the other inde-pendent inventors to fill the void. In reality, this is not a burden, but a tremendous opportunity.

In summary, you must do your homework, develop your inventions, carefully consider the market, prepare a presentation, and sell your inven-tions. Try to sell your inventions at the earliest possible stage and use a licensee's money and expertise to bring your invention to market. Your alternative is to more fully develop your own invention, build a small business, manufacture and sell products, and then, perhaps, sell the busi-ness to a large corporation.

Either approach could be immensely profitable.

17

Contracts

Contracts, like marriage, warrant careful consideration.

A contract is a legal document that defines the obligations of both parties who enter into an agreement. For a contract to be binding, there must be an offer, an acceptance, and some form of consideration. Nevertheless, a contract does not have to be written.

However, as an entrepreneur, you will want to reduce your agreements to writing. This doesn't mean that you need a complicated legal document. And at times, you won't even need a lawyer to review a contract. The forms of some contracts are extremely simple, in some cases, amounting to a short order form. It has been reported that the contract for Dr. Lister's secret formula and use of his name on "Listerine" was written on a single scrap of paper. That scrap of paper resulted in millions of dollars in royalty payments to Dr. Lister and his successors.

Nevertheless, in today's legally oriented society, contracts are typically more complex. For example, a simple consultant's agreement is included in Appendix J, and a typical license agreement is in Appendix D. These agreements are still relatively simple and do not approach the length or complexity of a joint venture or other complex document for the development or sale of a business. A typical joint venture agreement is included in Appendix H for comparison.

Before reviewing the details of a contract, consider the use of a letter of intent. Some business people, particularly those with foreign companies, use these letters. And even though these letters may not be legally binding, they do serve as a "gentlemen's agreement," and set forth the basic principles of a contract that have been agreed to. Their primary purpose is to define the business principles that will be incorporated in a contract.

So before you sign a letter of intent, make certain that you are committed to those principles, and don't expect to renegotiate them. Nevertheless, they are not cast in concrete, and if during subsequent negotiations you are unable to reach an agreement, you can always offer to concede a point, if the other party will also accept a change in the previously agreed to principles. For example, if you had agreed to a 3% royalty, and the other party later insisted that you take the responsibility for enforcing your patents against a third party infringer, you might agree to accept that responsibility if the royalty were increased. But please note that this is merely an example; it should not be construed as a suggestion that you accept the responsibility for future litigation.

17.1 KEY ISSUES

As an entrepreneur, identify the key issues before starting out to make a deal. Key issues usually involve money, so try to put a dollar value on each of your alternatives. For example, can you make more money by granting an exclusive license or by granting nonexclusive licenses to everyone in the industry?

And if you are willing to grant an exclusive license, are you willing to receive at least partial payment in the form of royalties as opposed to a lump sum payment? Without going into the details of taxation, there is usually a tax advantage in granting an exclusive license. Besides, most prospective licensees will demand an exclusive license before undertaking a development program. Those same licensees will usually oppose a large up-front payment, but will frequently accept a reasonable royalty provision.

As an entrepreneur, look beyond tax considerations to determine which approach will produce the maximum after-tax income for you. Ask yourself if an exclusive licensee will have the incentive to fully exploit your invention. In general, most companies prefer exclusive licenses; however, there are times when a company may be satisfied with a license for a single application. Just remember that, if you grant an exclusive license and your licensee fails to exploit a major application, you may suffer an irreparable loss.

There are times when you can enjoy the best of both worlds. You can do this by granting an exclusive license with a field of use restriction. For example, an inventor of a method for bonding metals might grant an exclusive license to the Boeing Aircraft Company to use the method in aircraft fabrication. Rights could then be offered for use in automobiles or boats. However, field of use restrictions are sometimes difficult to enforce, and should be granted with caution. Besides, you will need skillful legal drafting and consultation if you include a field of use restriction in your licenses.

Another approach to consider in an effort to maximize you income would be to suggest territorial restrictions. Such restrictions can lead to difficulty, however. In general, they are used to limit a licensee to a particular country. In fact, it is possible to grant an exclusive license to practice an invention in a particular state. But territorial restrictions often lead to problems and should be used only after consultation with your counsel.

There is one other alternative to an exclusive license to consider: grant an exclusive license for a limited period of time. For example, you might suggest an exclusive license for a three to five year term to give the licensee lead time in the market. Or you might try a common variation that is frequently easy to sell. Under this approach, you can provide that if sales do not reach certain levels, or drop below those levels, you have the right to convert the exclusive license to a nonexclusive license. You can also use other forms of diligence to assure that your licensee fully exploits your invention.

Now when you offer to sell an invention, ask for an initial fee. But be reasonable. Few companies will pay a million dollars up front for an unproven invention. And even though technical feasibility has been proven, the licensee still incurs risk in introducing a new product to the marketplace. For example, it was reported in an article in *Business Week* on Airwick Corporation that the development of new products is a high risk game, and that 80% of all new products fail.

The fact is that a company will not pay an exorbitant licensing fee. However, you can frequently obtain an initial payment of between $2000 and $25,000, particularly if your work will save the licensee more than that in engineering or other expenses. And it might be easier to sell this concept if you call for the payment in two steps. For example, ask for an initial payment of $2000 to $10,000 upon signing an agreement and an additional $10,000 to $15,000 at the end of the first year. As a further inducement for these payments, you can offer to treat them as an advance on royalties that are in excess of any minimum royalties.

In general, it is difficult to determine how much to ask and what is reasonable. But if you have actually introduced the product to the market and recorded annual sales of $100,000 or more, a substantial license fee would be reasonable. On the other hand, if you have a crude prototype that will require considerable development work by the licensee, the initial fee should be small. Just try to determine the value of the work. Ask yourself: How much would it cost a large corporation to reach this same state of development? Then a reasonable license fee would be slightly less than half of that sum.

17.2   ROYALTIES

Royalties are a key element in any contract. And royalties are usually based on the net sales prices of a product that is covered by the claims of your patent. Even though royalty rates vary, a 5% royalty is usually reasonable, except in high volume, low margin businesses. For example, the paint and automotive industries would argue for a royalty of 1% or even less. On the other hand, royalties in excess of 5% are difficult to justify in this country and would probably have a detrimental effect on sales. So if you expect a royalty in excess of 5%, you should be prepared to show the licensee that your proposal will result in unusual profits. It is true, however, that European companies frequently insist on an 8% to 10% royalty when granting a license, and are often willing to pay the same. However, such royalties are usually applied to products that have already been proven in the marketplace.

Now in determining royalties it is important to determine the royalty base, that is, what part or parts are subject to a royalty. You can be certain that if your invention relates to an aircraft landing gear that the manufacturer will refuse to pay a 5% royalty on the total price of an airplane. In general, royalties should be based on the value of the product covered by the claims in your patent. However, in at least one case an aircraft manufacturer did agree to pay a royalty based on the number of planes produced even though the patent covered only a portion of the plane. In that case, the royalty was a fixed dollar amount per plane, and the licensee selected the per plane basis for ease in accounting.

As an entrepreneur, you should be cautious about basing the royalty on the basis of a fixed price per unit or on the price or amount of some raw material that goes into the process or product. You are really interested in sharing in the value added by using your invention. Be reasonable, and think in terms of 20%−25% of any savings attributed to the invention. If you want to use a fixed amount per unit, include an escalator clause to compensate for inflation.

Also, when you discuss royalties, be prepared to accept a declining royalty, which is a rate that decreases as sales increase. This is based on the concept that if the licensee does a better job of marketing the invention, the licensee should receive a reward. An agreement of this type might typically provide for a 5% royalty on the first half million dollars in annual sale, 4% on the next million, and 3% on all sales in excess of that amount. There is a philosophical argument in favor of an ascending royalty; however, it is seldom acceptable to a licensee and probably works against your interest. Besides, an increased royalty may encourage your licensee to seek an alternative product to avoid the larger royalties.

Don't rely on the courts to renegotiate your license. You may have read in the newpapers that the courts awarded an employee of Sears Roebuck a very substantial sum of money because his agreement with Sears called for an unreasonably low royalty. The court concluded that during the negotiations Sears had defrauded the employee and had been less than candid in their dealings with him. However, this was a very unusual case and should not be relied upon.

To summarize, don't be greedy in negotiating royalties. Recognize that 3% of a very large sum is much better than 10% of nothing. Nevertheless, you are in a bit of a dilemma since you want to encourage your licensee to do a great job, and yet you want to maximize your own income.

17.3 MINIMUM ROYALTIES

Minimum royalties are almost as important as the royalty rate. They are important because you want your licensee to diligently develop your invention and bring it to the commercial stage within a reasonable time. Some entrepreneurs rely on a best efforts clause. While it is desirable to include a best efforts clause, you might do better with a minimum royalty. In fact, you should try to include both.

The advantage of minimum royalties is that they provide payments to you. Nevertheless, don't spend your money until you get it. Recognize that your licensee might terminate the agreement to avoid payment. Besides, you might have to waive any minimum royalties for the first year or two in order to give your licensee time to introduce a new product on the market. As a general rule, a minimum royalty of $10,000 or $20,000 in the third or fourth year is usually appropriate with an escalation to perhaps $50,000 per year by the seventh or eighth year. Recognize that this is only a general rule, which may not apply to your invention.

When you consider minimum royalties, recognize that the purpose of a minimum royalty is to prevent your licensee from sitting on your invention. You want to prevent the company from maintaining a license without putting forth a reasonable effort to promote it. On the other hand, some attorneys argue that large minimums are needed to force the licensee to obtain the maximum penetration in the marketplace. However, a licensee who has a profit incentive will do as much as possible to sell the product. And if the market is not profitable, a licensee will terminate. There are also cases where an invention has widespread appeal or represents a revolutionary advance in the art and justifies larger minimums. The problem is that such minimums are difficult to sell, and you may lose the whole deal over a point that might not be terribly important to your income.

Some entrepreneurs prefer a two-tier approach to minimum royalties. For example, a typical provision would provide that if royalties do not equal $50,000 per year within five years and each year thereafter, the licensee will lose their exclusivity, but will retain a nonexclusive license. Then a second provision would provide that if the sales do not produce a royalty of at least $25,000, you would have the right to terminate the license.

17.4   OTHER FORMS OF DILIGENCE

Your goal is to encourage a licensee to commercialize your invention. You should also recognize that there are other ways to assure yourself that your licensee is making their best efforts to make your product a success. One way to do this is by agreeing on how many people will be assigned to work on your project and what percentage of their time will be devoted to it.

As previously suggested, provide for a consulting agreement under which you will be employed by the company for one or more days each quarter. In this way you will receive some income, and at the same time, monitor your licensee's progress. You will also be able to make suggestions in the future development of your invention. However, don't expect to retain control of the project. If you want to control the project, you should continue to develop it on your own, and if necessary, seek venture capital. After all, a good licensee will have expertise in the area of new product development. If not, you have picked the wrong partner.

17.5   LEGAL ISSUES

Many of the legal provisions in a contract are closely entwined with business considerations. In other words, the legal provisions (including so-called "boiler plate") can make a significant impact on your earnings.

So when you write or review your contract, make certain that you define the key terms and assure yourself that you understand the obligations of both parties. Make certain that your invention as well as any improvements are clearly defined. For example, many license agreements include "improvement inventions" even though this term is subject to various interpretations. In your agreement, define what you mean.

And when you enter into an agreement, spell out who has the obligation to file and maintain any foreign patents. Usually, in an exclusive license, these fees are paid by the licensee with a provision that the licensor has the right to pay them if the licensee elects not to. A common provision is that, if the licensee elects not to pay maintainance fees in certain countries, then such countries will thereafter be excluded from the license.

The enforcement of your patents also presents a difficult philosophical problem. Patent litigation is expensive, with the cost of a single suit estimated at \$250,000 or more. Individuals and even small companies have difficulty in meeting these costs. Besides, experienced patent trial lawyers do not usually work for a contingent fee. Therefore, as an entrepreneur, a practical solution for you is to require your licensee to enforce your patents. The corresponding problem is that if your licensee sues on your patent and it is held invalid, the licensee will no longer have to pay royalties to you. This might, in some cases, provide the company's management with an incentive to lose the case or to exert less than a maximum effort in asserting your patent.

To solve the litigation problem, ask that the licensee pay for litigation expenses and that up to one half of the continuing royalties be applied to the costs. Then provide for joint control of any litigation, or at least for joint selection of counsel. This may lead to disputes and a substantial time period during which part of your royalties would be going to the lawyers. Nevertheless, it may be better than losing all of your future royalties.

Any enforcement provision should also provide for the right to grant a sublicense and a formula for sharing in any royalty produced under the sublicense. By and large, you will be better off with part of the royalty from a sublicensee than with risking your future income in a lawsuit.

Your licenses should also include a provision that spells out the terms of payment. Typically, payments should be made quarterly and within sixty days of the end of each calendar quarter. You will probably want payments in U.S. dollars and should provide for a basis for converting from foreign currency. You should also require a royalty report even if no royalty is due. This forces the licensee to issue a report and ascertains whether or not royalties are in fact due. It's a simple step that may avoid an oversight in paying you what is rightfully yours.

You may, like many entrepreneurs, also provide for arbitration as a way to resolve any differences between the parties. Arbitration can be expensive, but is probably a better solution than litigation for an individual.

However, when you provide for future litigation or arbitration between yourself and your licensee, use care in selecting the forum, that is, the place of resolving any disputes. You should also spell out the law to be followed in interpreting the agreement. In general, the laws of most states are acceptable; however, try for the law of your state. And avoid the law of a foreign country.

As an entrepreneur, you should also review any additional provisions of a contract with your attorney. Ask about the legal significance of each provision. Ask what effect it will have in dollars, and what alternatives the attorney suggests.

17.6   TIME IS OF THE ESSENCE

Many real estate brokers are critical of lawyers because they worry about losing a sale due to a lawyer's delay. They have learned that when someone is ready to buy, you close the deal before they change their minds.

This same philosophy is true in selling your invention to a corporation. Executives change jobs, business conditions and priorities change. So don't let a lawyer's delay kill your deal. Your lawyer may be busy, but if you work with and keep your lawyer advised of your progress, you should not have a problem. You can avoid many problems if you review your business proposal with your lawyer before entering into discussions with the other side. Then during discussions with the other side, you can accept some provisions subject to approval by your lawyer. In this way you can avoid making too many concessions. However, you might want to remember that you are negotiating a business agreement that has to make good business sense. In other word, don't lose the deal over a legal technicality.

One practical approach to any negotiation is to discuss the business principles and suggest that they have their lawyer prepare a proposed contract. It would be preferable to ask your lawyer to draft the initial proposal, but that would probably cost you more money. Besides, you can frequently speed up the process by having their lawyer draft the contract, because some companies insist on certain language. And if their preferred language is clear and equitable, why change it?

Now when you draft an agreement or revise the company's proposal, remember that this piece of paper will establish your legal rights and obligations. Don't rely on a relative who is a second year law student for legal advice, and don't try to cover every possible contingency.

17.7   FURTHER OBLIGATIONS

When you have a signed agreement, you are entitled to pat yourself on the back. However, your job isn't done. You should continue to work with your new partner. Advise the corporate management of proposed improvements in your invention and live up to all of your obligations. Remember that you have created a partnership, and do everything in your power to assure the success of your venture.

18

The Art of Negotiation

18.1 INTRODUCTION

The art of negotiation can be defined as the process of reaching an agreement by discussion and compromise. However, as an entrepreneur, you should recognize that there are numerous approaches to the negotiating process and that you must adopt an approach that is appropriate for the circumstances and that makes you comfortable.

Many individuals like to avoid confrontation. And you may be more successful if you avoid confrontation and work for a win-win solution. You can be successful if you analyze the negotiating processes and the respective interests of yourself and your customer. After all, your goal is to sell your invention, your proposal, or your services.

Now, consider the case of Mr. Lockwood (not his real name), who prided himself on his ability as a negotiator. He took a very aggressive approach and viewed every negotiation as a confrontation. He viewed negotiations as a win-lose situation, and was determined that he would be the winner.

Mr. Lockwood had approached my client, and asked for a license under one of our patents. In fact, he asked us to transfer all of our technology to him. He wanted my client to put him into business at little or no cost to him. He used a lot of negotiating tactics, but we terminated the discussions and Mr. Lockwood lost a business opportunity.

Nevertheless, Mr. Lockwood was successful in other negotiations. He was successful as a buyer because he only bought when he negotiated a low price. But what does this mean to you? It means that you will probably want to take a different approach. And it means that those of you who try to negotiate with someone like Mr. Lockwood will have to learn to deal with that approach. For example, you will have to learn to feed the other party's ego, to let an aggressive negotiator think he or she has won. Or you could look for another customer.

Before you approach a prospective customer, consider your own role as a negotiator. This role is actually an extension of your sales effort. Don't stop selling when you start negotiating.

18.2 SELLING: AN INTEGRAL PART OF NEGOTIATIONS

As an entrepreneur, your goal is to sell a product or process embodying your invention, or your services. And in most cases, you will not reach this goal until you have a signed contract.

Therefore, incorporate the ideas in Chapter 15 into your negotiating strategy. For example, prepare carefully for any negotiation and maintain a selling effort throughout your discussions. This effort may be subtle, perhaps an occasional reminder about the size of the market, or a statement like, "By working together we can have a commercial product on the market within a year." And throughout your negotiation, make suggestions that lead to a yes answer.

Now, as an entrepreneur, take a customer-oriented approach. Consider the needs of your customer and show how your proposal will meet those needs. Emphasize the reasonableness of your proposal and explain how it will lead to a mutually beneficial relationship. Keep selling and don't be greedy.

In any negotiation, just as in any sale, time is of the essence. Therefore, one of your goals is to complete the deal and get on with the important job of making money. In other words, focus your attention on closing the deal.

What this boils down to is that you should keep selling throughout the negotiation and finalize an agreement as soon as possible. And you can do this effectively if you develop a successful negotiating attitude.

18.3 DEVELOPING A SUCCESSFUL NEGOTIATING ATTITUDE

"Attitude is everything in negotiations," according to Emmett Murtha. Emmett knows a lot about negotiating attitudes since he is director of licensing for IBM. He said, "Negotiation is not bargaining. It is the interaction when two parties attempt to agree on a mutually acceptable outcome in a situation where their preferences for outcome are negatively related."

So what is a successful negotiating attitude? For an entrepreneur who is trying to sell an invention, a successful negotiating attitude is based on confidence in yourself and in your proposal. It includes a bit of enthusiasm and a commitment to work for a win-win solution.

One good approach for reaching a win/win solution is the pyramid approach. You start with a broad base, that is, you set forth all of the broad principles that will be readily agreed to. For example, you might say, "As a general principle both of us should make a reasonable return on our investment." And then you might suggest that each party assume certain obligations and spell out what they are.

The basic philosophy of this approach is to spell out in general terms as many things as you can in which there is little or no disagreement. And from there, try to become more specific. For example, you might indicate your willingness to accept a declining royalty rate in order to reward the company for their marketing efforts. You might also agree on the range of royalties, but reserve until later the decision on the level of sales required for a reduced royalty.

In this way you can reduce the differences to a minimum. And then, if you are flexible and consider the needs of your potential partner, you should be able to compromise on some of the remaining issues.

18.4   PREPARATION FOR NEGOTIATION

There is no substitute for adequate preparation for a negotiation. In fact, Emmett Murtha said, "Don't even discuss an issue for which you are not prepared."

Fortunately, there is a lot that you can do to prepare for a negotiation. First, "Think about what is in your best interest before approaching any negotiation." That is the advice from Stan Lieberstein. Stan emphasizes this advice in a course on negotiations that he has taught for the American Management Association, the Bureau of National Affairs, the Investors Association of New England, and so on.

Mr. Lieberstein said, "One individual came to me for help in licensing his invention. And then, as we talked, it became clear that licensing was not in his best interest." In fact, Stan said, "Sometimes, licensing is the worst approach for developing an invention."

In the previous example, Stan Lieberstein and his client developed a business plan. Stan said, "We developed a plan for developing his own business, for raising funds through a joint venture with distributors. For example, we appointed exclusive distributors in selected areas and gave each of the distributors a piece of the company for a certain amount of capital. We subcontracted the manufacturing of parts and subassemblies. And then, my client set up a small shop for final assembly."

Stan explained further, "In this way, we minimized the capital requirements, raised the necessary capital, and maintained control of the company." This example also illustrates the need to be flexible, to prepare for a negotiation, and to determine what is in your best interest.

Stan Lieberstein suggested a number of other considerations in preparing for a negotiation: "Before you approach a prospective partner, make certain that they have the capital needed for your proposal, a desire to invest that capital, a need for your product, and the means to distribute it." He added, "Some companies may build a new manufacturing facility for an untried product, but very few, if any, will create a new sales force."

According to Stan Lieberstein, "You should learn as much about your potential partner's planning as possible. Learn where they are headed, and where they anticipate growth. Then, when you understand their plans for growth, show them how your proposal fits in with their plans."

In preparing for any negotiation, try to anticipate what the other side wants. Be ready to show them how they will share in benefits from your proposal, and also how the parties will share in the downside risk.

In summary, identify areas of potential conflict, decide what is most important to you, analyze the needs of the other side, and develop a strategy for the negotiation. And while you are at it, develop a strategy that will help the other side to make the decisions that you want.

18.5   NEGOTIATIONS WITH A LARGE ORGANIZATION

"It is frequently difficult for an entrepreneur to get the same terms from a large corporation as those available to someone who is on equal footing with them," according to Stan Lieberstein. So if you want to take advantage of a large corporation's established distribution, capital resources, and the like, you may have to make a few concessions, you may have to accept a smaller royalty. But a small royalty on a high volume of sales can amount to more money than a large royalty on minimal sales.

Stan Lieberstein has one word of advice for those of you who want to work with a large company; the word is "motivation." Stan said, "As an entrepreneur, your key to success is to provide the motivation for them to sell your product."

Consider another point. In a way, licensing is like giving your child to someone else to raise. Therefore, strive for an appropriate degree of control over the activities of your licensee even though it may be a difficult point to sell. Try to structure the deal so that you have more than a bare license. Try to participate in the venture, to get some direct control over the impetus for selling.

Mr. Lieberstein suggested several other factors to consider before you negotiate with a large company. He said, "Try to establish a cooperative atmosphere in which the large company is motivated to sell a product which embodies your invention. To do this, do as much research as possible on the company, learn who the players are, what are their roles, and what are their needs."

Don't expect the impossible. Recognize that large companies have other commitments. No matter how much profit potential you can see in your product, they have commitments that they will not abandon. So what you need to do is to find the individual in the company who is most likely to be favorably disposed toward your proposal, and who has the authority to enter into an agreement.

Don't overlook another problem that is frequently associated with large companies. The problem is the N.I.H., or "not invented here," factor. Fortunately, there is a way to avoid this problem by dealing with someone from marketing. Not all marketing professionals will embrace new products; however, it is usually better to work with someone who wants something to sell, as opposed to working with a technologist who wants a new project to work on. Besides, the technologist would probably prefer to work on one of his or her own ideas.

Consider the case of Joan M., a vice president and general manager of a manufacturing company with annual sales in excess of $100 million. Joan liked new products and pushed the company's engineers to give her something to sell. She was impatient with engineering and believed that they would do research on a product forever, if permitted. Joan's desire was to push products to market; when she found a customer, she told the engineers to make the product.

18.6   DEALING WITH PEOPLE

All negotiations are with people. Therefore, all negotiations must be conducted at a personal level. And your proposal must be compatible with your potential partner's personal needs.

Consider the case of Richard, the director of new products for a major corporation. He had been ordered to find new products for one of the company's largest divisions, and to help them to increase their business.

At this time, an entrepreneur with a revolutionary filter approached Dick and offered him a license under the entrepreneur's patent. However, there were a number of problems associated with the filter. For example, the filter did not meet certain legal requirements, the patent was possibly invalid, and the entrepreneur was difficult to deal with and facing bankruptcy.

In spite of those problems, Dick promptly negotiated a deal with the entrepreneur because he thought that the entrepreneur would help the company to get a new product to the market quickly.

Emmett Murtha, the Director of Licensing at IBM, also emphasized the importance of working with people. He said, "Don't let the other party know how much you want the agreement." For example, in one situation where I acted as the negotiator for a large European company, the director general of that company and I discussed the case at length. Then we met with our counterparts in Switzerland. We continued the discussions late into the night, and on several occasions, were ready to break off the negotiations. But we finally reached an agreement.

After the agreement was signed, I learned how much my client wanted the agreement. Had I known earlier, I would have settled for less.

If you want to be successful in negotiations, don't cause the other party to lose face. Structure your deal so that everyone comes out a winner. And if you are reasonable, you can obtain important concessions without causing your potential partner to lose face. Keep in mind that you will probably be working together in the future, and may have to renegotiate the agreement at some future date.

When you deal with a large organization, be wary of the union technique in negotiations. This technique is also used by car dealers. For example, you negotiate what you feel is an acceptable agreement. But then the other party comes back and says, "I'm really sorry, but our president, executive vice president, or someone else, won't approve the deal, unless you make additional concessions."

In this case, you have three alternatives. You can say no, and be prepared to walk away from the deal. You can make the additional concessions. You would, of course, do this if the concessions are unimportant to you. Or you can say, "Okay, but I want something in return."

But don't forget that you may be far better off accepting a less satisfactory agreement than starting over with some other potential partner.

18.7   PATIENCE IN NEGOTIATIONS

There is no substitute for patience in negotiations. In fact, Emmett Murtha said, "Success comes to the negotiator with greater patience and staying power." He added, "Just remember that the other side, no matter how cool they appear, always has a deadline."

Far Eastern cultures often emphasize using patience as a negotiating tactic. For example, the Japanese couple patience with preparation. They frequently use a large team. In fact, during one negotiation in China, an associate asked the Chinese negotiator why they had so many chairs in the room. The Chinese negotiator answered, "We need them for negotiating with the Japanese because they always bring so many people." A few days later, we noticed a small bus outside of the office. My associate commented, "That is a taxi for one of the Japanese groups."

Patience is also one of the best techniques to use against the Doberman approach to negotiation. The Doberman approach is usually reserved for a true adversary situation. But I have encountered this technique when selling technology to a large company.

In essence, the Doberman approach is analogous to turning an attack-trained Doberman pinscher on your adversary, and after the dog has softened the other side up, you keep the dog barely under control and just out of reach of your adversary.

A negotiator who uses this technique starts the negotiations with outrageous demands, makes an incredible amount of noise, and acts as though you have done the negotiator some grave injustice. In addition, this individual acts as if it is up to you to compensate for some alleged wrongdoing. Such a negotiator continues in an aggressive manner to make demands on each issue.

In some cases, you can overcome the Doberman technique by calling their bluff. You slowly and quietly gather up your papers, put them into your briefcase, and extend your hand. Then you say something like, "I'm sorry, I thought that you were interested in working out a mutually beneficial arrangement. But since you obviously are not, I won't waste any more of your time."

Of course, you could fight fire with fire and take the same approach yourself. In reply to the aggressor's tirade, you could make equally outrageous demands, shout, and slam your fists on the table. This might work, but seems more likely to lead to high blood pressure than to a mutually beneficial agreement.

In one case, I saw one of my associates completely defuse a negotiator who tried to use the Doberman technique. My associate sat back and listened. And when his adversary paused, my associate said, "When you are finished with your theatrics, maybe we can get on with our discussions."

In my own experience, the best approach for dealing with an overly antagonistic negotiator is to use an overabundance of patience. You just have to stay calm and wait for your adversary to run down. Speak softly and slowly, but be firm. Take your time. Say something like, "I'm sorry if I upset you so much, but we don't see things that way at all." Sit back, relax, and realize that your adversary is merely acting like an ass.

18.8 DEVELOPING CREATIVE SOLUTIONS

Emmett Murtha said, "Don't let one bothersome issue deadlock your negotiations." When you come to a difficult issue, suggest moving on to other issues. However, be cautious in making this suggestion. For example, don't suggest a willingness to concede the issue. On the other hand, you might want to give in on this issue, if the other side concedes another.

According to Emmett Murtha, "The only kind of expertise required in most negotiations is the ability to ask intelligent questions." But then, "You should also be willing to be flexible."

Actually, most negotiations involve common sense resolutions of differences. For example, if you isolate what is most important to you from that which is most important to the other side, you can frequently accommodate the other side without making a serious sacrifice. However, when there is a direct conflict on a single issue, try to find a mutually beneficial solution that will lead to the commerical success of your invention. One simple approach that is frequently taken by Japanese and Chinese negotiators can often resolve issues that may develop into future problems. The solution is to provide that the issues will be mutually resolved when they become a problem.

Many lawyers would criticize this approach, arguing that it is better to resolve the matter during the courtship than to wait until after the honeymoon is over. Nevertheless, there are advantages in postponing the resolution of a difficult issue. First, the issue may never become a problem. Second, if the issue does become a problem, the parties will have worked together for a while and may be more amenable to compromise. Before accepting this solution, however, try to anticipate who will be in the better position in the future.

Before accepting a suggestion to postpone some matter until the future, review the entire agreement. Make certain that you are comfortable with the arrangement. Do you have a provision that assures you that your licensee will be diligent in commercializing your invention? Do you have a provision for arbitration? In each of the agreements I have negotiated with the Chinese and Japanese, we have included an arbitration provision. So if we are unable to agree on some action in the future, we have the mechanism to resolve it. But in over twenty-five years, I have never seen one of these (to be mutually agreed to) issues submitted to arbitration.

As a final example, consider the issue of royalties, an issue that comes up in most negotiations. Suppose the other party insists that 3% of the net sales price is the maximum acceptable royalty. And yet you feel that a 10% royalty is equitable in view of exceptional circumstances. Your proposal for a declining royalty based on sales volume is rejected.

In this case, you might compromise by accepting a 3% royalty on all products sold for the retail market, for example, all products sold in 2−8 oz.

containers. And then provide for a 10% royalty on all products sold in bulk containers. However, before proposing this type of solution, review it with counsel.

18.9   CLOSING THE SALE

Usually, you will want to finalize an agreement as soon as possible. This does not mean that you should make concessions easily, or that you should reduce pressure on the other side without obtaining some concession. It does mean that you can use a concession as a closing technique. For example, you might say, "If I concede this point, do we have an agreement?" Or, "I have a particular problem with one of the three remaining issues. If you will concede that point, I'll give you the other two, and we'll have an agreement."

Many concessions and settlements occur at or after a deadline to cut off further discussions. You should also realize that it is impossible to provide for every possible contingency. So what you want to do is negotiate a reasonable straightforward agreement, cover the important issues, and get on to business.

18.10   IMPLEMENTING AN AGREEMENT

The Chinese negotiators have a delightful custom; they have a large banquet to celebrate the conclusion of negotiations. They have these banquets even if the parties have failed to resolve all of the issues. In fact, I recall one banquet when the parties had agreed not to agree. And then, during the banquet, they reached an agreement.

The post-negotiation banquet is also common to others, to the Japanese, Russians, and Americans. I referred to the Chinese banquet because they seem to put more into them. Perhaps it is the sharing of so many plates of food, or the way it is shared. Whatever the reason, their banquets have a way of bringing the parties together. They have a way of developing a certain camaraderie.

During many negotiations, a certain amount of hostility develops. But if you recognize that all parties were doing their jobs to the best of their abilities, that all parties had certain interests to protect, you will be well on your way to working together for the mutual benefit of the parties.

So, when the agreement is signed, go beyond your obligations, and make your venture a successful business.

19

Litigation and the Entrepreneur

Entering the courtroom is like putting your head into the lion's mouth.

A CHINESE PROVERB

19.1 AN INTRODUCTION TO LITIGATION

Paul Jones (not his real name) was an ambitious engineer who had worked for the same company for over twelve years. In fact, he was a key employee and had started up several new chemical plants for the company.

Paul had done a good job in starting up those plants and thought that he should be promoted to plant manager. But he was passed over. He felt frustrated, and decided to leave the company.

Then an executive recruiter called Paul. The recruiter was looking for a director of manufacturing who would manage three plants. He was looking for someone to bring a new plant on stream, and to put his client in competition with Paul's present employer.

Paul accepted the new position. But before he gave notice, he did two things. He stayed late one night and copied his employer's engineering drawings. He also visited the company's newest plant and made a copy of their operations manual. And then Paul gave his notice that he was leaving.

When Paul's original employer learned that Paul's new company was about to enter into competition with them, they were concerned. They knew that it was difficult to produce their product, and did not want Paul to disclose their trade secrets to his new employer. So when a cleaning woman reported the late night copying, they filed suit.

Trade secret litigation is expensive. Paul's case was no exception. Each party entered into extensive discovery. Each issue was contested. A protective order under which the parties could review the other's documents was agreed to. Motions and countermotions were filed and argued. Two additional lawsuits were filed, and hundreds of thousands of dollars in legal fees were incurred by each side.

In addition, the employees of both companies spent many hours in depositions and at the trial. Finally, the parties agreed to settle. The costs had been enormous. Paul left his new job and found employment in another field.

Many corporate employees are destined to follow in Paul's footsteps. Some will start their own companies. Some will use a former employer's property through inadvertence. Some will act properly, and yet, they too may become involved in litigation.

So as an entrepreneur, one of your primary concerns should be to avoid litigation. And if you can't avoid litigation, consider the effect of litigation on you, your company, your customers, and on your adversary. You should also consider your alternatives.

19.2 LITIGATION AND THE LARGE CORPORATION

Many corporate executives are concerned about the high cost of litigation. They are concerned about the cost of outside counsel and expenses. They are also concerned about the amount of time required for their employees to gather documents, to testify, and to assist counsel.

Therefore a number of companies are relying on their internal staffs to do the work that had been done by outside counsel. But even more important, their in-house lawyers are doing a lot more before litigation is initiated. For example, they conduct a thorough review of the file history of the patent in issue, review the prior art, review company files, and do all that they can to make certain that there have been no prior publications, use, or an offer for sale that would invalidate their patent.

Of course, there are times when they do the same thing in an attempt to invalidate someone else's patent.

But before they assert one of their own patents, they review the evidence of infringement and compare the evidence with the claims in the patent. They consider the effect of any statements made during the patent prosecution and the question of equivalence, that is, whether an element in the potentially infringing article is equivalent to an element called for in the claim.

The in-house counsel often asks for a written, legal opinion on validity and infringement, taking into account all of the known evidence. This opinion is then discussed with management.

Consider the case of a general manager of a small manufacturing company. A competitor was infringing one of the company's patents, and the manager refused to give them a license. The manager sued the infringer, hoping to put the competitor out of business.

After many months of discovery, the manager asked for a thorough analysis of the case. The analysis showed that the competitor could make a minor change in design, and avoid infringement. In other words, if the court granted an injunction against further infringement, the competitor could modify the product and continue to sell the modified version.

As a result of this analysis, the general manager settled the lawsuit, and asked why someone had not explained the facts before the company incurred the expenses for litigation.

As an entrepreneur, it is up to you to gather all the facts, understand your alternatives, and make your own decisions.

You will also have to select counsel to prepare your case. One corporate counsel said, "When you select counsel, select an individual as opposed to a firm." For example, he selects an experienced litigator who has a technical background in his field of interest. He also insists that all depositions be taken by the lead counsel.

In one case in which I was involved, Clyde Willian of Willian, Brinks, Olds, Hofer, Gilson & Lione Ltd., of Chicago, Illinois, was taking a deposition. Clyde is one of the finest litigators that I know. In this case, he had spent over two days deposing an individual. He had approached several issues from different directions and finally uncovered evidence that invalidated the plaintiff's patent.

I doubt that many lawyers would have succeeded in eliciting this information from the witness, or that a less experienced lawyer would have had the skill or the persistence to uncover the information.

In selecting trial counsel, some corporate patent counsel select a general lawyer as opposed to a patent lawyer. They argue that the general lawyer will do a better job in explaining the technology to a judge or jury. They also use their in-house patent staff to work with the general lawyer. General lawyers, like Bernie Chanin of Wolfe, Block, Shorr, and Solis-Cohen in Philadelphia, Pennsylvania, do an outstanding job in explaining technology to the court. Of course, some corporate patent counsel select a patent litigation specialist as trial counsel. They base their selection on an individual's record, technical background, and approach to litigation.

Many corporate patent counsel agree on one point. They insist that a member of their in-house staff participate in all proceedings. They, or one of their associates, participate in the selection of witnesses, in preparing and answering interrogatories, in depositions, in formulating trial strategy, and in the trial and appeal. They do this because litigation requries a team effort.

As an entrepreneur, there are also things you can do to help keep litigation costs under control. For example, ask for the hourly rate charged by trial counsel, and any associates. And then ask for an estimate of how much time is anticipated for motions, discovery, and trial. Note that these estimates may vary substantially because of the actions taken by opposing counsel. However, by following the case closely, you can avoid surprises.

Corporate counsel are also concerned about how much the case will cost during each year. The timing of costs is more difficult to estimate, and yet it must be considered.

You should also try to anticipate what visual aids will be needed for trial. In one case, a plaintiff used model railroad components to construct a scale model of two plants for producing silicon carbide. These models helped counsel to clarify the issues. The scale models were expensive, but may have reduced the total costs for the lawsuit.

Next, consider what sort of litigation team you need. For example, you will need an experienced trial counsel, an associate counsel, and a technical expert. Just remember, if you, or your chief engineer, become a member of the team, you may not be available for other business.

Decide which claims you want to sue on. For example, one litigator suggests, "If you have 80 claims in a patent, you don't necessarily want to sue on all 80. Just select your best claims and focus your attention on your strongest case."

19.3 LITIGATION AND THE ENTREPRENEUR

You might ask: Why get involved in litigation? Actually, there are two good reasons. First, you may not have a choice; you may get sued. Second, it may make good business sense to sue on one of your patents.

Consider the case of a patent owner who had obtained a patent on a small sailboat. He had licensed two companies to manufacture boats under his patent. He owned one of the two companies.

When other companies manufactured similar boats, he sued them. And most of the infringers were too small to fight a lawsuit. They either took a license, or went out of business. In fact, two of the companies that challenged the patent went bankrupt.

But then, as the small boat business grew, two larger companies refused to honor the patent. The patent owner had to sue or lose his royalty income. Besides, as long as he took an aggressive approach toward any infringer, he could keep a number of smaller companies out of the business. And, if he won, he would collect damages.

Stan Lieberstein said, "Litigation is particularly difficult for a small company. It is difficult because they do not have an adequate staff to support trial counsel. Consequently, we spend a lot more time reviewing their records. At times, we have difficulty in finding the information that we need." In fact, Stan estimated, "Larger corporations can save 30 to 50% of the cost of litigating a patent because they have an internal staff that knows the facts or where to find them."

One of Stan's clients, the president of a small company, said, "Winning this suit could cost me my company." Stan explained that his company had more than enough capital to pay the legal fees, but could not spare their key executives to work with the lawyers. After all, if the president spent several weeks at trial, who would do his job?

19.4   DAMAGES

What happens if you win a lawsuit for patent infringement? Or, you might ask, what is my exposure if I lose?

There is a possibility that the patent owner will obtain an injunction. In that case, the infringer may be forced to sell an inferior product or could be put out of business. But what about monetary damages?

The patent statute, 35 USC 284, provides for damages that are adequate to compensate for the infringement, but not less than a reasonable royalty for the use of the invention. It also provides for interest and costs as fixed by the courts. And, when damages are not found by a jury, the court shall assess them. In addition, in certain unusual circumstances, the court may increase the damages up to three times the amount found or assessed.

In accordance with this section, the U.S. Court of Appeals for the Federal Circuit has identified six elements for establishing damages. They are:

1. Lost profits due to lost sales.
2. Lost profits on actual sales.
3. A reasonable royalty.
4. Prejudgment interest.
5. Attorney's fees.
6. Increased damages.

So, assuming that the plaintiff meets the burden of proof, and the patent is sustained, that plaintiff can look to these six elements for complete compensation for the defendant's infringing acts.

For example, the Court of Appeals for the Federal Circuit has held that to obtain lost profits on lost sales, it must be shown that "but for" the infringement the patent owner would have made those sales. In fact, in most cases where the patent owners have recovered lost profits on lost sales, there were only two suppliers, one of which was the patent owner. A recovery based on lost profits on actual sales is also usually limited to two-supplier markets.

What is a "reasonable royalty"? The district courts frequently turn to a hypothetical or arm's length negotiation as a basis for determining what is reasonable. As a result, the awards have varied, but frequently resemble the rates that are common to the industry in which the patent applies. In other words, if there is an established royalty rate within an industry, that rate will be applied. The district courts may also consider the rate by any other licensee under the same patent.

The Court of Appeals for the Federal Circuit has upheld an award for prejudgment interest in the absence of some specific justification for withholding such an award. So, if a patent suit takes three to seven years to reach final adjudication, and the prime rate increases during that time from 8 to 20%, damages could be substantial. In addition, a decision on whether to compound the interest is within the court's discretion.

The award of reasonable attorney's fees is also within the court's discretion. However, such discretion is limited to those cases in which there are exceptional circumstances. As a general rule, an award of attorney's fees will be limited to cases of willful infringement or cases involving some misconduct. For example, fraud in obtaining a patent, or a frivolous defense, might justify an award of reasonable attorney's fees.

Finally, a court may increase damages up to three times the amount found or assessed. The court can increase damages in the case of willful infringement, but will not do so if the infringer's actions were based on a reasonable doubt or upon the advice of counsel. Treble damages are unusual, and the facts that justify an increased award may vary. Therefore, it is suggested that you discuss this concept with counsel before you become involved in litigation.

19.5   REISSUES AND REEXAMINATION

As a patent owner, you can petition the U.S. Patent and Trademark Office to reexamine or reissue your patent before you file a lawsuit. You might elect to do this if you learn of prior art that might invalidate your patent.

Within two years of the issue date of your patent, you may apply for a reissue patent with broader claims. For example, you might amend your claims to call for "means for moving a car furnace" instead of "a transfer car," which had been defined as moving perpendicular to the track. You could do this if you wanted to broaden your claims to cover a railroad turntable.

Now, it is advantageous for a patent owner to have each patent reexamined in view of all of the known prior art. Then the owner can argue before a judge or jury that the patent examiner reviewed all of the pertinent references and concluded that the claims were patentable.

There are also times when a potential defendant may file a petition for reexamination of a patent. For example, if you are considering a license under the patent, you may be able to have some of the claims canceled, and avoid infringement. And the reexamination will be less expensive than litigation.

19.6   ALTERNATIVE FORMS OF DISPUTE RESOLUTION

As an entrepreneur, you could suggest an alternative form of dispute resolution in an attempt to avoid litigation. The alternative forms of dispute resolution range from arbitration to mini-trials.

Arbitration can be expensive. And you may incur some risk in following this approach. Nevertheless, it can be a relatively simple proceeding in which one or more issues are submitted to an arbitrator.

Arbitration and mini-trials have one common problem, which is that both parties have to agree to the procedure. Each party has to agree on matters such as discovery, format for the proceeding, and who will serve as judge.

In a mini-trial, each side presents its best case to a panel, which may include a senior executive from each company and a patent expert. Then the two executives meet to discuss settlement. If they can't agree, the patent expert issues an advisory ruling, telling the executives how the expert thinks a judge would rule based on the evidence presented. And then the executives try again to settle the matter.

If the parties can't agree, they litigate the issues.

Arbitration and mini-trials may offer an advantage to the patent owner if extensive discovery is avoided. The reason is that extensive discovery is helpful in preparing a defense.

There is one other weakness in nonbinding arbitration and mini-trials. In either case, you must rely on the reasonableness of a senior executive from each company. So if either of the executives is emotionally involved or irrational, the result may be an exercise in futility.

19.7   WHEN ALL ELSE FAILS

Unfortunately, you may have to litigate. For example, your alternatives may be to go out of business, file suit, defend a lawsuit, or perhaps, give your research and development to a competitor.

If you elect to file a suit or if you are sued, an attorney will prepare a complaint that charges the defendant with infringement or asks to have the patent declared invalid. In essence, the complaint forms the basis for the lawsuit. Then the complaint is served on the defendant. For example, a federal marshall may arrive on your doorstep and hand you a copy.

When you receive a complaint, the first thing to do is to read it. And then call your lawyer promptly, because some action must be taken, usually within twenty days. Do not call the other party or the other party's lawyer.

After receiving a complaint, the defendant's lawyer may file an answer or a motion to dismiss. The lawyer may argue that the suit was filed in the wrong jurisdiction or ask to have the suit transferred to a more convenient forum. The defendant's lawyer may also file a counterclaim. For example, in an action for patent infringement, the defendant usually asks the court to hold the patent invalid or unenforceable.

In patent litigation, both parties usually file one or more motions. These motions range from a motion to amend the complaint to a motion for summary judgment. In each case, the motion usually will be supported by a legal brief. Then the other party files a reply and the judge may ask for oral arguments on the issue. And as the litigation moves toward trial, both parties will become involved in the discovery process.

Discovery may begin with a set of interrogatories and a request for the production of documents. Some courts limit interrogatories to twenty, while other permit extensive use of this procedure. In either case, the interrogatories or questions are designed to elicit facts. In many cases, they are used as the basis for depositions.

"A deposition is testimony under oath," according to Clyde Willian. "It is a lot like testimony in a courtroom, but without the presence of the judge or jury."

Your lawyer should prepare you for your deposition. Together you should review any documents with respect to which you will likely be questioned. The lawyer should counsel you to give the facts as concisely and accurately as possible, and should advise you to answer only the questions asked, not to guess or speculate, and not to volunteer additional information.

When you are deposed, take your time in answering the questions. Think about what you're going to say, and give your lawyer an opportunity to object. Make certain that you understand the question before you answer, and do not let opposing counsel mislead you.

In one case, a witness had been deposed for the entire day. And, late in the afternoon, opposing counsel said, "This morning, you testified that . . ." Then the lawyer slightly distorted what the witness had said. The witness replied, "No, you have mistated what I said." Actually, your lawyer should protect you from this type of deception. However, you too should stay alert.

Clyde Willian cautions his clients, "Keep your answers simple and direct. Use a yes or no if the answer can be answered accurately in that manner. And if you don't know the answer, say "I don't know.' " Clyde also cautions witnesses against being baited. He said, "Don't get into an argument or give a careless answer."

In essence, there is no substitute for adequate preparation for a deposition. In fact, each witness should be personally prepared so that each knows what to expect. Even if you have been deposed before, your counsel should take the time to adequately prepare you for each deposition that you give.

Finally, after a lot of motions, depositions, and a number of conferences with the judge, your case will come to trial. And during the trial, witnesses, possibly you and a lot of others, will be called to testify. Just remember that the purpose of the trial is to present the facts to the court. In some cases, this is done in a few days. In other cases, the trial may take several weeks. In a few cases, the trial takes months.

If you have a jury trial, you will get a prompt decision. But in a nonjury trial, your lawyers may be asked to prepare post trial briefs and proposed findings of facts. And then you may have to wait for months for a decision. And this decision isn't final. Often, the loser will appeal.

In an appeal, counsel prepares a brief written argument and argues the case before the higher court. If you are before the U.S. Court of Appeals for the Federal Circuit with a patent case, you will receive a decision in about six to nine months from filing the appeal.

If you lose at this level, you might petition the U.S. Supreme Court for certiorari, but your chances of obtaining a review by the highest court are slim.

19.8 SETTLEMENT

You can always consider settlement before, during, or after a trial. In fact, many cases are settled on the steps of the courthouse, that is, immediately before trial. I recall one case that was settled after a decision by the Court of Appeals, but before filing a petition for certiorari.

But don't file a suit in the expectation of getting the other party's attention, that is, getting a quick settlement. You shouldn't do this because litigation tends to polarize the parties, and frequently costs a great deal of money before it is settled.

In summary, it is usually better to exhaust all means of avoiding litigation before filing suit.

20

Creativity—
A Valuable Asset

Creative individuals form the basis for technological leadership and success. Nevertheless, the role of an independent inventor is difficult. Inventors like Thomas Edison, Edward Achieson, and Chester Carlson all persevered and made major contributions to society. They succeeded because they went beyond the technical development of an invention. They believed in their ideas and convinced others that they were offering a business opportunity. They sold their inventions and themselves.

In today's society, you have an infinite number of opportunities. And, business managers are eager to capitalize on your inventions, provided that you demonstrate the profit potential of your proposal But your success as an entrepreneur is dependent on your ability to communicate, and your ability to convince someone else that your proposal is valuable.

Having read the previous chapters, you should have all the information you need to begin your own business. It's natural to feel a bit hesitant. Nevertheless, think optimistically and succeed. Don't turn back because of some preconceived notion that you can't "sell." There is no magic in selling, just an honest and sincere effort coupled with a little preparation.

Anyone who just can't summon up the courage to sell a project can look for a partner who is capable of making a presentation to a potential buyer. Besides, most presentations are more effective if handled by two people. Nevertheless, care should be used in selecting a partner for sales, and you should have an understanding in writing before you begin to work together.

Ray Kroc, who promoted MacDonald's and made it what it is today, was 52 years old when he entered into business to develop a fast food franchise. He recognized the potential for a small fast food business with a limited menu. He believed in an idea and did something about it. The world did not beat a path to his door until he cleared the path with a lot of hard work and provided good quality at a reasonable price. Mr. Kroc devoted his entire effort to MacDonald's. He based those efforts on a single successful operation and overcame a number of difficulties before his chain became so successful.

There is one caveat. That caveat is to be cautious. Technical developments tend to take time before achieving commercial success. And the costs for proceeding from a prototype to commercial success will often involve hundreds of thousands of dollars. Nevertheless, don't be discouraged, since most of these sums may be paid by your licensee. Just don't quit your job in the expectations of immediate riches.

And don't overlook the one major advantage in the invention development business. The advantage is that you can devote your efforts to your favorite project, and then you can operate on a part-time basis. In this way, you can avoid the frustrations of a corporate bureaucracy and enjoy working on a number of challenging and stimulating projects that are made up of your own ideas.

So if you are a self-starter, a highly motivated individual, and believe in your own ideas, you will be successful. And you may become wealthy. Even if you don't get rich, you can produce extra income and enjoy your work. Self-satisfaction is a reward in itself.

21

Getting Started

Everyone has good ideas. It is what you do with them that separates the successful entrepreneur from the idle dreamer.

As an entrepreneur, you know that you have a good invention. By now you should have some idea as to its value. You should have evaluated its potential, and formulated a plan for its further development. You should also recognize what it will take to convert your invention into a business.

And if you want to convert your invention into a successful business, you will follow the two most important lessons in this book. First, do it now. Don't reread the book; get started. Rereading the book would amount to procrastination. Nevertheless, you may want to use the book as a reference and refer to the various sections as your work commences.

Second, don't get discouraged or think that the whole process is too complicated. The process of developing your invention should be fun. It should be a lot like writing a book. You just take one step at a time.

And if you take one step at a time, and have perseverance, you may become a successful entrepreneur.

APPENDIXES

The agreements included in these appendixes are based on negotiated contracts. They are not suitable for an initial proposal and may not be appropriate for your purposes. They do illustrate what other parties have done.

Invention Submission Letter

John Doe
Development Enterprises

July 20, 1985

Mr. Alfred Smith
Vice President
U.S. Indian Motorcycle Corp.
North Bend, Indiana

Dear Mr. Smith:

As one of the leading marketers of motorcycles and motorcycle accessories, you may be interested in a business opportunity developed by one of our clients.

Our client, an experienced executive, is seeking an exclusive distributor for a series of motorcycle educational programs. These programs will generate sales in excess of $20 million dollars annually with a profit of 30–40%.

The really exciting thing about these programs is that they will create a new market for 100,000 Indian motorcycles annually.

I plan to be in your area on August 11–12, and would like to discuss this matter with you at that time. I will call you within the next two weeks to confirm a time.

Very truly yours,

Invention Submission Form

DISCLOSURE SUBMISSION CONDITIONS
TO THOSE WHO SUBMIT DISCLOSURES TO ABC COMPANY

While this company is anxious to take every opportunity to improve its products and add profitable ones to its line, it has found certain precautions necessary in accepting disclosures. For example, its employees have varied and numerous ideas of their own, worked out in the past, or now being worked out, for the purpose of improving or adding to its many lines of products. Some of these ideas might, by chance, be similar to your own. Hence, in order to avoid any possible future confusion between your ideas and its own, and to prevent any misunderstanding as to what the rights and obligations of the inventor and the company are, the company's policies as to considering inventions are set forth below:

1. The company cannot agree to hold your disclosure in confidence for the reason, among others, that it must disclose the invention to various employees and sometimes even to those outside of its employ, to determine its value to it, and because agreements to hold in confidence have been found to entail other obligations not intended by either the submitter or the company. It is understood, therefore, that no confidential relationship or agreement to compensate is entered into by reason of the company considering your disclosure.

2. A full written disclosure, preferably the patent application, drawing, and specification, if there are such, or if not, a sketch or drawing (which need not be anything but a rough one, provided it illustrates the invention so one skilled in the art can understand it), must be furnished to the company, as the company will otherwise have no way of telling whether or not it will be interested in your ideas.

3. The company cannot ordinarily return any descriptions, drawings, or other disclosures sent to it, since otherwise it has no record of what was disclosed to it, though it may sometimes do so if allowed to make a copy. Therefore, you should keep a duplicate of any disclosure sent to the company.

4. The company is not under any obligation to reveal to you information of its own in the general or specific field to which the disclosure relates.

5. The company wishes you to be satisfied that your interests are fully safeguarded as, for instance, by having filed an application for U.S. patent. If no such application has been filed, you should have the copy of your drawings that you retain signed, dated, and witnessed.

6. Any disclosure to this company is made on the understanding that the company assumes no obligation to do more than consider the disclosure so far as in its judgment the disclosure merits and to indicate whether or not it is interested and that you rely only on your rights under the patent laws.

7. The company receives no rights hereby, or as a result of considering this disclosure, under any patent rights you have or may acquire to the subject matter of the disclosure.

8. The foregoing applies to any additional or supplemental disclosures relating to the same subject matter.

TO: ABC COMPANY

I am submitting herewith a disclosure of

_____

on the conditions set forth above.

Signed this _____ day of _____, 1986.

_____

(Signature)

Confidential Agreement

CONFIDENTIAL AGREEMENT

The ABC Manufacturing Company of Weston, Connecticut 06883, U.S.A., (hereinafter referred to as MANUFACTURER) possesses technical information relating to the design, manufacture, and sale of equipment for retreading radial tires, herein called APPARATUS. Your company, the Oxford Products Company of London, England (hereinafter referred to as COMPANY), will be discussing with MANUFACTURER matters of possible mutual interest relating to said APPARATUS, and may obtain from MANUFACTURER technical information relating thereto.

MANUFACTURER is willing to make available to COMPANY such of its technical information as in MANUFACTURER's opinion would be useful to COMPANY for the aforesaid purpose on the following basis:

1. COMPANY and its employees agree to hold in confidence for a period of ten (10) years from the date of this agreement any and all technical information disclosed, directly or indirectly, to COMPANY by MANUFACTURER relating to said APPARATUS, except:

technical information that at the time of disclosure is in the public domain;

technical information that after disclosure is published or otherwise becomes part of the public domain through no fault of COMPANY (but only after it is published or otherwise becomes part of the public domain);

techical information that COMPANY can show was in its possession at the time of disclosure and was not acquired by COMPANY, directly or indirectly, from MANUFACTURER or from a third party who is under an obligation of confidence to MANUFACTURER not to disclose said technical information; and technical information that COMPANY can show was received by its after the time of disclosure by MANUFAC-TURER from a third party who did not acquire it, directly or indirectly, from MANUFACTURER or its affiliates under an obligation of confidence.

(a) For the purpose of the provisions of this Paragraph 1, any combination of features shall not be deemed to be within the foregoing exceptions merely because the individual features are in the public domain or in the possesion of COMPANY unless the combination itself and its principle of operation are in the public domain or in the possession of COMPANY.

(b) All written technical information disclosed by MANUFACTURER shall be marked CONFIDENTIAL at the time of disclosure, and all oral technical information that is stated to be confidential at the time of disclosure shall be reduced to writing within thirty (30) days of disclosure and confirmed as confidential to recipient.

2.   COMPANY agrees that it will not, without the prior written permission of MANUFACTURER, use the technical information to be held in confidence by COMPANY under Paragraph 1 hereof for any purpose other than to enable COMPANY to determine whether to enter into, or to fulfill, a contractual relationship with MANUFACTURER.

3.   If COMPANY will be testing and evaluating MANUFACTURER's APPARATUS, COMPANY agrees that all test data, test results, and evaluations conducted and arrived at by COMPANY and/or by MANUFACTURER will be held in confidence and will not be made available to or disclosed to anyone other than MANUFACTURER without its prior written approval. If after said testing and evaluation, or before, no contractual relationship is entered into between MANUFACTURER and COMPANY with regard to said APPARATUS, COMPANY agrees to turn over to MANUFACTURER all technical information, test data, test results, and evaluations and will retain none of them, or any copies thereof, for itself or for any person or firm.

ACCEPTED AND AGREED TO:

By: _____   By: _____
Title: _____   Title: _____
Date: _____   Date: _____

License Agreement (Exclusive)

LICENSE AGREEMENT

THIS AGREEMENT made and entered into on the _____ day of _____, 1986, by and between

GILBERT R. JONES of _____ No. Street, _____ City, State _____, Zip _____, herein called "JONES"; and

ABC Brown Division of ABC Incorporated, having its principal place of business at _____ No. Street, _____ City, _____ State, _____ Zip, herein called "ABC";

WITNESSETH THAT:

In consideration of the mutual covenants herein contained and intending to be legally bound hereby, the parties agree as follows:

1. Definitions

As used herein, the following terms shall have the meanings set forth below:

A. *Inventions* means the widget as disclosed and claimed in United States Patent No. 0,000,000, additional patent applications and improvement inventions of JONES.

B. *Patents* means United States and foreign patents covering the Inventions, patents to be issued pursuant thereto, and all divisions, continuations, reissues, and extensions thereof.

C. *Technical Information* means the information and data in the possession of JONES that JONES has the right to disclose relating to the *Inventions*.

2. License

JONES hereby grants to ABC an exclusive worldwide license, including the right to grant sublicenses, to make, have made, use and sell products embodying the *Inventions* under the *Patents*; and to use the *Technical Information* in practicing the *Inventions*.

3. Information—Patents

A. JONES shall make available to ABC for its use all *Technical Information* in his possession concerning the *Inventions* and shall promptly disclose to ABC on a nonconfidential basis all discoveries, developments, and patents pertinent thereto. JONES shall have the sole right to prosecute domestic and foreign patents on the *Inventions* and shall have the right to determine whether or not to file any patent application, to abandon the prosecution of any patent, or to discontinue the maintenance of any patent. JONES shall notify ABC in writing of his intent not to file a patent application, to abandon the prosecution of any application, or to discontinue maintenance of any patent in force on any improvements of the *Inventions* at least forty-five (45) days prior to the last day on which action is required to preserve such application from abandonment or to maintain such patent in force and upon written request shall promptly furnish to ABC all papers pertaining to such application or patent, so that ABC may have the option, at its own expense, to take the required action.

B.   ABC shall notify JONES on or before December 31, 1986 of its findings with respect to its market evaluation and whether or not it elects to continue with the License. If ABC notifies JONES that it has no further interest in a license, this agreement is terminated.

4.   Litigation

A.   JONES shall notify ABC of any suspected infringement of the *Patents*. The sole right to institute a suit for infringement rests with ABC. JONES agrees to cooperate with ABC in all respects, to testify when requested by ABC, and to make available any records, papers, information, specimens, and the like. Up to one half of any royalty earned or minimum accrued during the pendency of such litigation shall be applied to the cost for such litigation. Any recovery received pursuant to such suit shall be applied first to reimburse ABC for its expenses and thereafter divided in proportion to JONES' royalties to ABC's profits.

B.   In the event that any patent infringement action is threatened or commenced against ABC or any of its sublicenses or customers as a result of the manufacture, use, or sale of products embodying the *Inventions*, ABC may terminate this Agreement upon the giving of thirty (30) days written notice to JONES unless JONES shall undertake to hold ABC harmless and defend or settle such a threat or action.

5.   Royalties

A.   ABC shall pay to JONES Five Thousand Dollars ($5000) within thirty (30) days of the execution of this agreement. Such $5000 payment shall be applied as an advance against future royalty payments that are in excess of minimums.

B.   ABC shall pay to JONES a royalty of five percent (5%) of the net sales price of all products sold under the licenses granted under Article 2 hereof, provided, however, that after December 31, 1990, no royalty shall be accrued or payable to JONES unless the product is covered by the claim of an unexpired patent in the country of manufacture or sale. In computing the net sales price, ABC may deduct any sales commission paid to its sales representatives.

6.   Minimum Royalties

ABC shall pay to JONES royalties as stated in Article 5, but in no event shall annual royalties be less than the following minimum royalties in each of the calendar years indicated.

Calendar Year	Minimum Royalties
1987	$5,000
1988	15,000
1989*	25,000

*and each calendar year thereafter during the term of this Agreement

7.   Payments

A.   Not later than the last day of February, ABC shall furnish to JONES a written statement of all amounts accrued hereunder during the annual period ended the last day of the preceding December and shall pay to JONES all amounts due to JONES. In addition, ABC shall pay to JONES on such last day of February the minimum royalty obligation for the present year. Such minimum royalty shall be applied as an advance against earned royalties for that year.

B.   If this Agreement is for any reason terminated before all of the payments herein provided for have been made, ABC shall immediately pay to JONES any remaining unpaid balance even though the due date as above provided has not been reached.

8.   Records

ABC shall keep accurate records of all operations affecting payments hereunder, and shall permit a mutually agreed to Certified Public Accountant to inspect such records during regular business hours throughout the term of this Agreement provided, however, that no more than one inspection per year shall be permitted and that all costs associated with the audit shall be paid by JONES.

9. Warranties

A. JONES warrants that he has the right to grant all of the rights granted herein.

B. Nothing in this Agreement shall be deemed to be a representation or warranty by JONES of the validity of any of the *Patents*.

C. JONES warrants that he has no information indicating that any of the claims of the *Patents* are invalid.

10. Termination

A. This agreement shall end upon the expiration of the last to expire of the *Patents* included herein, or upon the abandonment of the last to be abandoned of any patent applications included herein, whichever is later, unless this Agreement is sooner terminated.

B. ABC may terminate this Agreement at the end of any calendar year upon thirty (30) days written notice in advance to JONES or at any time after the expiration of any patent included herein or a final adjudication of invalidity of any patent included herein by written notice in advance to JONES.

C. If either party shall be in default of any obligation hereunder, or shall be adjudged bankrupt, or become insolvent, or make an assignment for the benefit of creditors, or be placed in the hands of a receiver or a trustee in bankruptcy, the other party may terminate this Agreement by giving thirty (30) days notice by Registered Mail to the party at fault, specifying the basis for termination. If within thirty (30) days after the receipt of such notice, the party at fault shall remedy the condition forming the basis for termination, such notice shall cease to be operative and this Agreement shall continue in full force.

11. Nonassignability

ABC shall not assign any right hereunder without the written consent of JONES, except to the extent necessary to transfer the rights to a purchaser or successor of the entire business related to *Inventions*.

12. Reform

The parties agree that if any part, term, or provision of this Agreement shall be found illegal or in conflict with any State or Federal law, the validity of the remaining provisions shall not be affected thereby.

13. Waiver and Alteration

A. The waiver of a breach hereunder may be effected only by a writing signed by the waiving party and shall not constitute a waiver of any other breach.

B. A provision of this Agreement may be altered only by a writing signed by both parties.

14. Implementation

Each party shall execute any instruments reasonably believed by the other party to be necessary to implement the provisions of this Agreement.

15. Construction

This Agreement shall be construed in accordance with the laws of the State of New York of the United States of America and in the English language.

16. Entire Understanding

This Agreement represents the entire understanding between the parties, and supersedes all other agreements, express or implied, between the parties concerning the *Inventions*.

17. Addresses

For the purpose of all written communications between the parties, their addresses shall be:

> GILBERT R. JONES
> COMPANY NAME
> NUMBER AND STREET
> CITY, STATE AND ZIP CODE

ABC BROWN DIVISION
NUMBER AND STREET
CITY, STATE AND ZIP CODE

IN WITNESS WHEREOF the parties have caused this Agreement to be executed by their duly authorized officers on the respective dates and at the respective places hereinafter set forth.

ATTEST: GILBERT R. JONES
By: _____   By: _____
Signed at: _____   Date: _____

ATTEST   ABC INCORPORATED
By: _____   By: _____
Signed at: _____   Date: _____

License Agreement
(Nonexclusive)

NONEXCLUSIVE LICENSE AGREEMENT

THIS AGREEMENT made and entered into this ___ day of _____, 1986, by and between ABC INCORPORATED, a New York corporation, having a principal place of business at _____ (hereinafter called ABC) and AMERICAN PRODUCTS CO., INCORPORATED, a _____ corporation having a principal place of business at _____ (hereinafter called LICENSEE).

WHEREAS, ABC owns the entire rights, title, and interest in and to United States Patent No. _____ entitled: _____; and

WHEREAS, LICENSEE is desirous of obtaining a license under the ABC Patent on terms and conditions hereinafter set forth;

NOW, THEREFORE, in consideration of the mutual covenants herein the parties hereto agree as follows:

Article I   Definitions

A.   Patent—shall mean United States Letters Patent No. _____ issued on _____.

B.   Products—shall mean _____ covered by the claims of the Patent.

Article II   Grant

ABC hereby grants to LICENSEE a nonexclusive, nontransferable license, without right to sublicense to make, sell, and use products that are covered by a claim or claims of the Patent.

Article III   Consideration

LICENSEE agrees to pay to ABC a royalty in the amount of Five Dollars ($5.00) for each product made and sold by LICENSEE from the effective date and for the term of this License Agreement.

Article IV   Payment and Reports

A.   LICENSEE shall pay to ABC or its designee a nonrefundable advance on royalties of Two Thousand Five Hundred Dollars ($2,500.00) within thirty (30) days of the effective date of this License Agreement and prior to the beginning of each year thereafter during the term of this

License Agreement (each year thereafter beginning on the anniversary of the effective date of this License Agreement).

    B.   LICENSEE agrees to keep, as of the effective date of this License Agreement, true and accurate books and accounts and records showing the quantities of products made and sold and to provide to ABC or its designee a report listing the quantities of such products made and sold during each calendar quarter during the term of this License Agreement.

    C.   Royalties that are in excess of the advance on royalties called for in Part A of this Article shall be due and payable to ABC within thirty (30) days following the end of each calendar quarter for which said products are made and sold and shall accompany the report required by Part B of this Article.

Article V   Inspection

ABC shall have the right during the term of this License Agreement to have LICENSEE's books and records relating to manufacture and sale of products audited at ABC's expense at reasonable intervals, not greater than once per year, during normal business hours.

Article VI   Term

    A.   The term of this License Agreement shall be for a period of one (1) year beginning on the effective date of this License Agreement.

    B.   LICENSEE has the option to extend the term of this License Agreement for additional and successive one (1) year periods by providing notice to ABC along with the advance on royalties called for in Article IV, Part A, herein, prior to the expiration of the previous term provided, however, that the term of this License Agreement shall not extend beyond the life of the Patent.

    C.   Upon the expiration of the term of this License Agreement without an election by LICENSEE to extend the term accompanied by the required advance or royalties, the license granted in Article II herein shall be immediately revoked and canceled.

Article VII   Termination for Cause

Upon default of any provision herein by either party, the injured party may give to the defaulting party written notice of intent to terminate this License Agreement, and if the existing default is not cured within ninety

(90) days after receipt of such notice, the injured party may terminate this License Agreement forthwith by written notice to the defaulting party. Termination for cause shall not relieve LICENSEE of the obligation to pay all royalties accrued up to the effective date of termination.

Article VIII Notices

Notices hereunder may be given by registered or express mail to the party to be notified at its designated address unless such address has been changed by such party by prior notice.

Article IX Governing Law

This License Agreement shall be construed in accordance with and governed by the laws of the State of New York in the English language.

Article X Entire Agreement

This License Agreement represents the entire understanding between the parties and supersedes all other agreements, express or implied, between the parties.

In witnesseth whereof, the parties hereto have respectively caused this instrument to be executed on the dates hereinafter indicated. The below signers swear that they are authorized to represent and sign this Agreement in the capacity indicated.

By: _____

Title: _____

Date: _____

By: _____

Title: _____

Date: _____

Manufacturing, Sales, and Trademark Agreement

Australia and New Zealand

MANUFACTURING, SALES, AND TRADEMARK LICENSE AGREEMENT

This Agreement, subject to the approval of the Reserve Bank of Australia, is made effective as of the 1st day of July, 1986.

between

ABC Incorporated
a corporation of the State of New York of the U.S.A.
with an office at its

_____

_____

_____

(hereinafter called "ABC")

and

Sea Breeze Mfg., Pty. Limited
an Australian proprietary limited company with offices at

_____

_____

_____

(hereinafter called "Licensee")

WITNESSETH

WHEREAS ABC's Boat Division of _____, U.S.A. is a manufacturer and worldwide marketer of fiberglass sailboats sold under the trademark "Brandshatch," which have a universal reputation for quality, styling and performance and Licensee, which has facilities in Australia for manufacturing fiberglass sailboats and marketing them in Australia and New Zealand, wishes to acquire a license to manufacture Brandshatch model 35, 41, and 43 sailboats in Australia and sell them in Australia, New Zealand, New Caledonia, the Solomons, Fiji, New Guinea, and Tahiti, which ABC is willing to grant.

NOW THEREFORE

In consideration of the mutual covenants and agreements hereinafter set forth, the parties hereby covenant and agree as follows:

I. Information, Molds, Components, and Services Supplied

(a) *Technical Information:* ABC, after the effective date of this Agreement given above, shall disclose and make available in confidence to Licensee a technical data package containing the technical know-how and other information in existence at the date of this Agreement, including specifications, drawings, designs, standards of quality and performance, and molding and assembly information relating to the manufacture of Brandshatch sailboats, models 35, 41, and 43 sold by ABC's Brandshatch Division, all such information being hereinafter called "tangible technical information."

ABC agrees to supply Licensee in confidence upon written request with updated information of the same character in ABC's possession at the date of this Agreement that it has the right to disclose and that will enable Licensee to manufacture sailboats according to the current manufacturing processes of ABC's Brandshatch Division. This information and additional information of the same character relating to other ABC Brandshatch Division sailboats that may be added to this Agreement by written amendment according to Article VIII shall thereupon be tangible technical information and subject to the same conditions.

(b) *Reinforced Fiberglass Parts and Associated Tooling:* ABC shall also supply in confidence to Licensee crated reinforced parts of Brandshatch 35, 41, and 43 sailboats needed to fabricate molds conforming to ABC Brandshatch Divisions quality requirements and associated tooling including patterns, jigs, and fixtures. The tangible information supplied by ABC under paragraph I(a) and a set of reinforced parts and tooling supplied under this paragraph I(b) plus due care in their use by qualified workers is all that in ABC's opinion is reasonably required to properly manufacture Brandshatch model 35, 41, and 43 sailboats to meet ABC's specifications, but ABC will, as provided in paragraphs I(d) and I(e), make qualified technical representatives available to render any assistance Licensee may reasonably require.

(c) *Sailboat Components:* ABC agrees to have its ABC Brandshatch Division sell to Licensee at Division's commercial export prices and terms and subject to its production schedules at the time, components for Brandshatch model 35, 41, and 43 sailboats.

(d) *Visits of Licensee's Personnel to ABC's Brandshatch Division Premises:* ABC, upon the written request of Licensee, to the extent of governmental restrictions, shall arrange for reasonable numbers of technical representatives of Licensee to visit appropriate plants of ABC's Brandshatch Division for reasonable periods to consult with AMF Brandshatch Division engineers and observe manufacturing practices employed on Brandshatch sailboats. Such visits shall be at Licensee's expense and shall be scheduled and conducted in a manner that in ABC's opinion will not interfere with current operations.

(e) *Visits of ABC Brandshatch Division Engineers to Licensee's Premises:* ABC, upon the written request of Licensee, shall make available for reasonable periods at the Australian plants of Licensee qualified technical representatives to consult with, advise, and assist Licensee in using the set of molds and tooling provided under paragraph I(b) and in molding and assembling Brandshatch model 35, 41, and 43 sailboats. Licensee will be responsible for obtaining any necessary visas or entry permits needed for the ABC representatives.

(f) *Licensee's Improvements:* Licensee agrees to disclose promptly in writing to ABC's Brandshatch Division at its Weston, Connecticut, U.S.A., address given above, any and all inventions, improvements, and modifications acquired or developed by Licensee during the period of this Agreement relating to sailboats, similar to the Brandshatch model 35, 41, and 43 sailboats and any other ABC Brandshatch sailboats that may be added to this Agreement by written amendment after their commercial reduction to practice.

II. Trademarks and Markings

(a) *Registration:* Licensee agrees to cooperate with ABC in registering this Agreement with appropriate governmental authorities where registration is required in the countries set forth in paragraph III(a). Licensee agrees to execute any other proper documents that ABC may require for the full protection and enforcement of ABC's trademark properties, including the execution of Registered User Agreements in Australia and New Zealand.

(b) *Trademark Use to Benefit ABC:* Any use by Licensee of a trademark on a product licensed or to be licensed under this Agreement shall inure to the benefit of ABC as the Proprietor for a registration of such trademark. Licensee agrees to cooperate with ABC in the prosecution of any application for trademark registration for such products that ABC may wish to file, and for that purpose Licensee shall supply to ABC from time to time such specimens, photographs, labels, and similar material as may reasonably be required in connection with any such application. No trademark other than a trademark licensed or to be licensed under this Agreement shall be used on products licensed or to be licensed under this Agreement without ABC's written approval.

(c) *Nonlicensed Marks:* It is expressly understood and agreed that no license is granted with respect to the tradename and trademark "ABC" either alone or in combination with any other name or geometric configuration. Such tradename and trademark or any names or marks confusingly similar thereto, except for the license notice provided for in paragraph II(e) below, shall not be used in connection with any product manufactured or sold by Licensee except for those so marked by ABC's Brandshatch Division and purchased for resale unchanged by Licensee.

(d) *Quality Control:* Licensee covenants that sailboats manufactured, assembled, and sold or leased under the trademark "Brandshatch" or any other trademark to be licensed under this Agreement or any combination of them shall conform to ABC's requirements, including tangible technical information, standards, quality, and being molded on molds produced from ABC Brandshatch Division reinforced fiberglass parts as described in paragraph I(b) and no others. In the event of any failure to so conform, ABC may withdraw permission to use these trademarks until ABC is satisfied that Licensee is conforming with ABC's requirements, and Licensee receives ABC's permission to commence or resume such use. Upon reasonable notice, Licensee shall permit ABC access to its plants and to those of its suppliers and dealers to inspect and verify such conformance.

(e) *License Notice:* Licensee shall affix to all sailboats licensed or that may be licensed under this Agreement a marking plate bearing the inscription "Manufactured and Distributed from Australia by Sea Breeze Mfg. Pty. Limited under licenese from ABC INCORPORATED through its ABC Brandshatch Division, Weston, Connecticut, U.S.A."

III. Licenses Granted

ABC hereby grants and agrees to grant to Licensee for the term of this Agreement as it may be extended from time to time, unless sooner terminated as provided hereinafter, the following licenses:

(a) *Know-How License:* An exclusive license to make Brandshatch 35, 41, and 43 sailboats and components therefor with the confidential use of the tangible technical information and ABC Brandshatch Division reinforced fiberglass parts as described in paragraph I(b), patterns, jigs, and fixtures in Australia only and to sell the products so made in Australia, New Zealand, Fiji, New Caledonia, the Solomons, New Guinea, and Tahiti. Licensee convenants to use such tangible technical information only for Brandshatch 35, 41, and 43 sailboats made in Australia and not to use it in any boats made outside of Australia.

(b) *Trademark License:* A license to use the trademark "Brandshatch" in connection with Brandshatch 35, 41, and 43 sailboats made in Australia with the confidential use of the tangible technical information and the molds and tooling supplied under paragraph I(b) for sale in the countries listed in paragraph III(a) under the appropriate trademark registrations and subject to the conditions set forth in Article II hereof.

(c) *Restriction on Other Licenses:* ABC covenants not to grant a license to any other party to use the Brandshatch trademark for this product in the countries listed in paragraph III(a) during the term of this Agreement.

IV. Compensation

In consideration for the rights and licenses granted and to be granted and the confidential use of the tangible technical information, the sets of molds and tooling and technical services furnished and to be furnished to it hereunder, Licensee shall pay or have paid in United States currency to ABC at its ABC Brandshatch Division, the following:

(a) *For the Technical Data Package of Paragraph I(a):* $50,000 (U.S.).

(b) *For the Updated Information of Paragraph I(a):* Prices and terms to be negotiated.

(c) *For the Reinforced Fiberglass Parts of Paragraph I(b) and Associated Tooling:*

1. Set of reinforced fiberglass parts: $75,000 (U.S.) f.o.b., Weston, Connecticut.
2. Set of patterns: $25,000 (U.S.) f.o.b., Weston, Connecticut.
3. Set of jigs and fixtures: $75,000 (U.S.) f.o.b., Weston, Connecticut.

(d) *Shipping Expenses:* ABC will prepay shipping papers, consular invoice certification, and insurance costs for Licensee's account to
_____.

(e) *Percentage Royalty:* A percentage royalty in the amount of three and one-half percent (3½%) of Licensee's bona fide gross selling price on all sales of Brandshatch sailboats and component parts therefor produced with the use of the tangible technical information or of the ABC Brandshatch Division supplied reinforced fiberglass parts of paragraph I(b) and tooling or with the use of the trademark "Brandshatch" or confusingly similar variations. Percentage royalties on transactions with parties controlled by, controlling, or otherwise related to Licensee or its employees shall be based upon the bona fide, arms length gross selling price of the same type of item to unrelated third parties.

(f) *Minimum Royalties:* If percentage royalties to be paid under paragraph IV(e) do not, after taxes if any are deducted, total or exceed after conversion to United States currency as provided in paragraph V(d) a minimum royalty of $5,000 in the first full year following the date of this Agreement, $10,000 in the second year thereafter, and $20,000 in the third year thereafter that this Agreement is in effect, then Licensee shall pay to ABC in addition to the percentage royalties, the difference between the $5,000, $10,000, or $20,000 minimum royalty as applicable and the total of percentage royalties due for that year. These sums are minimum guaranteed, annual royalties and each one as applicable becomes due for each year following the date of this Agreement or in total for any part of the respective year before termination if terminated because of a breach of Licensee.

(g) *Fee for Technical Assistance at Licensee's Plants:* Two Hundred United States Dollars (U.S. $200.00) for each day or part thereof including travel time for each technical representative made available by ABC to render services as provided in paragraph I(e), plus living and travelling expenses for such representative, including business-class round trip air transportation via the most direct, timely route between ABC's place of business at which the representative is regularly based and Licensee's plant.

V.   Payments and Statements

(a) *For Technical Data Package, Molds, Tooling, and Prepaid Shipping Expenses:* Payable to ABC ninety (90) days after shipment and presentation of the invoice, consular certificate, bill of lading, evidence of insurance, and a draft for the invoice amount in favor of ABC Brandshatch Division of ABC INCORPORATED or to its order, from an irrevocable confirmed letter of credit for _____ Dollars in United States Currency (U.S. $) to be established at the Guaranty Trust Company, New York, New York, U.S.A., ninety (90) days before the shipping dates as advised by ABC.

(b) *Updated Information of Paragraph I(a):* Thirty (30) days after the invoice date.

(c) *Royalty Payment:* Licensee within thirty (30) days after each complete three month period following the effective date of this Agreement, and after each complete three month period thereafter that this Agreement is in effect, shall render to ABC's Brandshatch Division on behalf of ABC, unless otherwise specified in writing by ABC, a written statement certified to be correct by an officer of Licensee itemizing the products licensed under this Agreement that were sold during the period from the effective date through the first complete three month period following, and during each complete three month period thereafter, stating the currency exchange rate applied, according to paragraph V(d), including receipts for withholding taxes paid, if any, and giving any other data that is necessary or convenient in ABC's opinion to substantiate the propriety of each royalty computation and payment. Payment of the corresponding royalty from the effective date of this Agreement, including any amount to make up the minimum royalties of paragraph IV(f), shall be made with each statement or as soon after the first statement as the Licensee ascertains from the Australian Commission of Taxation the amount, if any, to be retained in respect of tax due, or which may become due on the payment, and obtains from the Reserve Bank of Australia the requisite authority of that Bank to the making of such payments. The Licensee agrees to take prompt steps to ascertain the foregoing amounts from the bank. Any withholding or other taxes assessed and to be retained under the Australian tax laws on or in respect of royalties remitted under this Agreement shall be deducted from the payment due before remittance and paid by the Licensee or its paying agent to the tax authority on behalf of the payee.

(d) *Currency Conversion:*   Conversion of foreign currency into United States Dollars for all payments due under this Agreement shall be computed at the selling rate for United States Currency in terms of the foreign currency prevailing at the National Bank of Australia Limited at the close of business on the business day preceding the time of remittance; provided that at ABC's discretion, late payments shall bear interest at the rate of twelve percent (12%) compounded quarterly from the due date with the conversion made as described, but at the selling rate in effect on the due date.

VI.   Records and Audit

Licensee shall keep and permit to be examined by ABC during the period of this Agreement as it may be extended and for two years thereafter books and records containing complete and accurate data to enable determination of the amounts payable and information to be supplied under this Agreement.

VII.   Reserve Bank of Australia Approval of this Agreement

This Agreement is subject to and conditioned upon the approval of the Reserve Bank of Australia Exchange Control Authority being obtained within ninety (90) days of the date of execution on behalf of ABC set forth below, unless extended by written notice from ABC; otherwise it shall be void and of no effect. Licensee agrees to submit this Agreement for the approval, pay any approval fee for its own account, and give ABC prompt written notice of the final approval and effective approval date, or disapproval of the Exchange Control Authority for the full performance of this Agreement, or of the Authority's approval subject to any required changes, and enclose a copy of the approving document, if approved. ABC's letter accepting the approval of the Exchange Control Authority for performance of this Agreement on any changed terms shall constitute ABC's ratification.

VIII.   Term and Termination

(a) *License Period:*   This Agreement shall continue in full force and effect for a period of three (3) years from the date of this Agreement set forth above, provided that if Licensee sells a total of twenty-five (25) Brandshatch sailboats in the third full year, pays the associated royalties when due, and complies with all of the other terms of this Agreement, it shall have an option exercisable upon written notice to ABC sixty (60) days prior to the anniversary date to continue this Agreement for a fourth full year, and if the Agreement is so continued and Licensee sells a total of twenty-five (25) Brandshatch sailboats in the fourth year, pays the associated royalties when due, and complies with all the terms of this Agreement, it shall have a similar option to continue this Agreement for a fifth full year, unless in all cases it is terminated as set forth below.

(b) *Insolvency or Default Termination:*   ABC may also elect to terminate this Agreement at any time by giving written notice if the Licensee shall enter into compulsory or voluntary liquidation or winding up, or shall take the benefit of any act in force, for the relief of insolvent debtors, or shall make a composition with its creditors, or shall do any thing whereby it shall become subject to the provisions of any bankruptcy laws, or if its business shall be assumed or taken over by any government or governmental authority, or in the event that the Licensee shall neglect or fail to perform or discharge any obligation or to correct any substantial breach or default under this Agreement.

(c) *Failure to Make Payments:* ABC, without relieving Licensee of its obligation to make the payments, may also terminate this Agreement upon thirty (30) days written notice if Licensee does not make the percentage or minimum royalty payments set forth in paragraphs IV(e) and IV(f).

(d) *Licenses Ceased upon Termination:* Upon termination of the Agreement all licenses and rights granted by ABC will promptly terminate, and the right of Licensee to make any use of tangible technical information or any trademark licensed under this Agreement or to be licensed under this Agreement shall cease forthwith except to the extent provided for in paragraph VIII(g). Licensee thereupon agrees to promptly return or cause to be promptly returned to ABC all tangible technical information, and other information supplied or that may be supplied by ABC hereunder and all copies thereof, whether in the possession of Licensee, its employees, suppliers, or customers.

(e) *Repurchase of Molds:* ABC shall have the option (but not the obligation), upon any termination of this Agreement, to repurchase any or all of the molds built with the use of the reinforced fiberglass parts of paragraph I(b) at the net price of _____ in U.S. Currency, less full depreciation for normal usage based on _____ parts per mold; provided that the figure used for parts molded shall not be less than a minimum quantity of _____ per year per mold or pro rata portion thereof from the elapsed period when the mold was available for use.

(f) *No Effect on Prior Obligations:* Termination of this Agreement for any reason shall not relieve either party of any obligation accruing prior to such termination and shall be without prejudice to any other remedies arising from any breach, default, or failure to perform.

(g) *Work in Process:* No termination hereunder shall prevent Licensee from delivering any Brandshatch sailboats and any other sail boats that may be licensed under this Agreement in process of manufacture or on order hereunder at the date of such termination, provided that ABC's quality requirements set forth in paragraph II(d) are maintained. The compensation due ABC upon delivery of such sailboats shall be payable as if this Agreement were not terminated.

IX. Other ABC Brandshatch Division Sailboats

In the event that Licensee complies with all the terms of this Agreement, and ABC decides to license during the remaining term of this Agreement the manufacture and sale of ABC Brandshatch Division sailboats other than the models 35, 41, and 43 in the countries listed in paragraph III(a), ABC agrees to offer Licensee the right of first refusal of any license agreement it proposes for such other sailboats in these countries.

X.   Other Provisions

(a)   *Best Efforts:*   Licensee shall exert its bona fide best efforts to obtain sales of and further the distribution of Brandshatch 35, 41, and 43 sailboats and any other sailboats that by written amendment may be added to the licenses of this Agreement throughout the countries listed in paragraph III(a) and to effectuate the purpose of this Agreement.

(b)   *Assignment Restrictions:*   This Agreement shall be binding upon and inure to the benefit of ABC and Licensee and to the succesors of ABC's business of which this is a part. This Agreement shall not be assigned or transferred by Licensee in whole or in part without the prior written consent of ABC, and any attempted assignment or transfer by Licensee otherwise shall be invalid.

(c)   *Notices:*   Any notice, statement, or payment provided for in this Agreement shall be in or accompanied by a writing and shall be deemed duly given when deposited in the mail properly sealed to be sent air mail, postage prepaid to the parties at the post office addresses set forth above, unless other addresses are substituted therefor by written notice or it may be duly given by telex communication or cable if promptly confirmed by airmail. Where a notice period is specified it shall run from the date posted or the date sent from the telex communication or cable transmitting office.

(d)   *Independent Contractor Relationship:*   It is understood that neither ABC nor any of its divisions shall bear any responsibility to Licensee or any third party arising out of the implementation of this Agreement, as amended. Nothing contained herein shall create any relationship between Licensee and either ABC or any of its divisions other than that of independent contractors.

(e)   *All Lawsuits to Require ABC's Consent:*   Licensee agrees that it will not make ABC a party to any lawsuit, infringement action, or regulatory action it might initiate pursuant to this Agreement without ABC's prior written consent.

(f)   *Merging of Prior Understandings:*   This Agreement and any Registered User Agreements as provided for in paragraph II(a) constitute the entire agreement and understanding between the parties concerning the making and selling of Brandshatch 35, 41, and 43 sailboats and any other sailboats to be licensed under this Agreement under ABC's tangible technical information, molds, tools, and trademarks in the countries listed in paragraph III(a) and supersedes any previous agreements and understandings between the parties relating to the same subject matter. No modifications or claimed waiver of any of the provisions hereof shall be valid unless in writing and signed by authorized officers of the party to be charged.

(g) *Law:* This Agreement has been made in contemplation of the laws of the State of New York of the United States of America, and its validity and construction shall be governed by the laws of the State of New York except that disputes concerning trademarks shall be decided under the trademark law of the respective trademark issuing country.

XI. U.S. Department of Commerce Mandated Regulations

In further consideration of the license granted, Licensee covenants that it will not export or transfer or knowingly permit the export or transfer of the tangible technical information, reinforced fiberglass parts, or tooling, supplied by or on behalf of ABC, or of related information and data based upon or utilizing these items, or of products or materials incorporating these items, related information and data to North Korea, Vietnam, Kampuchea, Cuba, or other country where authorization is required without obtaining the prior authorization of the Office of Export Control Authorization of the United States Department of Commerce.

IN WITNESS WHEREOF, the parties hereto have caused this Agreement to be made and executed by their duly authorized officers as of the date first above written.

ATTEST: ABC INCORPORATED

_____   By: _____

ATTEST: SEA BREEZE
                                             MANUFACTURING PTY.
_____   LIMITED

                                         By: _____

Joint Development Agreement

JOINT DEVELOPMENT AGREEMENT

This Agreement made this _____ day of _____, 1985 between XYZ Products Company of London, England (hereinafter called XYZ) and ABC INCORPORATED of Weston, Connecticut (hereinafter called ABC).

WITNESSETH

WHEREAS, ABC is engaged in the business of developing, manufacturing, and selling filter media for the processing of liquids.

WHEREAS, XYZ is engaged in the sales and distribution of such media.

WHEREAS, it would be beneficial for ABC and XYZ to jointly develop filter media and products for purification of interferon.

Now, therefore, it is mutually agreed as follows:

Article I.   Definitions

(a)   JOINT DEVELOPMENT PROGRAM shall mean the efforts of ABC and XYZ to assist each other in developing commercially viable products for the purification of interferon.

(b)   INFORMATION shall mean information, know-how, and materials resulting from the JOINT DEVELOPMENT PROGRAM.

(c)   INVENTIONS shall mean all inventions and improvements arising out of the JOINT DEVELOPMENT PROGRAM.

(d)   PATENT RIGHTS shall mean any patent applications filed or patents issuing on the INVENTIONS.

(e)   PRODUCT shall mean the media including cartridges, associated hardware, equipment, and instrumentation developed through the JOINT DEVELOPMENT PROGRAM and deemed commercially feasible for purification of interferon.

(f)   COSTS shall mean all direct costs expended by XYZ and ABC during the JOINT DEVELOPMENT PROGRAM, including costs for PATENT RIGHTS and pro rata costs incurred by ABC and XYZ for employees, but excluding overhead.

Article II.   Joint Development Program

ABC and XYZ agree to use reasonable efforts in the JOINT DEVELOPMENT PROGRAM to develop a PRODUCT. All COSTS shall be shared equally between ABC and XYZ.

Article III. Confidential Information

In the course of the JOINT DEVELOPMENT PROGRAM a party may receive proprietary information. Therefore, each party agrees to treat as confidential all information received from the other party hereunder for a period of five (5) years from the date of this Agreement. This obligation of confidence shall not apply to INFORMATION which:

   (a)   at the time of receipt is in the public domain

   (b)   after receipt becomes part of the public domain by publication, sale of the PRODUCT or otherwise; provided that the information did not enter the public domain by breach of this Agreement by the receiving party;

   (c)   the receiving party can establish by competent written proof dated before the date of this Agreement was in its possession at the time of disclosure and was not acquired, directly or indirectly, from the other party or the JOINT DEVELOPMENT PROGRAM; and

   (d)   is rightfully obtained without restriction by the receiving party from a third party having a legal right to disclose the same.

ABC and XYZ agree that such INFORMATION to which the obligation of confidence applies shall only be used by the receiving party in the JOINT DEVELOPMENT PROGRAM, to effectively develop, manufacture, and sell the PRODUCT or to obtain PATENT RIGHTS.

Article IV. Inventions and Patent Rights

   (a)   ABC and XYZ agree to promptly communicate and disclose to each other all INVENTIONS.

   (b)   ABC and XYZ agree to asset each other in obtaining appropriate PATENT RIGHTS for all patentable INVENTIONS and agree to provide to each other all necessary INFORMATION in their possession in order to obtain such patent rights.

   (c)   A party shall send copies of all proposed U.S. patent applications on INVENTIONS to the other party within thirty (30) days of filing any application.

   (d)   Each party shall retain the ownership of and the right to apply for and obtain PATENT RIGHTS on INVENTIONS of their employees. If an INVENTION is made jointly by employees from both parties, each party shall retain their respective ownership in the PATENT RIGHTS for such INVENTION and the parties shall mutually agree upon the party responsible for obtaining such PATENT RIGHTS.

(e)   A party shall have a nonexclusive, royalty-free license, with the right to sublicense, all PATENT RIGHTS, not owned or jointly owned by that party.

(f)   All foreign filings for PATENT RIGHTS and maintenance thereof are to be mutually agreed upon by the parties.

(g)   All filing, maintenance, and associated costs for PATENT RIGHTS, regardless of ownership, are to be shared equally by the parties.

(h)   If a party does not agree to file and/or maintain a particular PATENT RIGHT, pursuant to paragraph (f) herein; or pay the share of costs, pursuant to paragraph (g) herein, the party forfeits all rights of ownership and license pursuant to paragraphs (d) and (e) herein and said PATENT RIGHT, and shall, if requested by the party, assign said PATENT RIGHT to the other party.

Article V.   Sale and Distribution of Product

(a)   Upon the development of any PRODUCT hereunder, such PRODUCT shall be manufactured exclusively by ABC and sold exclusively by XYZ provided that XYZ issues orders for $100,000 worth of PRODUCT from ABC within one (1) year.

(b)   If within one (1) year of ABC's notification that a PRODUCT developed hereunder is available, XYZ does not proceed pursuant to Article V(a) herein, ABC shall be free to distribute and sell said PRODUCT to anyone.

(c)   If within six (6) months of ABC's notification that a PRODUCT hereunder is available and neither XYZ or ABC is distributing and selling said PRODUCT, the rights to said PRODUCT, including any PATENT RIGHTS covering it, may be licensed or assigned to a third party, providing both ABC and XYZ agree.

Article VI.   Consideration and Costs

(a)   In consideration of the technical and manufacturing expertise of ABC, the exclusive marketing rights granted herein and as contribution toward the costs of the JOINT DEVELOPMENT PROJECT already incurred by ABC, XYZ shall pay to ABC $100,000 upon execution of this Agreement.

(b)   During January and July of each year, the parties shall meet and agree upon the COSTS incurred for the previous six (6) months and an amount agreed upon which one party shall pay the other in conformance with the requirements of Article II.

Article VII.   Term

This Agreement shall begin on July 1, 1986 and continue in full force and effect for two (2) years thereafter; provided that each party continues to exert its reasonable efforts under Article II herein. The provisions of Articles III, IV, and V shall survive any termination of this Agreement.

Article VIII.   Notice

Any notice or other communication under this Agreement shall be sufficiently given if sent in writing by certified or registered mail, postage prepaid, or by telegram, addressed as follows:

To XYZ: _____
                                              _____
                                              _____

To ABC: _____
                                              _____
                                              _____

Either party may change the address set forth above from time to time by written notice given to the other party.

Article IX.   Entire Agreement

This document sets forth the entire agreement between the parties relating to the JOINT DEVELOPMENT PROGRAM and constitutes the only agreement in force and effect between the parties relating to such and it supersedes all other agreements, oral or written, heretofore made between the parties relating to the JOINT DEVELOPMENT PROGRAM. No alterations, modifications, or variations of the terms of this Agreement shall be valid unless made in writing and signed by duly authorized agents of the parties hereto.

Article X.   Applicable Law—Disputes

This Agreement shall be governed by and construed in accordance with the laws of England.

Any dispute or claim concerning the validity, scope, meaning, construction, interpretation, or application of this Agreement shall be finally settled by arbitration in accordance with the regulations in force for the Arbitration Institute of the London Chamber of Commerce and enforceable in any court having jurisdiction thereof.

IN WITNESS WHEREOF, each of the parties hereto has caused this Agreement to be executed on its behalf by its duly authorized officer as of the day and year first above written.

XYZ PRODUCTS COMPANY

By: _____

Title: _____

ABC INCORPORATED

By: _____

Title: _____

Joint Venture Agreement

JOINT VENTURE AGREEMENT

This Agreement, after approval of the Government of Sweden, is made effective as of the 1st day of January, 1986.

between

Biological Testing and Manufacturing Company
a corporation of the State of Delaware, of the U.S.A. with offices at

_____

(hereinafter called "BTM")

and

Stockholm Supply Company
a Swedish company with offices at
Stockholm, Sweden
(hereinafter called "SSC")

WITNESSETH

WHEREAS, BTM has a business in the United States of developing and producing biological chemicals for health related purposes, and SSC has a business in Europe of marketing biological chemicals for health related purposes to clinical institutions and industrial firms in the health field with expertise in commercial packaging of these chemicals, and

WHEREAS, the parties wish to undertake a joint venture within the structure of a European corporation in which each party owns equal shares to import BTM's products, repackage them in accordance with local regulations, and market them throughout European countries, and SSC owns all the stock of a Swedish corporation which the parties wish to use for their operating entity.

NOW, THEREFORE

In consideration of the mutual covenants and agreements hereinafter set forth, BTM and SSC hereby covenant and agree as follows:

I. SSC's Warranties

SSC hereby represents and warrants to BTM that it owns all of the outstanding share capital, represented by shares of _____, which is a joint stock company, validly incorporated and presently existing under the laws of Sweden, but only in the form of a corporate shell without operations (hereinafter called the "Shell Corporation"), that all of the issued shares have been regularly issued and are fully paid and nonassessable, and that the Shell Corporation has no debts, unpaid taxes, unpaid capital reserve requirements, liens, encumbrances, claims, or any other liabilities, actual or contingent, against it. SSC also represents and warrants that there have been no changes in these papers as of the effective date and that it will not permit any changes to be made thereafter except as provided herein.

II. Issuance of Shell Corporation Stock to BTM

SSC agrees within _____ days of the effective date of this Agreement and in consideration of BTM's obligations under it, to transfer to BTM, one-half of all outstanding shares of the Shell Corporation, all of which are now held by SSC, or in the alternative to cause the Shell Corporation, in consideration of it being a beneficiary under this Agreement, to issue the same number of shares to BTM as are outstanding before this issuance. In the event that the shares presently outstanding plus the shares to be issued to BTM exceed the shares that the Shell Corporation is authorized to issue under its present Articles of Incorporation, SSC agrees to cause the Shell Corporation to amend its Articles to provide for the increase in the number of outstanding shares. All of these shares shall be fully paid and nonassessable. SSC agrees that it will not permit any additional shares to be issued except as provided herein.

III. Initial Joint Venture Stockholders Meeting and Election of Directors

Within ____ days after BTM receives one-half of the then outstanding shares of the Shell Corporation, BTM and SSC agree to waive notice and meet at a duly constituted stockholders meeting to be held at SSC's offices set forth above to implement the joint venture. At or before this meeting SSC agrees to cause all of the existing directors to submit their written resignations to the stockholders. Thereafter, BTM and SSC each agree to nominate an equal number of directors, not less than three nor more than five for a total of not less than six nor more than ten directors and to vote them into office. Unless one or more of the BTM nominees are residents of Sweden, or are European Economic Community citizens, the residency requirements for directors, if any, shall be satisfied by the SSC nominee directors.

IV. Articles of Incorporation

At the initial stockholder's meeting, BTM and SSC shall vote to change and cause their nominee directors to implement the changes to the Articles of Incorporation in a form substantially following customary forms in Sweden, and as agreed upon between BTM and SSC, which articles shall, however, include express provisions to the following effect:

(a) To change the name of the Shell Corporation to _____, (hereinafter called the "Joint Venture Company").

(b) To set forth as a main purpose of the Joint Venture Company the importation, repackaging, and marketing of BTM's products in Western Europe.

(c) To provide for the same number of directors as determined and elected under paragraph III. Each director shall serve for a term of two (2) years,provided that during that term, a director may be removed with or without cause and replaced by majority vote of the shares of the party that nominated that director, upon written notice to the Joint Venture Company, Attention of the President, all of the directors and the other stockholders without calling a special or regular stockholders meeting.

(d) Control of the management and policies of the Joint Venture Company shall be vested in its Board of Directors. No decision of the Board shall be made except by resolution in respect of which a majority of the directors, including at least two nominees of BTM and of SSC, shall have recorded an affirmative vote.

(e) To increase the authorized equity capital of the Joint Venture Company to _____ consisting of _____ shares of _____ par value, the increase in the number of shares over the amount issued and outstanding to BTM and SSC at the time of the meeting to be subscribed to in equal shares by BTM and SSC, with the Board of Directors to decide when and in what increments the capital shall be paid in by each of the parties.

(f) Further increases in equity capital will only be made to the extent necessary to permit increased borrowings by the Joint Venture Company for the purpose of financing its business of distributing BTM's products in Western Europe.

(g) Any additional issues of stock to be made by the Joint Venture Company shall be offered in the first instance to the initial stockholders in proportion to their holdings of stock at the initial joint venture stockholders meeting set forth in paragraph III.

(h)   All shares issued by the Joint Venture Company shall carry equal voting rights. Each share shall have one vote.

(i)   The Board of Directors shall hold a meeting at least once in every six (6) months following the effective date.

(j)   All amendments to the Articles of Incorporation shall require the affirmative vote of at least three-quarters ($\frac{3}{4}$) of all outstanding shares.

(k)   Shares of the Joint Venture Company shall not be transferable by a shareholder without initially offering them to BTM or SSC at the same price at which it is proposed that such shares be sold to the nonshareholder. The offeree shall have thirty (30) days in which to decide whether or not to accept such offer. In the event that the offeree does not accept such offer, then the offering shareholder shall be free to sell such shares to the nonshareholder at the price specified, provided that such sale shall take place within ninety (90) days of the date on which the offer is first made to BTM or SSC, always provided, however, that a shareholder may always transfer its shares to a wholly owned subsidiary or BTM may transfer its shares to its parent corporation of New York, New York.

V.   Appointment of Officers

The Board of Directors of the Joint Venture Company will appoint all of its officers and auditors. The parties agree to instruct their nominee directors to vote for a Chairman of the Board who is acceptable to both parties, to vote for a BTM nominee director designated by BTM as President and Chief Executive Officer and for an SSC nominee for Executive Vice President for Sales and Marketing. The parties agree to cause each of their nominee directors to vote for two (2) auditors with equal capacity for the Joint Venture Company, one designated by BTM, one by SSC. Both parties agree to consult with each other regarding such appointments prior to making a definite decision.

VI.   Distributor Agreement

The parties agree to cause their nominee directors to approve and instruct the officers to accept and execute Exhibit A on behalf of the Joint Venture Company. BTM agrees to have Exhibit A executed on its behalf.

VII.   Confidential Obligations

It is anticipated that during the implementation of the Distributor Agreement of paragraph VI, technical information that the parties consider to be proprietary and trade secrets will be disclosed to each other. Each party agrees to hold in confidence technical information received from the other party or from the Joint Venture Company for a period that is the later of the termination of the Distribution Agreement or seven (7) years after disclosure, provided that this confidential obligation shall not apply to:

(a) information readily available to the public in the same form, either at the time of disclosure or after by publication except by breach of this Agreement.

(b) information that can be shown by written evidence dated before the disclosure to have been in the receiving party's possession before the disclosure, and

(c) information received by a third party who did not breach a confidential obligation by disclosing it to the receiving party.

VIII. Financing

(a) It is also anticipated that in the normal course of events, the authorized capital to be paid in by BTM and SSC under paragraph IV(d) will be sufficent for the purchase, importation, repackaging, and distribution of BTM's products throughout European countries and the associated organizing and administration expenses for a period long enough for the Joint Venture Company to build up a surplus that will enable it to finance its own activities thereafter, either wholly through its surplus and earnings or with the addition of borrowings.

(b) In the event that circumstances in the opinion of at least three-quarters ($\frac{3}{4}$) of the directors justify borrowings of some kind to further finance the continuance of the business of distributing BTM's products in Europe, BTM and SSC shall be equally responsible for the debt incurred, if incurred in the normal course of business according to this Agreement.

(c) It shall be the responsibility of SSC to assist the Joint Venture Company in obtaining Swedish borrowings authorized by the directors and of BTM to assist the Joint Venture Company in obtaining Dollar borrowings, provided that the other party shall furnish any reasonable amount of support to the assisting party in negotiating the loans.

(d) In the event that the loans are made by BTM and SSC, the interest rate that each shall charge shall be at the prime or base rate on corporate loans at the close of business on the last business day preceding the date of the loan at large New York City and Stockholm money center commercial banks, respectively, plus two percent (2%).

(e) In the event that loans made to the Joint Venture Company by third parties require a guaranty of payment, BTM and SSC agree that they shall be guaranteed by BTM and SSC on a joint and several basis. Accordingly, in the event of nonpayment by the Joint Venture Company, the lender shall be entitled to obtain full payment under the guaranty either from BTM or SSC and such guarantor making such payment shall be entitled to obtain fifty percent (50%) of such amount from the other guarantor.

IX. Credit Information and Hiring Assistance

(a) SSC shall upon request of the Joint Venture Company furnish general financial advice and available credit rating information regarding prospective customers as well as making credit investigation of specific proposed customers where it has no credit rating information available.

(b) SSC shall also, upon request, assist the Joint Venture Company in recruiting personnel other than as provided for above, in developing customer contacts and setting up regional sales offices, if required, and in making necessary contacts with national and local government officials for the purpose of introducing and promoting BTM's products throughout the countries of Europe.

X. Governmental Approval

SSC agrees, to the extent required, to submit this Agreement promptly to the Ministry of Commerce for an investment permit to BTM. SSC agrees to give BTM prompt notice of the Ministry's approval accompanied by the permit or of the Ministry's disapproval. If this Agreement in its entirety is not approved by the Ministry of Commerce by November 30, 1986, then the Agreement shall be void and of no further effect, unless BTM gives SSC written notice of any extension of time or changed conditions to obtain the approval.

XI. Dividend Policy of Joint Venture Company

It is agreed that after an earned surplus of   has been accumulated, fifty percent (50%) of the net profits of the Joint Venture Company (after payment of applicable taxes and satisfaction of the legal reserve requirement) in each year shall thereafter be distributed by way of dividends to the stockholders unless otherwise agreed.

XII. Termination of Distributor Agreement

Upon any termination or expiration of the Distributor Agreement of paragraph VI, the parties agree to dissolve the Joint Venture Company and distribute its assets to the stockholders.

XIII. Liquidation

If the Joint Venture Company has any liabilities or debts at the time of its dissolution and its assets are not sufficient to discharge them in full, then BTM and SSC shall each pay in any unpaid portion of the capital of the Joint Venture Company previously subscribed by it and such liabilities and debts shall be discharged and paid out of the assets of the Joint Venture Company before any distribution of capital is made to BTM and SSC. SSC agrees to assist BTM in obtaining repatriation of BTM's share of any distribution.

In witness whereof the parties hereto have caused this Agreement to be made and executed by their duly authorized officers as of the day first above written.

BIOLOGICAL TESTING AND MANUFACTURING COMPANY

STOCKHOLM SUPPLY COMPANY

Distributor Agreement

DISTRIBUTOR AGREEMENT

This Agreement is made effective as of the 1st day of January, 1986.

between

Biological Testing and Manufacturing Company
a State of Delaware, United States of America Corporation
with offices at:

(hereinafter called "BTM")

and

Stockholm Supply Company
a Swedish company with offices at:
Stockholm, Sweden
(hereinafter called "Distributor")

WITNESSETH

WHEREAS, BTM is in the business in the United States of developing and producing biological chemicals for health related purposes and the Distributor, which has been organized for the business of marketing biological chemicals for health related purposes to clinical institutions and industrial firms in the health field in Europe, wishes to distribute BTM's product line in European countries, which is a market that BTM wishes to supply.

NOW, THEREFORE

In consideration of the premises and of the mutual terms and conditions hereinafter set forth, BTM and the Distributor hereby covenant and agree as follows:

1.   Distributorship Appointment and Territory: BTM hereby appoints the Distributor and the Distributor hereby accepts the appointment as BTM's exclusive distributor subject to the exception of paragraph 11(d) in Austria, Belgium, Denmark, The Federal Republic of Germany, Finland, France, Greece, Ireland, Italy, Lichtenstein, Luxembourg, Monaco, the Netherlands, Norway, Portugal, Spain, Sweden, Switzerland, and the United Kingdom but not elsewhere, (hereinafter called the "Sales Terri-

tory") for sales of the BTM products described in the BTM Catalog Price Schedule effective December 1985 (hereinafter called "Special Product(s)"), as the list may be amended by written notice from time to time.

2. Sales Policy: The market for Special Products appears to be essentially for medical research by industrial firms, universities, and clinical institutions and for treatment of patients by clinical institutions. Since approval of Special Products for patient treatment, human and animal, by the individual pharmaceutical regulatory authorities within the jurisdictions of the Sales Territory is anticipated to involve individual time consuming procedures and tests, which are not anticipated for research uses, the main thrust of the sales effort for Special Products should be directed towards medical research.

3. Quality Control: Special Products are manufactured to high quality standards consistent with their intended purpose in the health related field. Most of them have a definite shelf life both before and after being radioactively activated or "labeled" after which they should not be used. BTM agrees to inform the Distributor of those products which do have a definite shelf life and its duration before and after being activated. The Distributor agrees to refrain from altering or tampering with Special Products in any way other than with respect to their packaging and labeling and to withdraw from sale any Special Products that cannot be reasonably used within the shelf life specified by BTM, and to dispose of them in accordance with all applicable regulations for the disposal of chemical and nuclear waste including those of the European Economic Community, "EEC," and of the European Free Trade Association, "EFTA." The Distributor upon reasonable notice shall grant BTM or its representatives access to the facilities used by Distributor and its agents for the manufacture, storage, sale and disposal of Special Products to inspect them and verify their condition.

4. Safety, Health, and Other Regulations: It is understood that safety, health, pharmaceutical, and other regulations in the various jurisdictions of the Sales Territory including the EEC and EFTA as well as language and measurement systems differ from those in the United States and to some extent throughout the Sales Territory. The Distributor agrees to comply with all such regulations concerning the sale, use and disposal of Special Products in the Sales Territory and hold BTM harmless from any litigation and claims that may be instituted for failure to comply therewith. For protection of each of the parties in that respect, the Distributor will procure and maintain general liability insurance in the sum of One Million Dollars in U.S. currency ($1,000,000) combined single limit for

bodily injury and/or property damage each occurrence with BTM named as a co-insured under the policy. The Distributor further agrees to procure for BTM a certificate of insurance evidencing such coverage and expressly undertakes to maintain and not to cancel such coverage except upon thirty (30) days notice to BTM.

5. Notice of Regulations: The Distributor shall keep BTM informed in writing of all administrative, technical, pharmaceutical, and other health related laws and regulations applicable to the Special Products in the Sales Territory, including those of the EEC and EFTA, together with its recommendations on how to comply with them on sales of Special Products in each jurisdiction. BTM, however, shall be the sole judge of whether or not it will modify any of the Special Products or components therefor in order to conform with the Distributor's interpretation of such laws and regulations, and BTM shall be under no obligation to modify any of such Special Products or components, provided that the Distributor may refuse to sell a specific Special Product in a jurisdiction if it in good faith believes based upon substantiated evidence that a Special Product does not comply with the jurisdiction's regulations.

6. Trademarks:

(a) BTM and the Distributor shall agree upon the form and usage of a new trademark to be applied to the packages of all Special Products to be resold in Europe under this Agreement, hereinafter called the "Licensed Trademark.") The Distributor agrees that BTM or BTM's designee shall be the proprietor of the Licensed Trademark, subject to a license to the Distributor to apply it to the packaging.

(b) The Distributor agrees for itself, its subdistributors, dealers, representatives, and successors that any use by it of a trademark on a Special Product, other than the Distributor's name and designation as distributor, shall inure to the benefit of BTM or BTM's designee as the proprietor both at common law and under the civil law and for registration of the trademark and that it and they will not assert any proprietorship rights of its own to, nor do anything adversely affecting the value of such trademarks.

(c) The Distributor agrees that it will assist BTM or its designee in making applications for registration of the Distributor as a registered user of the Licensed Trademark and any other trademarks used on Special Products in countries that have registered user requirements and execute or have executed upon written request of

BTM or its designee, proper documents prepared by BTM or its designee to accomplish this and protect and enforce these trademarks.

7. Repackaging: The Distributor shall, as required, repackage the Special Products or modify the packaging in its packaging facility to show the shelf life, bear the Licensed Trademark, conform to each local, EEC, and EFTA regulation in the Sales Territory, and to indicate the Distributor as the distributor of the Special Products, provided that except for the tradename and trademark "Biological Testing and Manufacturing Company" as the manufacturer, which shall remain on a modified package or be added to a new package, all other BTM trademarks, if any, shall be deleted from the packages. The Distributor shall obtain BTM's prior written consent, which shall not be unreasonably withheld, to all new and modified packages including the labels and printing.

8. Confidential Obligations: The Distributor acknowledges that all technical information and know-how relating to Special Products disclosed to the Distributor under this Agreement is proprietary information owned by BTM and constitutes trade secrets of BTM. The Distributor agrees to have all of this technical information, except that which is readily available to the public in the same form in which it is disclosed to the Distributor, held in confidence, and use it only for the purpose of carrying out this Agreement. This obligation shall survive any termination or expiration of this Agreement.

9. Subdistributors and Dealers: The Distributor's rights under paragraph 1 are not assignable or otherwise transferable, provided, however, that the Distributor may appoint subdistributors and dealers in the Sales Territory for the purpose of selling and distributing Special Products. The Distributor agrees to advise BTM of the names and addresses of any proposed subdistributors or dealers and the appointment thereof shall be subject to the approval of BTM in writing. The Distributor agrees to enter into written, enforceable contracts with any subdistributor and dealer to perform or put the Distributor in position to perform all of the obligations of the Distributor to BTM under this Agreement. Upon execution of such agreements, true copies shall be promptly sent to BTM for its approval, which approval shall not be unreasonably withheld. The agreements shall provide that they shall not take effect until approved by BTM. The Distributor further agrees that unless BTM otherwise instructs the Distributor, all orders to BTM for Special Products shall be placed through the Distrib-

utor, and the Distributor shall be responsible for payment therefor. The Distributor shall not create or imply any obligation whatsoever of BTM to any such subdistributor or dealer.

10. Marketing Duties of the Distributor: The Distributor hereby agrees:

(a) to exert its best efforts starting on the Effective Date to solicit sales from all potential purchasers in the Sales Territory through a sufficient staff of qualified, financially sound, reliable employees, subdistributors, dealers, and other representatives, and to build up the use of the Special Products and displace any competitive products in the Sales Territory.

(b) to establish and maintain a suitable place or places of business within the Sales Territory to efficiently serve the entire territory.

(c) to purchase Special Products and repackage them strictly in accordance with the terms and conditions of this Agreement, so as to conform with the regulations of each country of the Sales Territory where they are distributed and of the EEC and EFTA and conduct its business in accordance with the highest business standards refraining from any act that may reflect adversely upon the business, integrity, and goodwill of BTM.

(d) to provide instructional and other necessary services for all Special Products in the Sales Territory through technically qualified and responsible personnel in accordance with practices, procedures, and standards that may be established by BTM and communicated to the Distributor from time to time through various instructional communications.

(e) to purchase and maintain in the proper environment, a sufficient quantity and variety of Special Products with due consideration for shelf lives, and to provide prompt and efficient service on all orders for Special Products in the Sales Territory.

(f) to obtain all proper and necessary clearances, exemptions, permits, import and nuclear licenses, and other approvals, if any, required by any agency of the governments or multinational authorities in the Sales Territory in which this Agreement is to operate in connection with the performance of this Agreement there (other than Registered User Agreements) and any work and residence permits required for BTM technical personnel who are requested by the

Distributor to lend technical and sales support in the Sales Territory. The Distributor agrees to register this Agreement with the EEC and any country of the Sales Territory, whose registration is required, and to give BTM prompt written notice of the final approvals of any approvals so required with their effective dates. In the event that any of the terms of this Agreement are disallowed in any country of the Sales Territory or by any of the multinational authorities, the Distributor shall forward to BTM a true copy of the disallowing document, with an English translation if in some other language.

(g) to submit copies of all published and proposed advertising and other promotional literature, quarterly reports of the needs of customers for the Special Products, a review of the sales details including prices for the preceding quarter, the proposed sales activity for the next quarter with an updated forecast of sales for the next twelve months, the current inventory and shelf lives, and any other information that is likely to be of interest to BTM in relation to the marketing of the Special Products.

11. BTM's Marketing Assistance:

(a) BTM agrees to provide the Distributor, to the extent available, with reasonable quantities of sales literature, promotional materials, instructional manuals, and other technical and descriptive data relating to the Special Products.

(b) BTM may from time to time give the Distributor notice of additions to its product lines and upon the Distributor's written request they shall be deemed added to Schedule I, which shall be amended to such extent without further action, and they shall become Special Products.

(c) BTM, upon written request of the Distributor, shall make available for reasonable periods in Europe a qualified technical representative to consult with, advise, and assist the Distributor in making sales of Special Products. The Distributor shall pay BTM Two Hundred Fifty Dollars ($250.00) in U.S. currency for each day or part thereof including travel time for each such BTM representative plus living and traveling expenses including first-class round trip air transportation. These amounts shall be payable within thirty (30) days of the date of the invoice billing for the services.

(d) BTM will refer to the Distributor inquiries and orders concerning the Special Products received directly from customers in the Sales Territory, provided that should a customer in the Sales Territory express a strong preference to deal directly with BTM on one or more Special Products, BTM may make the sale, subject to a service commission in U.S. currency to be paid to the Distributor within sixty (60) days of the sale, of ten percent (10%) of BTM's international sales price f.o.b. loading dock, City, State, U.S.A. charged to the customer, with a copy of a pro forma setting forth the sale. In such event, the Distributor agrees to lend support to the customer in the use of the Special Product in the Sales Territory according to its regular marketing procedures.

12. Special Product Prices: The prices of Special Products to the Distributor shall be determined by subtracting a _____ percent (___%) from the price f.o.b. loading dock, City, State, U.S.A. set forth in the catalog and brochures of Schedule I and by adding the cost of export packaging. BTM will prepay for Special Product's account any taxes, freight, shipping papers, consular fees, and insurance to Stockholm. The prices for Special Products are subject to change on the date determined in BTM's sole discretion, but the changes shall only be effective with respect to this Agreement after written notice to the Distributor on the later of the date of the invoice or the date on which the change is stated by BTM in the notice to be effective. All orders that are received by BTM prior to the effective date of the change so determined and that specify shipment within ninety (90) days thereafter shall be invoiced to the Distributor at a value determined by applying the _____percent discount to the last previous effective price.

13. Purchase Orders:

(a) The Distributor shall submit its purchase orders for Special Products in writing to BTM at its City, State, U.S.A. address given in the heading of this Agreement.

(b) The Distributor may at its option place orders by telex communication, provided that they are promptly confirmed by a mailed writing.

(c) Purchase orders shall be subject to written acceptance by BTM at City, State, U.S.A., and BTM shall promptly process the accepted orders.

(d) Due to the nature of the product, delivery schedules stated by BTM upon acceptance of an order are estimates and not binding and any delay in delivery shall not give rise to any damages whatsoever nor require BTM to take back any Special Product so delivered. However, a specific delivery schedule may be required by the Distributor for a particular order and, once explicitly accepted as such by BTM, it shall be binding upon BTM, provided that BTM shall not be responsible for delays caused by strikes, shortage of materials, civil strife, acts of God, or any events or acts beyond the control of BTM.

(e) Cancellation or modification of any orders or portions of orders after acceptance by BTM shall only be with BTM's written consent and if allowed will be subject to reasonable reassay and handling charges according to BTM's International Sales Policy at the time.

(f) BTM will endeavor to make Special Products available in the quantities and at the times specified by the Distributor in its purchase orders, but in case of a shortage in the Products, BTM reserves the right to allocate available supplies to its various distributors and customers in such a way as it may reasonably determine.

(g) BTM may at any time in its sole discretion limit, change, or discontinue the manufacture and supply of any of the Special Products without prior notice to the Distributor but will inform the Distributor of the discontinuance.

14.   Payments for Distributorship Products: The Distributor shall make payment for Special Products to BTM at its address above in United States Dollars upon delivery, port of entry, Sweden or upon such other terms as are agreed to in writing from time to time between the parties.

15.   Audit: The Distributor shall keep and permit to be examined by BTM or its representatives at all reasonable times during the period of this Agreement and for two years thereafter, books and records containing complete and accurate data, which may be extracted and copied, to enable determination of the amounts payable and information to be supplied and other such particulars as may be reasonably required by BTM to determine the operation of the Distributor under this Agreement.

16.   Termination and Effective Date:

(a) Unless sooner terminated as provided below, this Agreement shall begin on the effective date first set forth above, subject to the final approval of any approvals, if required, by the EEC, EFTA, and of the individual governments of the Sales Territory and continue until December 31, 1990, and if not terminated by either party before then, shall continue thereafter for two year periods until terminated upon ninety (90) days written notice prior to the end of any such two year periods by either party for any reason whatsoever, unless otherwise terminated as provided below.

(b)   This Agreement shall terminate immediately upon the Distributor becoming insolvent, being adjudicated bankrupt, liquidating, taking the benefit of any act in force or legally permissable procedure for the relief of insolvent debtors, upon the recision of any approvals provided for in this Agreement, upon the nationalization of the Distributor by any governmental authority or of any part of its stock or assets, upon any of the exports or transfer to the prohibited countries set forth in paragraph 18, without the required authorization, or upon written notice to the Distributor by BTM if the Distributor ceases active and diligent promotion of sales of Special Products throughout the sales territory, or following any other breach such as failure to pay invoices or to submit reports when due that is not corrected within thirty (30) days after written notice of the breach is given to the Distributor.

(c)   Upon termination of this Agreement the Distributor covenants to return all of the technical information relating to Special Products and all copies thereof and make no further use of them and to take all action required to remove any reference to BTM from all advertising, signs, letterheads, offices, and all other materials bearing it.

(d)   Termination of this Agreement for any reason shall not relieve either party of any obligation accruing prior to termination. Accrued invoice amounts due shall be paid as though this Agreement were not terminated.

17.   Blocked Currency: In the event that foreign exchange restrictions or government recision or expiration of the approvals for the remittances provided for in this Agreement, or any other reason makes it impossible to make remittance in United States Currency, the obligations for which have accrued according to the terms of this Agreement, then the Distributor shall promptly notify BTM of such event with full particulars and deposit all moneys due, to the credit of BTM or another BTM designee,

in the local currency in an interest bearing account at a banking branch of any United States Bank or Trust Company.

18.   Assignment: This Agreement shall be binding upon and inure to the benefit of BTM and to the assigns and the successors of that part of the business of BTM to which it pertains but shall not be assignable by the Distributor nor pass by operation of law to the Distributor's successors or representatives in liquidation or bankruptcy without BTM's prior written consent. Any proposed assignment of this Agreement by the Distributor or succession to its rights otherwise than with BTM's written consent shall be void and of no effect.

19.   U.S. Department of Commerce Mandated Regulations: In further consideration of the distributorship appointment, the Distributor covenants that it will not export or transfer or knowingly permit the export or transfer of the Special Products or any technical information relating to Special Products that may be supplied to it or that may be supplied by BTM, or of related information and data based upon or utilizing this information or of products or materials incorporating this information to North Korea, Vietnam, Cambodia, Cuba, or other country where authorization is required without obtaining the prior authorization of the Office of Export Control Authorization of the United States Department of Commerce.

20.   Law of Agreement: This Agreement has been made in contemplation of the laws of the state of New York of the United States of America and shall be construed in accordance with and governed by such laws.

21.   Notices: All notices, submissions, delivered, approvals, statements, and payments provided for in this Agreement, subject to the provisions of paragraph 13(b) with respect to purchase orders, shall be in or be accompanied by a writing and be effective as of the fifth (5th) day following the day on which they are deposited with the postal authorities concerned to be sent air mail, postage prepaid, to the address of the parties set forth at the start of this Agreement or at such other address as they may designate upon like notice. If a notice period is specified herein, it shall run from the fifth day following the date deposited with the postal authorities as described in this paragraph.

22.   Agreement Changes: This Agreement and the Joint Venture Agreement between BTM and Stockholm Supply Company of Stockholm, Sweden constitute the entire agreement and understanding of the parties and supersede all prior agreements and understandings with respect to the

subject matter hereof, whether written or oral. No modification or claimed waive of any of the provisions hereof shall be valid unless in writing and signed by authorized representatives of the party against whom such modification or waiver is sought to be enforced.

IN WITNESS WHEREOF, the parties hereto have caused this Agreement to be made and executed by their duly authorized officers as of the date first above written.

Biological Testing & Manufacturing Co.

_____

Stockholm Supply Company

_____

Consultant's Agreement

CONSULTANT'S AGREEMENT

This AGREEMENT is executed as of _____, 1986, between GIL-BERT JONES (hereinafter called CONSULTANT) and ABC BROWN DIVISION (hereinafter called ABC).

WHEREAS, the parties desire to cooperate in the development and marketing of the Jones' basketball practice system under the terms of a license agreement between the parties of even date herewith.

NOW, THEREFORE, in consideration of the mutual covenants and promises herein contained, the parties hereto agree as follows:

Article I.   Statement of Work

CONSULTANT shall to the best of his abilities cooperate with ABC consulting on the design and marketing of the Jones basketball practice system and basketball throwing machines (these services hereinafter called the WORK.)

Article II.   Payment

For performing the WORK, CONSULTANT shall be paid $200.00 per day for the days he spend in actual work authorized by ABC plus a royalty as provided in the aforementioned license agreement and ABC shall reimburse CONSULTANT for his actual expenses that are approved in advance in writing by ABC.

Article III.   Term

The term of this Agreement shall be one year from its effective date of January 1, 1986, unless sooner terminated as provided herein, or extended by mutual agreement in writing. Any other modification of the term of this Agreement shall not be binding upon ABC unless accomplished by a formal written supplement to this Agreement.

Article IV.   Reports

CONSULTANT shall furnish reports to ABC concerning the work and activities of CONSULTANT under this Agreement. Said reports shall be in such form and at such times as agreed upon by the parties hereto.

Article V.   Personal Services

A.   The WORK provided for herein shall be performed personally by CONSULTANT and no other person shall be engaged by CONSULTANT for such WORK. Provided, however, that this paragraph shall not apply to incidental services needed by CONSULTANT to assist him in performance of this Agreement and provided at his own expense unless such expense is approved in writing in advance by ABC.

B.   Neither this Agreement, nor any interest herein or claim hereunder, shall be assigned or transferred by CONSULTANT to any party or parties without the written authorization of ABC.

C.   This Agreement is made with the understanding that CONSULTANT is an independent contractor and not an employee of ABC.

Article VI.   Patent, Copyright, and Data Rights

A.   CONSULTANT shall promptly disclose in writing to ABC all ideas, inventions, improvements, and developments relative to the Jones basketball practice system and ball throwing machine that are originated by him in connection with his WORK under this Agreement. CONSULTANT further agrees that all such ideas, inventions, improvements, and developments shall be included in the aforementioned license agreement.

B.   In respect to all copyrightable material, first produced or composed by him in connection with the performance of his WORK under this Agreement, CONSULTANT hereby conveys to ABC the sole and exclusive right to transfer or obtain for itself or its designee any and all rights to such copyrightable material as it shall deem appropriate in its sole and exclusive discretion, agrees to and hereby assents to all such transfers, and agrees to assist in the registration and/or transfer of all such copyrights by ABC or its designee in any manner as aforesaid.

Article VII.   Termination

This Agreement may be terminated by either party by giving to the other party thirty (30) days written notice. Such termination shall be addressed to CONSULTANT at: _____

_____

_____

Upon such termination, CONSULTANT shall be reimbursed for all his approved expenses incurred prior to such termination. Termination shall not affect CONSULTANTS obligations under Articles IV, VI, and VII.

Article VIII.   Secrecy

CONSULTANT agrees that for a period of five (5) years after conclusion of this Agreement, he will keep confidential any confidential information of ABC Brown Division obtained by him during the period in which this Agreement is in force and will refrain from using, publishing or revealing such information acquired by him in the course of this WORK without the written consent of ABC, excepting only information (1) that was known to CONSULTANT prior to its disclosure by ABC, (2) that becomes known to the public without fault of CONSULTANT, (3) that is disclosed to CONSULTANT by a third party in good faith, or (4) that is specifically released from confidential status by ABC.

IN WITNESS WHEREOF, the parties hereto have executed this Agreement as of the date and year first above written.

By: _____
Gilbert Jones

By: _____
ABC Brown Division

Index

Abandoned inventions, 84
Abstract of disclosure, 144
Addition, 83
Advanced Refractory Technologies Inc., 4, 5
Affidavits, under sections 8 & 15, 189
Aggregation, 82
A. J. Associates, 76
Amendment, 164
American Intellectual Property Law Assoc.,
    19
American National Standards Institute,
    139
AMF American, 9
AMF Wyatt, 9
Anatomy of patent, 89
Antecedents, 124
Application:
  continuation, 167
  divisional, 167
Arbitrary marks, 188
Arbitrary word, 184
Arbitration, 232
Assignment search, 72
Attorney, when to use, 22
Attorney-client interview, 23
Attorney's fees, 250

Background of invention, 93, 146
Bacon, F. R., Jr., 56
Bacon and Thomas, 67
Baner, Don, 65
Banner, Donald, 33, 34, 35, 37
Banner, Birch, McKie and Becket, 33
Battelle Development Corporation, 5, 64

Best embodiment, 152
Best mode, 153
Blakely, Keith, 4, 6
Broad coverage, importance of, 32
Brownell, Karl, 5
Bureau of the Census, 58
Business negotiations, 211
Business plan, 55, 61
Business Week, 214
Butler, Thomas W., Jr., 52, 54, 56, 60

Cancellation, 190
Carborundum Company, 4, 5, 34, 84, 205,
    216, 220
Carlson, Chester, 5, 6
Celanese Corporation, 74
Cepuritis, Talivaldis, 81, 118, 120, 124,
    125, 129, 130
Chanin, Bernie, 248
Claims, 99
  dependent, 124
  drafting, 116
  form of, 108
  formal requirements, 117
  generic, 44, 121
  Jepson, 112
  Markush, 113, 121
  method, 78
  purpose of, 104
  scope of, 103
  species, 44, 121
  subcombination, 127
  types of, 109
  varying scope, 129

Classification, 160
Closing the sale, 244
Coined word, 184
Collection search, 71
Combination claims, 111
Compere, Richard H., 182, 183, 185, 187, 188, 191
Composition of matter, 78
Computer search, 72
Concurrent proceeding, 191
Confidential:
    agreement, 269
    information, 46
Conflicts with competitors, 185
Connecticut Venture Management Corp., 61
Constructive reduction to practice, 45
Consultants' agreement, 323–326
Continuation application, 167
Continuation-in-part, 162
Contracts, 225
    employment, 45
    government, 45
    key issues, 226
Contractual negotiations, 180
Contributions, others, 48
Convention period, 86
Copyrights, 15
Cost effectiveness, 177
Court of Appeals for the Federal Circuit, 31
Creativity, 255
Cushman, Darby and Cushman, 161
Customer-oriented, 237

Damages, 250
Dann, C. Marshall, 13, 14, 19
Dann, Dorfman, Herrell and Skillman, 13, 19
Dealing with people, 240
Debriefing, 209
Declaration, 155
Declining royalty, 229
Dependent claims, 124
Deposition, 253
Description of alternatives, 153
Description of drawings, 151
Description of your invention, 151
Descriptive marks, 184, 188
Design patents, 79, 138
Determining patentability, 75
Deutsch, Franz, 9

Developing a team, 177
Development and Use of Patent Classification Systems, 160
"Directory of Registered Patent Attorneys and Agents," 20
Discounted cash flow, 52
Discovery, 253
Dispute resolution, 252
    alternative forms, 252
Distinctive mark, 184
Distributor agreement, 311–322
Divisional application, 167
Doberman approach, 242
Drafting claims, 116
Drawings, formal requirements, 135
Dressler, Goldsmith, Shore, Sutker & Milnamow, 81
Dun & Bradstreet, 201
DuPont, 4

Electrical symbols, 139
Elements, indispensable, 119
Embodiment, preferred, 63
Employer's facilities, use of, 47
Employment contracts, 45
Enforcement of your patent, 232
Engineering notebook, 7, 40
Environment:
    and large corporation, 215
    for small business, 214
Environmental influence, 213
Erlandson, Paul, 61
Examiner, interview with, 165
Ex parte Marga Faulstick, 81
Experimental use, 85

Fanciful marks, 188
Federal trademark, 15
Ferris, John, 82
Fie, Larry, 9
File wrapper estoppel, 163
Filing receipts, 159
Final fee, 169
Final rejection, 166
Fisher, Clarence M., 98, 148
Flow charts, 138
Foreign filing, 172
Forms of diligence, 231
Fraud, effect of, 170
From Technical Professional to Corporate Manager, 36
Functional language, 120

General description of invention, 149
Generic claim, 44
Generic marks, 187
Gentner, John, 9
Gerber, Dr. H. Joseph, 30, 33
Gerber Scientific Inc., 30
Getting appointment, 206
Getting started, 259
Gilson, Jerome, 192
Girard, Joe, 56
Government contracts, 45
Graham, Betty, 10
Graham v. *John Deere*, 80
"Guidelines for the Preparation of Patent
    Abstracts," 146

Holt, William, 83
Howe, H. Gordon, 197, 199, 202
How to Sell Anything to Anybody, 56
Hymo, Lawrence A., 161, 163, 165, 166

Identifying and evaluating ideas, 7
Implementing agreement, 244
Incontestability, 190
Increased damages, 250
Indispensable elements, 119
Information disclosure, 161
Infringement search, 70
Initial approach, 205
Initial interview, 207
Initial presentation, 201
Innovation, 52
Integrity, rule of, 37
Interference, 44, 167
Interrogatories, 253
Intrapreneuring, 202
Introduction:
    definite, 123
    indefinite, 123
Invention, 5
    abandoned, 84
    assignment of, 46
    developing your, 35
    nonstatutory, 113
Inventions and Their Protection, 101
Invention submission form, 265
Invention submission letter, 263
Issuance of patent, 170

Jackson, Auzville, Jr., 76, 77, 78, 80, 86
Jackson, John, 34
Jepson claim, 112

Joint development agreement, 297–302
Joint venture agreement, 303–310

Kennecott Copper Company, 4
Kenney, J. Ernest, 67, 69, 70, 71, 72
Key elements for success, 212
Klitzman, Maurice H., 44
Kreidl, Dr. Norbert, 81
Kroc, Ray, 256

Lacey, William, 134, 135
Lawyer(s), 17
    anatomy of, 18
    how to select, 19
Lee, Smith and Zickert, 90
Lee, William Marshall, 90, 91, 92, 96, 98,
    100, 101
Legal Care for Your Software, 16
Legal issues, 231
Letters Patent, 11
License agreement:
    exclusive, 273
    nonexclusive, 281
Lieberstein, Stanley H., 20, 39, 40, 41, 42,
    43, 45, 46, 47, 48, 49, 177, 238, 239,
    249
Likelihood of confusion, 186
Liquid Paper, 11
Listerine, 226
Litigation, 245
    and entrepreneur, 249
    and large corporation, 247
Little, Larry, 10, 222
Lost profits, 250
Luedeka and Neely, 76

Machine, 78
Management techniques, 51
Managing new development, 54
Manual of Patent Classification, 60, 65, 66,
    68
Manufacture, 78
Manufacturing, sales and trademark
    agreement, 285
Market evaluation, 55
Market research, 56
Markush claim, 113, 121
Martindale Hubbell, 20
Means plus function, 111
Meltzer, Robert, 82
Method claims, 78
Meyer Blanke Company, 10, 222

Miccioli, Bruno, 184
Minimum royalties, 230
Mini-trial, 252
Modern Plastics, 198
Moody's International Index, 197
Murtha, Emmett, 237, 238, 240, 241, 243
Murtz, Hari M., 110

Negotiating attitude, 237
Negotiation:
   approaches to, 236
   art of, 235
   creative solutions to, 242
   preparation for, 238
Nonobviousness, 80
Nonstatutory inventions, 113
Norton Company, 21
Notebook, engineering, 40
Notice of allowance, 7, 40

Oath, 155
Objects of invention, 98, 150
Obligations, contractual, 233
Official action, 161
Official Gazette, 60
Operation of invention, 154
Order of elements, 123
Ownership, 40

Participation in sale of invention, 179
Patent(s), 11
   design, 79
   importance of, 30
   narrow, 34
   plant, 79
   title, 92
Patentability:
   determining, 75
   tests for, 79
Patentable, 12
Patent agent, 18
Patent application:
   filing and prosecution of, 157
   formalities of, 158
   preparation of, 178
Patent drawings, 133
Patentee Index, 72
Patent evaluation, 64
Patent Interference Law and Practice, 44
Patent lawyer, 18
Patent searcher, 67
Patent specification, 141

Patience in negotiations, 241
Pennie & Edmunds, 82
Photographs, 138
Pinchot, Gifford, 202
Planned Innovation, 52, 56
Plant patents, 79
Poissant, Brian, 82
Poms, Smith, Lande and Rose, 176
Post issuance fees, 171
Practicing Law Institute, 177
Preamble, 117
Preferred embodiment, 63
Prejudgement interest, 250
Preliminary search, 66, 68
Preliminary search and opinion, 178
Price determination, 58
Prior art, 127
   problem with, 127
Proof, required, 44
Prosecution of application, 179
Protecting your investment, 87
Public use, 85

Qualifying a prospect, 199

Raymark Inc., 216
Reasonable royalty, 250
Reconnaissance in selling, 221
Records, written, 40
Reduction to practice, 44, 168
   constructive, 45
Reexamination, 171, 251
Registering a trademark, 188
Reissues, 171, 251
Remer, Daniel, 16
Requirements, statutory, 77, 90
Research Corporation, 197
Return on investment, 52
Rights, establishing, 39
Robertshaw Controls, 76
Rose, Alan, 176, 177, 178, 179, 180
Ross, Frederick J., 216
Royalties, 228

Sale, 85
Scientific Advances Inc., 10
Scott's Liquid Gold, 59
Search:
   assignment, 72
   collection, 71
   computer, 72

conducting your own, 72
infringement, 70
novelty, 66
preliminary, 66, 68
validity, 69
Second presentation, 209
Selecting:
  licensee, 199
  right individual, 201
  target, 197
  trademark, 183
Selling:
  ideas, 193
  inventions, 195
  part of negotiations, 236
Settlement, 254
Shaffer, Peter, 4, 5, 6, 7, 8, 40, 53, 57, 73
Sharp, Walter, 9, 15
Shelcone Inc. v. *Durham Industries*, 82
Shotgun method, 200
Sophisticated buyer, 192
Species claim, 44
Specification, 91
Square D Company, 34
Standard & Poor's Directory, 197
Statistics, U.S. government, 57
Statutory bar, 85
Statutory requirements, 77, 90
Strategic information, 218
Strategic planning, 213, 217
Strategy for R & D, 219
Strength of trademark, 187
Structuring a presentation, 203
Subcombination claims, 127
Substitution, 83
  of materials, 83
Suggestive marks, 188
Summary of invention, 96, 149
Synergism, 82

Tactics in selling, 221
Tappan Company, 33
Technical evaluation, 60
Terms of payment, 232
Territorial restrictions, 227
Tests for patentability, 79
Thomas' Register, 56, 197
Time, of the essence, 233
Timing, importance of, 37

Title:
  of invention, 143
  patent, 92
Trade associations, 57
Trademark(s), 15, 181
  cancellation, 190
  infringement, 185
  oppositions, 189
  prosecution, 189
  search, 185
  strength of, 187
Trademark Protection and Practice, 192
Trade secret(s), 9, 73
Trade secret litigation, 246
Treble damages, 251
Trilon Discovery Corporation, 196
TYROLIA, 9

U.S. environment, 222
U.S. government statistics, 57
U.S./USSR Technology and Licensing, 176
Use of consultant, 200

Validity search, 69
Vargady, Leslie O., 36, 82, 142

Webb, Burden, Robinson & Webb, P.A., 105
Webb, William H., 38, 105, 106, 114
Welton, Ted, 220
Whipple, Robert P., 64
Whipple International, 64
Who Owns What's In Your Head, 20, 49
Willian Brinks Olds Hofer Gilson & Lione
  Ltd., 182, 248
Willian, Clyde, 248, 253, 254
Witnessed and understood, 43
Witnesses, 43
Wolf, Blacke, Shorr and Solis-Cohen, 248
Woodling, George V., 101
Words and phrases, 130
Working with your attorney, 175
Written records, 40

Xerography, 6
Xerox Corporation, 218

Young, Edgar D., 196, 198